D1596388

CANADIAN BRASS

STEPHEN J. HARRIS

Canadian Brass:
The Making of a Professional
Army, 1860–1939

UNIVERSITY OF TORONTO PRESS
Toronto Buffalo London

© University of Toronto Press 1988
Toronto Buffalo London
Printed in Canada

ISBN 0-8020-5765-9

Printed on acid-free paper

Canadian Cataloguing in Publication Data

Harris, Stephen John
Canadian brass

Includes bibliographical references.
ISBN 0-8020-5765-9

1. Canada. Canadian Army – History. 2. Military
education – Canada – History. 3. Canada – History,
Military. I. Title.

UA600.H37 1988   355.3′1′0971   C88-093266-X

This book has been published with the help of a grant
from the Social Science Federation of Canada, using funds
provided by the Social Sciences and Humanities Research
Council of Canada.

To the Three Js

Contents

Preface

This book grew out of a series of questions that occupied my thoughts while I was on staff at the Canadian Forces College, Toronto, between 1970 and 1974. In general, they pertained to the history of that institution and how it had changed over time. More specifically, they involved the nature of a professional military education and what, if anything, was unique about it in Canada.

I found no satisfactory answers. Three friends and colleagues – Mr Ross Allen, Professor John Campbell, and the late Dr W.T. (Tom) Traynor – convinced me that these questions deserved more serious study. As a result, when the opportunity arose to enter the PHD program at Duke University I seized it without delay. There Dick Preston and Ted Ropp set me on my course, let me make mistakes, and when necessary, steered me in the right direction again. I can never repay my debt to them.

Now that I am at the Directorate of History, National Defence Headquarters, I have as colleagues some of the best critics in the world: Alec Douglas, Ben Greenhous, Norm Hillmer, Roger Sarty, Owen Cooke, and Bill McAndrew. Each in his own way has helped me change this manuscript from a thesis to a book. I thank them and Diane Mew, my editor, for making it better than it was. If it is not even better, the responsibility is mine, and mine alone.

For their invaluable guidance through mazes of documents, books, and private papers I am grateful to all the librarians and archivists who have helped me, especially those at the Public Archives of Canada and the Directorate of History, National Defence Headquarters. Barbara Wilson at the Public Archives of Canada I will single out, as has every other Canadian military historian. Her knowledge I respect deeply, while her enthusiasm helped see me through many months of research in Ottawa.

For the foundation on which all else is built, and for their unflagging moral support, I thank my parents. For keeping me sane over all the years I credit friends and fellow bandsmen in Burlington, Toronto, and Ottawa. For keeping me happy (and honest), I thank my wife, Joey.

S.J.H.
Aylmer, Quebec

B Battery, School of Gunnery, Royal Canadian Artillery, based in Quebec, crossing the St Lawrence River near St Helen's Island, 1873

The Infantry School Corps in front of the Officers' Barracks, Fredericton, New Brunswick

'Having found the enemy, the advance party signals for their horses.' An obviously posed portrait of members of the Royal School of Mounted Infantry, Winnipeg

Major-General E.T.H. Hutton (4th from left) and Colonel W.D. Otter (3rd) at the Old Fort, Toronto 1898, prior to the Staff Ride

Officers of the Staff Ride, Niagara 1898: included, in the front row, are Lieutenant-Colonel Sam Hughes (4th from left), Lieutenant-Colonel Hubert Foster (5th), Lieutenant-Colonel W.D. Gordon (6th), Major-General E.T.H. Hutton (8th), Lieutenant-Colonel W.D. Otter (9th), and Lieutenant-Colonel F. Lessard (10th)

Major-General the Earl of Dundonald

Major-General Colin Mackenzie

Sir Frederick Borden, minister of militia and defence, July 1905

Major-General Percy Lake, chief of the general staff, July 1905

Lieutenant-General Sir Sam Hughes

Sir George Perley

Major-General S.C. Mewburn, Sir Robert Borden, and Sir Edward Kemp

Lieutenant-General Arthur Currie and Brigadier-General J.H. MacBrien at
the front, September 1917

Lieutenant-Colonel H.D.G. Crerar (3rd from left), Brigadier-General
A.G.L. McNaughton (4th), and the staff, Canadian Corps Heavy Artillery,
January 1919, Bonn, Germany

Canadian 'spies,' 1921–3: Lieutenant-Colonel F.O. Hodgins, Lieutenant-Colonel J.M. Prower, and Colonel James Sutherland Brown (right) on a reconnaissance of strategic points in Vermont and New York State: on the road between Keene and Upper Jay

Brown's party on the road in the Ausable Valley west of Lake Placid

The Royal Canadian Dragoons, with pith helmets and swords, practise anti-aircraft drill, Camp Borden 1937

The RCD, in cavalry cloaks and gas masks, with their simulated armoured fighting vehicle, Camp Borden 1937

Partial mechanization: horses and the signals truck fording a stream; the RCD at Camp Borden 1937

RCD armoured cars and horses, Camp Borden 1937

Major-General E.C. Ashton

Major-General T.V. Anderson

Ian Mackenzie, minister of national defence

CANADIAN BRASS

Introduction:
Military professionalism

The idea that the military should rank with such traditional professions as medicine, law, and the church is of recent origin. Although most career officers in the American and continental European armies probably considered themselves to be professionals by the 1930s (the proportion in the British army may have been smaller), their status as such was not universally accepted. Indeed, the first serious study of professions and professionalism, admittedly the work of two English academics who may have been influenced by the popular image of British officers as public school dilettantes, excluded the armed forces from consideration.[1]

Times have changed. Today the military's status as a profession is secure, and the literature of history and sociology is replete with case studies illustrating the extent to which particular armies, navies, and air forces meet the criteria of professionalism developed over the past five decades.[2] The language used to describe and explain these criteria has, of course, changed in these fifty years. But the most important attributes of professionalism – expertise, corporateness, and responsibility – have remained constant.

Expertise is best defined as specialized knowledge and skills, learned through study and practice, and capable of being tested according to universal standards, that allow an individual to carry out his or her work. In the case of the military profession this expertise has been described as 'the management of violence'[3] or 'the ordered application of force in the resolution of a social problem.'[4] At one level it refers to the soldier's technical competence on the battlefield: the ability to make the best use of his arms and equipment and lead others according to a sound tactical or strategic plan to defeat the enemy.

But soldiers are not always at war, and professional competence cannot be defined solely as their facility at winning battles. In a peacetime environment, therefore, expertise suggests the soldier's ability to learn the appropriate lessons from past mistakes and successes; to identify the kinds of weapons and equipment likely to be important in the future; to translate these into a practical doctrine; and to measure, as far as possible, the changing capabilities of potential enemies. The competent army is one which, having engaged in this critical study and thinking, successfully prepares for the next war, not the last, does a better job than its opponent of marrying new technologies with tactics that will exploit them, and is ready for the specific conflict in which it finds itself. Trevor Dupuy calls all this 'a genius for war,' where 'the ability to perform in accordance with theory [is] so thoroughly ingrained in all leaders – and the soldiers too – that they will automatically perform their wartime tasks intelligently and flexibly.'[5]

Corporateness describes the internal ordering of the profession, its sense of exclusivity, and the feeling that its members form a 'sacred band' distinct from the community they serve and distinct from both citizen militias and wartime conscript armies. It derives from the view that since professional expertise is the product of prolonged study and repeated practice, only those who have made the military a career, have undertaken a serious study of their profession, and have received the requisite training are qualified to judge the competence of others within the profession. Entrance to and status (promotion) within the profession should therefore be governed by regulations set down by the profession itself, according to its own criteria of merit, which in turn should be based on the expertise, knowledge, and skills an individual has displayed. It follows that such extraneous considerations as socio-economic status, religion, ethnic origin, or party political affiliation are not, in and of themselves, indications of merit and should, as a result, have no bearing on the assessment of an individual's professional qualifications. Nor should they be imposed from the outside as the main criteria for entry to or advancement within the profession.[6]

The notion that a profession has a monopoly over the specialized knowledge and skills involved in performing its task (and is alone competent to judge when this expertise has been acquired) suggests that it must have a certain independence from external influences. Accordingly, professional armies contend that it is their prerogative to test the mettle of officer candidates at military academies and colleges, and to require that officers pass promotion exams and attend staff and war colleges before they are promoted to senior rank and hold the most important command and staff appointments. Similarly, it is argued that because the military profession's advice to government on military matters is tendered by those most qualified to do so its credibility and objectivity need not be doubted. Indeed, some ask, where, outside the military profession, is the body of knowledge and expertise that can reasonably or usefully be asked to corroborate or contradict the validity of professional military opinion on purely military matters?

Responsibility, the last of the three attributes of professionalism, refers to the profession's relationship with its clients. It reflects the view that professionals should use their knowledge and power only for the benefit of the client, and not for selfish or self-serving reasons. Since the state is the military profession's client, it follows that the army serves the state and that the political power – the government – enjoys paramount authority. The government makes policy; the army carries it out. This is the doctrine of civilian control of the military.

Government has the responsibility to provide security for the state through policies which establish the scope of military activity, but it lacks the specific expertise to determine what may reasonably be asked of the military and what is best for it. The military profession, on the other hand, has the requisite knowledge to provide advice on what may and ought to be done but has no power to legislate. Moreover, the military profession has no grounds for assuming that it understands better than the politicians what is possible from the perspective of popular opinion. Armies, navies, and air forces are not alone in making claims on the treasury. 'The fact that war has its own grammar,' Samuel P. Huntington has declared, 'requires that military professionals be permitted to develop their expertise at this grammar without extraneous interference ... [But] no commonly accepted political values exist by which the military officer can prove to reasonable men that his political judgement is preferable to that of the statesman. The superior wisdom of the statesman must be accepted as fact.'[7]

Co-operation and trust therefore seem essential for the existence of a healthy civil-military relationship. When governments can be sure that the advice they receive from their military staffs is objective and competent, is based upon professional knowledge and expertise, and serves the interests of the state and not just those of the armed forces, they are more likely to take it seriously and arrive at sound military policies. Similarly, armies are well served when they know that the government has done its utmost to provide them with the resources they must have to do their job. The degree of harmony is greatest when army and government agree as to the nature of the job to be done, when politicians expect, as a matter of course, that the best solutions to the country's military problems will emerge from within the military profession, and when soldiers sense that the politicians will not pursue unrealistic military policies beyond the capabilities of the profession or exploit military policies and internal military affairs for political gain.

This book will look at these three attributes – expertise, corporateness, and responsibility – in the context of the historical development of the Canadian military profession. It argues that the permanent force which emerged between 1871 and 1914 – the genesis of today's professional Canadian army – did so in an atmosphere of disharmony and dissonance which retarded the inculcation of these three attributes within the profession. For most of this period there was confusion about the need for regular soldiers, what they should do, how they should be managed, and who should be appointed and promoted. The doubt reflected a feeling that Canada had few enemies, that the militia of part-time citizen soldiers perceived to have won the War of 1812 was sufficient defence, and that, in the worst case, the Dominion could always rely upon the British army.

Canada's political traditions also influenced the management of the regular army. Appointments to and promotions within the part-time militia had formed an integral part of the government's patronage network – a practice that was easily carried over to the permanent force after it was authorized. Accordingly, the demand that this should be a professional army in which merit was a prerequisite for advancement was unwelcome in political quarters because it threatened the government's freedom to use a national institution for political gain.

Finally, the period before the Great War was one in which amateur soldiers flourished. When, as was often the case, they entered politics, they carried with them the belief that they were at least equal, if not superior, to the regular army in all areas except the latter's adherence to red tape. As a result, these amateur soldier-politicians were reluctant to concede greater knowledge and expertise to the permanent force, and they had the power to ignore its advice and to thwart its every attempt to assert professional independence.

All these factors influenced the pace at which military professionalism developed before the Great War. Despite the best efforts of the British officers sent to command and reform the army, Canada's regular soldiers were told repeatedly and forcefully that they should aspire to nothing more than teaching the militia, and that to do this they need not worry about preparing themselves to fight in the next war. At the same time party political loyalties often determined who would become regular officers, and who would be promoted.

These factors also established the kind of behaviour that would be tolerated from Canada's professional army. Taken as a whole, the permanent force was generally lacking in expertise, corporate loyalty, and the sense that its primary responsibility was to its client. The circle had been closed. Having been born into a hostile environment in which the need for a professional army was questioned, the regulars perpetuated the sense of doubt and hostility. They could not, by their own efforts, win credibility as a professional body or persuade Canadians to demand the reforms needed to make the army more professional. In short, they lived up to the very limited expectations most Canadians had of them, and in so doing forfeited the respect professionals might anticipate.

It was only during the Great War that opinion began to change – when regulars, militiamen, and civilians alike began to realize that a military system which did not demand professional expertise and knowledge could produce casualties. The post-war army was therefore determined not only to preserve what it had learned from four years' fighting at the front, but also to ensure that Canadians and their governments did not forget. As it turned out, the return to peace, closer ties and friendlier relations with the United States, and the depression of the 1930s made it easy for most Canadians to ignore the lessons of 1914–18 or to declare them irrelevant. That set the stage for a sustained struggle on the part of senior officers, the 'Canadian Brass' of the title, to win respect as professionals, and to secure the Canadian army's professional identity and independence. The book concludes that this struggle was not over when Canada went to war again in 1939.

A note on terminology is in order. Most armies number only commissioned career officers among the members of the military profession. Non-commissioned officers and private soldiers, generally considered to be the technicians, are excluded because they do not have the same kind of professional education and training and because they do not shoulder the same kinds of burdens and responsibilities. Officers in the reserve, militia, or citizen army, are excluded because they have not made the military a career and so cannot devote themselves full-time to study and training. I accept this reasoning, and use 'professional' and 'military profession' only to refer to career officers individually or as a corps.

It should also be noted that Canada's land forces have had a bewildering array of official titles over the years, some of them quite misleading. 'Active militia,' for example, designated the part-time force of citizen-soldiers who never trained. Although 'Canadian Army' as a proper name has existed only since the Second World War, I have used 'Canadian army' as a generic term for land forces. 'Regular(s)' and 'permanent force' are employed to describe the professional, full-time army and its officers. 'Volunteer(s),' 'militia,' 'reserve,' and 'citizen' denote the part-time, non-professional army.

PART I

MILITARY EDUCATION AND TRAINING, 1860–1914

I

Beginnings: The militia schools and the creation of the permanent force, 1860–1883

'With so few troops at my disposal,' lamented General Sir Hastings Doyle, 'I must naturally in case of sudden invasion, look to the Militia of these Provinces for assistance, but we should look in vain.'[1] With these words the commander of the British garrison at Halifax described the problem confronting him in 1861 as he contemplated the difficult task of defending the Atlantic provinces of British North America against an attack from the United States. A report filed three years later by Lieutenant-General Sir William Fenwick Williams, general officer commanding British forces in Canada, indicated that little had changed. The presence of an enlarged British garrison in North America had not strengthened local military spirit whatsoever. Instead, Fenwick Williams grumbled, the Canadians seemed 'to look on their coming dangers with the eye of a child, under the protection of a Parent who is bound to fight, whilst they pursue their ordinary business, or agitate themselves by fruitless party politics and parliamentary conflicts.'[2]

Both Doyle and Fenwick Williams had good reason to be concerned about the state of the colonial militias. British policy since the Crimean War in the mid-1850s had aimed at reducing the mother country's commitments to imperial defence, especially in colonies enjoying responsible self-government, to allow for the strengthening of the army closer to home. Local forces were to take up the slack. The outbreak of the Civil War in the United States in 1861 did force London to change course and reinforce its North American garrison significantly in case the conflict spilled over the border. Nevertheless, this was conceded (by London, at least) to be an interim measure, to last only until the Americans had resolved their problem and formulated a stable foreign policy. At that point, the withdrawal of the British army could be considered again.

Given the military potential of the United States, it was unrealistic to expect British North America to defend itself without help from the imperial power.

As it was, the less than enthusiastic response of Canadians towards organizing their own defence upset British planning. Neither Doyle nor Fenwick Williams was sure that his regulars were sufficient to repel any invasion from south of the border. It was crucial, therefore, to somehow shake Canadians out of their lethargy and convince them to reform their military institutions.[3]

Unhappily, the inefficient colonial military systems of the 1860s were by and large popular, having been credited with the defeat of the Americans fifty years before, and of Papineau's and Mackenzie's rebels in 1837–8. Out of these victories there had grown up a Canadian myth that an unpaid militia, theoretically a levée en masse, organized into battalions for administrative purposes and liable to call-out in times of crisis, was the only army Canada needed. Little thought was given to training these battalions between emergencies, and by the 1850s even the practice of holding a yearly muster parade, if only for accounting purposes, had faded away.

Reform was attempted in the two Canadas in 1855, when the Militia Act, itself a product of a British troop withdrawal, incorporated a handful of volunteer companies into the order of battle. Yet despite the prospect of receiving payment for drill – there was no financial reward for militia service per se – the initial enthusiasm for these volunteer units soon dwindled. It was only in 1860 that the surviving companies began to be brought together into battalions, and some consideration was given to their training. Even so, neither the militia levée en masse nor these volunteer battalions could be regarded as a potential field army. They lacked all forms of logistical support – medical, ordnance, and transport services – while only a small minority of the officers and men who had at one time served in the British army had any recent experience of battle. There was no staff organization to speak of, either to make plans or to supply the army, and no officer was called upon to qualify for his rank and appointment. Instead, local prominence and influence were the main criteria for promotion, the logic being that men of standing would have an easy time convincing neighbours to fulfil their military obligation. Slightly more was expected of an officer in a volunteer unit since he might have to conduct drill in the local town square, but this did not extend to formal qualifications. Indeed, in the early years some volunteer companies had actually elected their officers.[4]

Reform, of a sort, was more acceptable in the Maritime colonies, and in particular in Nova Scotia. Volunteer companies had been authorized in 1859, and staff officers and drill sergeants from the British garrison were employed to conduct basic training. In 1862, however, the colony chose to rejuvenate its sedentary militia, demanding that it train for five days a year and prescribing an additional twenty-eight three-hour drill session for officers, to be supervised by officers from the British garrison. But this was training at a low level, and the instruction given to the militia officers was not sophisticated or comprehensive.[5]

The fact that the Canadian provinces did nothing to train their military officers was by no means unique, however, as the British army of the 1860s still clung to an essentially amateur ethos. Seniority and purchase were the keys to advancement, especially in the cavalry and infantry. Moreover, this was not resented; the idea of introducing compulsory examinations to test an officer's fitness to command before he was promoted had actually been rejected in the 1850s. The American army was no more professional.[6]

Still, there were significant differences between these services and the Canadian militia. A British officer could learn the basic elements of his trade on active duty in India, Africa, and elsewhere in the empire, while the American army regularly fought in the West. And by 1865, of course, almost all American officers had served in the Civil War. In Canada, by contrast, there was nothing to raise the militia and volunteers above the level of an armed mob. Proof of this came at the 'battle' of Ridgeway in 1866, when an outnumbered and poorly organized force of Irish-American Fenians dispersed the Canadians sent to oppose them. Fortunately, the Fenians also ran.[7]

Quite simply, the Canadian militia was not good enough to defend its borders, and had no obvious opportunity to become good enough. The British officers in Canada knew this, but short of a complete revolution in Canadian policy there was little they could do beyond instituting incremental reforms and inducements to improve. By 1860 they were providing musketry and drill instructors to the militia (after extensive haggling with Canadian officials over who would bear the cost) and were contemplating the dispatch of an artillery battery to North America to serve as a model for the struggling provincial gunners. But such palliative measures could accomplish only part of what was required.[8]

In February 1862 it seemed that, at long last, substantial reform of the Canadian military system was in the offing. Worried by the *Trent* affair, which had soured Anglo-American relations, and persuaded that the militia and volunteers were 'altogether insufficient and defective,' John A. Macdonald committed the government to a thorough-going review of defence policy. The commission which he appointed to review military questions – and which he himself chaired – returned with the recommendation that Canada should maintain a fully trained militia of fifty thousand men, and that all officers should be compelled to pass proficiency examinations set and marked by the British army upon their first appointment and before every promotion.[9] If these recommendations had been accepted and implemented as proposed,

Canada would have created the foundation for a sound citizen military force.

But in the midst of difficult financial and economic times, Canadians did not want to spend the estimated one million dollars a year this army was expected to cost, and they were loath to break with long-standing militia traditions. George Taylor Denison, commanding a Toronto cavalry troop, was especially hostile to the suggestion that British officers alone were competent to assess the credentials of colonial soldiers. He was familiar enough with them, he told Macdonald, that he 'should be sorry to have them considered as even equals to the majority of ... Volunteer officers either in intellect, education, military capacity, talent, or military knowledge.'[10] Beset by turmoil within his own administration, Macdonald lacked the strength to force the bill through the legislature. The militia bill was defeated in May 1862, and the government fell.

The new premier, John Sandfield Macdonald, had consistently opposed any increase in Canadian expenditure for defence on the grounds that the province's security was an imperial, not a local, responsibility. It was for the British to pay, since the British government had full authority over foreign policy. But urged on by Governor General Lord Monck, and after conducting a poll of senior militia officers, Sandfield Macdonald was convinced that the militia officer corps had to be improved. In particular, he wanted to weed out the octogenarians who were neglecting even the simplest of their custodial duties. They would be retired. For the rest, he declared, selection on the basis of merit would replace seniority as the criterion for promotion, and all officers would have to satisfy minimum educational standards before their appointments could be confirmed.[11]

This was a start at reform, but only just. These regulations were not meant to apply to officers in the volunteer companies, while there was no provision to train those in the militia. As it happened, others were already considering this problem. Shortly after Sandfield Macdonald's interests became known General Fenwick Williams proposed the creation of an artillery school in conjunction with a British battery.[12] At about the same time Lieutenant-Colonel Walker Powell, deputy adjutant general of militia – and more importantly, a Canadian – recommended that the British infantry battalions in the North American garrisons be used to instruct the city volunteer regiments.[13] H.B. Willson, a lawyer, journalist, land speculator, and sometime proponent of annexation to the United States, went further, suggesting that all the British units and sub-units in the country could serve as model schools for the militia and volunteers alike.[14]

Willson's idea was practical, politic, and worthy of both British and Canadian support. It promised to improve the Canadian army, thereby satisfying British requirements, but it was also much cheaper and much less traumatic for Canadians than the establishment of a fifty-thousand-man permanent militia. In March 1863, then, Sandfield Macdonald outlined his government's policy, adhering closely to Willson's outline. The scattered companies of the Royal Canadian Rifles, a British garrison regiment stationed permanently in British North America, would provide schools of instruction to prepare militia (but not volunteer) officers for compulsory qualifying exams. The three-month courses being proposed, the premier announced, would remove those who were 'devoid of all military knowledge and fit only to lead men to massacre.'[15]

The British were ready to assist, but they had reservations about the Canadian plan. Asked by Lord Monck for his comments, Lieutenant-Colonel George Peacocke of the 16th Foot, then stationed in Toronto, replied that British officers would have to supervise all examinations to ensure that they were conducted and marked with suitable rigour. In addition, successful candidates should spend some time with regular detachments of the British army to experience army routine at its fullest.[16] The Duke of Cambridge, commander-in-chief of the army, and the secretary of state for war agreed with Peacocke in principle; to protect standards further they stipulated that all schools should be located at battalion headquarters rather than at company outposts. Like Peacocke, they feared that the quality of instruction would be diluted, and maybe even undermined, if it were removed from the control of relatively senior British officers.[17]

Sandfield Macdonald included these suggestions in his militia bill and presented his revised program to the legislature on 16 September 1863. Beginning the next year, he told the Assembly, any man aspiring to a commission in the militia would have to attend a school of instruction at a British battalion headquarters in Toronto or Quebec for not less than three months in order to learn company drill and administration. An additional three months would be required to qualify for command of a battalion. British officers would set and supervise the examinations at both levels, thereby setting the militia's professional standards, but the final selection of candidates would remain a local Canadian prerogative.

Debate on this proposal was surprisingly restrained given the turmoil of the previous months and the defeat of John A. Macdonald's government. Questions about the program's cost came early, and were easily turned aside; the only financial commitment made by Canada was the payment of travel expenses to the schools and a fifty-dollar bounty for each examination passed successfully. Still, some amendments were necessary to satisfy the legitimate complaint that farmers would be unable to find time to travel to Quebec or Toronto for three months at a time. As the rural legislators pointed out, this influential and important segment of society would soon be ineligible to serve as militia officers, and when that happened – and country units began to be commanded by outsiders who lived closer to the schools – the territorially based esprit de corps that was the hallmark of the rural militia would soon disappear. The demise of the farm regiments would follow soon after.

This was an important problem, and one which Sandfield Macdonald had already recognized when he first thought of using the scattered companies of the Royal Canadian Rifles as the basis of his military schools organization. But now that the British, fearing watered-down standards, were refusing to make these available and demanded instead that the schools be located in Toronto and Quebec, the premier had to find another solution. Arguing that testing military knowledge and expertise, however acquired, was his sole object, Sandfield Macdonald withdrew the provision demanding three months' attendance at the schools and substituted the simple requirement that officer candidates pass the final exam set by the British staff. If they could do this without leaving home until the last few days of a course, so much the better. This proved acceptable to all concerned, but as a result the province's system of military education was neither uniform nor universal.[18]

Sandfield Macdonald's program was an instant success. The schools established in Toronto and Quebec in 1864 proved so popular there was an immediate demand for more. The British, welcoming this enthusiasm, quickly offered to train infantry officers in Hamilton, London, Kingston, and Montreal, and to add cavalry instruction to the schools in Toronto and Montreal. The new schools in Hamilton and London closed soon afterward because of a shortage of students, but the rest flourished, producing on average five hundred trained cadets a year.[19] Although these graduates were far from being ready to lead men into battle, they at least had some familiarity with their duties, a fact which British officers serving in Canada lost no time in pointing out.[20]

Perhaps more important, the military schools won widespread civilian support. *The Volunteer Review*, a local journal traditionally hostile to anything that smacked of regular army pipe-clay and red tape, applauded the officer training system as the only worthwhile feature of Sandfield Macdonald's militia policy.[21] Indeed, the response to the schools was so favourable that when John A. Macdonald returned to power in 1864 he promoted the creation of even more than the existing four, and his government hastened to extend the system to Nova Scotia and New Brunswick following Confederation in 1867.

Yet within three years most of the British schools had closed, victims of the penultimate imperial military withdrawal from Canada. Only the Halifax garrison remained, but it was too far from Quebec and Ontario to serve the majority of militia and volunteer officers. Anxious that military instruction continue, the British officers still in Canada implored the Dominion government to establish a permanent force to serve as a training cadre for the militia before imperial troops left for the last time. The British government went even further, offering to transfer the Royal Canadian Rifles to Canadian service en masse as a ready-made regular regiment, but Ottawa refused, preferring not to bear that kind of expense. Instead, it was decided, Canada would set up small schools in each of the military districts that had been established across the country, employing the local militia staff as instructors assisted by two or three British army sergeants.[22]

That Canada refused to create a regular army in 1870, or even one full-strength instructional battalion of infantry, should not have surprised the British. John A. Macdonald had already been embarrassed by similar proposals only eight years before, and the sentiments that had caused his defeat then had changed hardly at all: Canadians still clung to the belief that defence was an imperial problem to be financed by the British Treasury because control over foreign policy rested in London, not Ottawa. And, it was clear, they continued to place great faith in the military prowess of the part-time militia and volunteers, and so wanted nothing to do with an unnecessary standing army.

The prime minister was also influenced by doubts as to whether the military schools system established in 1864 actually served Canadian interests as well as he had first believed. For one thing, the British-run schools had never served the francophone population well, despite efforts to provide translators and time for students to become familiar with English-language publications. French Canadians had responded accordingly: few attended these essentially unilingual institutions, fewer qualified, and fewer still came forward to provide the instructional staff for a Canadian school to operate in French. Following the British model, there was even less hope of finding enough francophones to provide the full other-ranks establishment necessary if officer trainees were to practise what they had been taught.[23] Beyond this, the military schools had begun to lose popularity with the English-speaking militia and volunteers because they had inadvertently invaded the preserve of established social hierarchies. The sons of the old militia élite found to their dismay and disgust that many of their fellow officer cadets came from the ranks of the seasonally unemployed and had joined up simply to collect whatever bonuses were available to those who passed their examinations. Whether such men would make good officers was irrelevant: to the scions of old Toronto and Montreal families, these interlopers were simply not gentlemen.[24]

Finally, the entire military schools system continued to draw heavy criticism from the rural districts. Despite Sandfield Macdonald's attempt to ease the burden on farmers, many prominent men from the country were failing the basic general education tests for officer cadets, while those who did pass still found the time involved in qualifying thoroughly inconvenient. Bowing to this pressure, John A. Macdonald's government waived all pre-admission tests for the new, Canadian-run schools, and continued Sandfield Macdonald's practice of demanding only a pass on the final examination. As a result, potential officers did not have to undergo instruction on a day-to-day basis, and few chose to.[25]

Only the artillery retained anything like the British model. The techniques of modern gunnery had advanced so far that they were difficult for part-time officers to learn, and as a result the Canadian government readily accepted British advice to use the former imperial fortresses at Kingston and Quebec as training schools complete with a staff of professional officers seconded from the Royal Artillery. Colonels Thomas Bland Strange and G.A. French were hired to command what would become the Canadian artillery's A and B batteries, manned by militiamen on short-service call-out until 1873, and by permanent gunners thereafter.[26]

The schools at Kingston and Quebec flourished under their British officers, in part because they were the only route to a commission in the artillery, but also because they had immediate credibility: the British had left behind most of their equipment, each battery included an appropriate number of private soldiers, and the fortresses were seen to be an important contribution to the Dominion's defence. By comparison, the Canadian-run militia schools had no equipment, lacked qualified instructors, and were forced to offer a totally theoretical curriculum since they had no troops attached to them. Furthermore, as one critic charged, 'the most complete incapacity was no barrier' to qualifying because direction of the schools was entirely in Canadian hands.[27] Examiners simply approved the work of their friends whether or not it met the standard. Protests about the degree of political favouritism at the schools were voiced time and again but to no avail, and eventually the militia officers themselves rendered judgment, voting with their feet. By 1874 all the district military schools had closed, recognized for what they had been – tenth-rate institutions of little value.

The success of the artillery batteries and the failure of the militia schools reawakened hopes that permanent units of infantry and cavalry might yet be established to provide the country's basic system of officer education. In 1873 Colonel H.C. Fletcher, a British officer serving as an aide to the governor general, submitted a proposal for the creation of all-arms 'brigade' schools in each military district; they would be commanded by British army staff college graduates and include a permanent other-ranks establishment.[28] Colonel Strange and Colonel Robertson-Ross, the adjutant general of militia, agreed with Fletcher, as did Major-General Edward Selby Smyth when he arrived to take up the new appointment of general officer commanding (GOC) after Robertson-Ross's departure. More important, the long-serving Colonel Walker Powell, responsible now for administration as adjutant general under Smyth, admitted that Fletcher's plan had merit, but cautioned that it was too ambitious. Support was likely for only one such school; however, he added, the government must be made to realize that a worthwhile system of officer education and training depended upon the existence of regular units of infantry and cavalry as well as artillery.[29]

Implementation of these recommendations was unlikely so long as the Conservatives remained in office. Once Alexander Mackenzie's Liberals won power in 1873 the soldiers had an opportunity to start afresh. However, in addition to their call for regular infantry and cavalry regiments, Colonels Fletcher, Strange, and Walker Powell had all pointed to the value of establishing a Canadian military academy or college modelled on Sandhurst or West Point. Walker Powell went so far as to argue that a permanent instructional brigade should be no more than a temporary expedient until the proposed military college was producing officers in sufficient numbers to staff all the militia battalions. Mackenzie listened closely and opted for the military college, putting off any decision to authorize the formation of regular companies of infantry and cavalry. The prime minister, it appears, was persuaded that only a military college could prepare officers for higher command and staff appointments – by virtue of an extensive academic program and access to current British doctrine. But that was not the only reason for his choice. Since the Royal Military College would offer sophisticated technical instruction, especially in the field of engineering, as with West Point its graduates could serve the civilian community as well as the military; and it was likely that this would turn critics away from commenting on what was, after all, a significant addition to the defence budget.[30] New units of infantry and cavalry could not have been defended so easily in the House of Commons, or in front of militia officers sure to regard them as rivals.

However, since nothing was done to dissuade militia officers from following the existing path to a commission – which involved much less work than the military college course – and as RMC made no pretence of being a staff college, all the prime minister had accomplished was to furnish yet another means by which to qualify as an officer. Furthermore, because the student body was kept small and its graduates were not compelled to join the militia, the military college failed to meet Walker Powell's criterion: RMC did not – would not – provide the Canadian militia with its trained officer corps of the future.

Selby Smyth had not objected to the creation of RMC, but the GOC knew that it was going to take more than a military college to make the militia efficient. Within the year he was again urging the government to authorize the formation of three regular infantry battalions (of five hundred men each) to serve as schools of instruction and to protect Canada from 'communism' and labour unrest.[31] The government refused. Trying another tack, he sought permission to direct the Royal Military College to offer a more sophisticated course for senior officers in order to lay the groundwork for an administrative and operations staff at headquarters and in the military districts. Once again the politicians demurred.[32] Then, when the government reacted sharply to the popular fear of an impending war with Russia in 1878, he tried again.[33] With the report of a Russian cruiser off the east coast, even the prime minister was shaken, confiding to the governor general that he was at last convinced that Canada must have a regular army of its own. But, Mackenzie added, 'the impatience of our people with respect to a standing army' and the depressed economic conditions were forcing him to move slowly.[34] As it turned out, he was too slow. Within months his government was defeated in a general election, and Sir John A. Macdonald returned to office.

Although Macdonald and his colleagues had proved time and again that they were no friends of a regular army, Selby Smyth was not to be put off. Carefully reworking his previous submissions to remove the doubts he had once expressed about the ability of Canadian officers to command regular units, the GOC eventually convinced the minister of militia, Alexander Campbell, of the need to maintain a permanent force in the Dominion. Campbell, however, had no luck with his cabinet colleagues. Even though the prime minister was sympathetic, admitting the value of regular soldiers in combating internal unrest, the proposal met stiff opposition and the matter was dropped.[35] Still, by the time he left Canada in 1880 Selby Smyth had engineered two major reforms: the two artillery schools had begun to train infantry and cavalry officers, while RMC was offering a nine-month 'long course' which introduced militia officers to the study of military history, tactics, strategy, and the more complex aspects of field engineering, none of which were taught elsewhere in the Dominion.

Major-General Richard Amherst Luard, the new general officer commanding in 1880, began where his predecessor left off. 'Much impressed with the ignorance of [the] officers' he met on his first inspection tour, and recognizing the folly of attempting to train rural officers in only five days of drill each year, he immediately urged the creation of infantry schools across the country, including a permanent French-speaking company in Montreal.[36] Again the minister was receptive, actually recommending drastic reductions in the number of militiamen to be trained each year in order to free funds for these schools. But as before cabinet refused even to consider his suggestion; it was much too dangerous, from the political point of view, to do anything that upset the country's citizen soldiers. Campbell then put forward the simple alternative of adding infantry, cavalry, and engineer platoons to each of the two artillery batteries to improve their instruction for these arms; but even this compromise failed to win the approval of cabinet.[37] Popular antipathy to the idea of standing armies, and the expense involved in maintaining additional regular units, were powerful arguments in favour of the status quo.

When Adolphe Caron replaced Alexander Campbell as militia minister later in the year Luard was certain that he had lost all opportunity to improve the militia and expand the regular force. Not only had Campbell been the government's strongest advocate of a standing army, but the new minister also heralded a return to the tried and true practice of managing the part-time militia for political advantage regardless of its impact on military efficiency. For patronage was Caron's forte, and political favouritism did not fit with Luard's view that military promotions and appointments must be made according to merit, and merit alone.

For three years Luard's expectations proved accurate. Nothing was said about a permanent force, while the traffic in militia commissions was appalling. In June 1883, however, Caron put before cabinet a proposal to create infantry and cavalry schools at Toronto, Montreal, and Fredericton, and to require all militia officers to attend the appropriate school to qualify for their appointments. The government agreed, and the policy was implemented in a general reform of the Militia Act. In theory, the Dominion had found its officer education system by returning to the model of the 1860s. In theory, too, Canada had given birth to its own military profession by the creation of regular, standing units of the three combat arms.

Why this sudden and dramatic shift in policy occurred is not entirely clear. One explanation is that, in a nice parallel with 1863, the government made a symbolic gesture to offset its refusal to assume complete responsibility for the defence of Halifax, something the British sought eagerly.[38] Another possibility is that the idea of establishing a small regular force was one whose time had finally arrived. The Russian war scare of 1878 undoubtedly played a part in this, but it seems likely that Colonel Walker Powell's conversion was crucial. He was one soldier at headquarters whom the politicians could approach secure in the knowledge that his loyalty was to Ottawa, not London; moreover, he understood the militia, and could be counted upon to warn the government against any innovation likely to upset the citizen soldiers.[39] For Caron, therefore, the creation of infantry and cavalry schools in 1883 may well have appeared to be a safe, uncontroversial measure. For Luard, it marked the first step in achieving what London had been after for years: Canada's commitment to defend itself with an army that could fight.

2

The permanent force and 'real soldiering,'
1883–1914

Caron's reforms had far less impact than Luard anticipated. Although the schools created in 1883 would inevitably help the militia, there was a crucial difference between them and the artillery batteries at Quebec and Kingston. In addition to their instructional duties, the latter were also quasi-operational units responsible for the upkeep and defence of their fortresses, and they practised this role even while they trained militia gunners. The same could not be said of the infantry and cavalry schools. Indeed, when the Liberals criticized the government for breaking with tradition and creating a standing army, Caron rightly retorted that this was not at all the case. The school companies, he explained, were much too small to be considered the nucleus of a field army; and besides, their job was not to fight, but to instruct the militia. For better or worse, then, the officers and men who joined the infantry and cavalry school corps would be teachers in uniform.[1]

Just how far removed from 'real soldiering' life in the permanent force would be was soon evident. Although the commanding officers originally appointed to these units were sent to England to spend time with the British army (the rest trained at Halifax), they were left more or less on their own once they returned home. There were no promotion examinations to pass, and few tests of their military competence. Furthermore, the courses offered to the militia demanded very little of the regulars. Based on British guidelines prepared in the 1860s, the curriculum consisted in the main of lectures presenting repetitive lists of the duties involved in rudimentary administration, with some time for parade square drill. Tactics, and field operations in general, received little or no attention, either as part of the militia course of instruction or to improve the practical knowledge of the instructional staff.[2]

Indeed, the permanent force probably became less experienced as the years passed. A few of the new subalterns appointed each year attended the Royal

Military College, but many joined the infantry and cavalry with no previous military background or, at best, a few score parades with their local militia unit. And since these officers were not sent to England or Halifax for training, the only place they could learn their trade was within the school itself, where the level of military knowledge and experience was already low. By all accounts, moreover, superiors rarely delegated authority to their younger lieutenants and captains, leaving them with little opportunity to learn even the habit of command or the fundamentals of military administration. Finally, apart from those lucky enough to see active service during the Riel Rebellion in 1885, few had a chance to practise tactics and fieldcraft; they were either preoccupied with their own essential upkeep and administration – feeding and clothing the men; looking after horses and equipment; supervising the orderly room, drill, and picquets; and holding disciplinary parades – or such training was prohibited. Yet, because there were no promotion examinations, these untrained junior officers could count upon being promoted eventually to the rank of lieutenant-colonel, at which point they would be responsible for training the next generation of subalterns. Given such a cycle of mediocrity, conditions could get only worse.[3]

These developments should have come as no surprise to anyone who, during the summer of 1883, paid close attention to the way Caron had set out to man the infantry and cavalry schools in the first place. Unknown to the minister, since early 1881 General Luard had been compiling a list of British army veterans and RMC graduates suitable for permanent employment against the day when a regular army would be established in Canada. But when he forwarded this list to Caron in June 1883, its receipt was not even acknowledged. Instead, as the weeks passed by and the press discussed the candidates under serious consideration, it appeared that blatant political jobbery was playing a major part in the selection process.[4] Appalled that patronage should loom so large in the regular force's crucial formative years, Luard pleaded with Caron to protect the army's credibility by rigorous application of the merit principle, but again received no reply.[5] Now desperate, the GOC turned to the governor general and Colonel Walter Powell for help, but their efforts were equally fruitless.[6] In the end, Caron made his choice without once speaking to Luard and even announced his decision while the GOC was away from Ottawa on an inspection tour. Taken to task for this by Walker Powell, Caron justified the affront with the disingenuous remark that the matter had been delayed long enough.[7]

Luard was horrified when he saw the minister's selection. Although some of the twenty-one nominees had the GOC's approval – Colonel W.D. Otter of the Queen's Own Rifles was one, as were six RMC graduates – some seemed entirely unworthy of their appointment. Nine had no military experience and had undoubtedly been put forward to ensure that the officer corps enjoyed a balanced regional representation. Others had served in the militia but had not done well, and their appointment could only be explained in terms of their political or social connection. Captain Charles J.Q. Coursol, for example, who had been arrested for drunkenness while on a course at A Battery, was the son of a member of Parliament and the grandson of Sir Etienne Taché, a former premier and father of Confederation. It was not the best of beginnings.[8] Still, things could have been worse. Three officers – B.A. Vidal, G.J. Maunsell, and J. Freer – had British experience, and J.F. Turnbull, in the militia since 1855, had attended cavalry manoeuvres in Europe at his own expense several times during his career. Moreover, the prime minister had already forced Caron to remove even more objectionable candidates from his original list, and to stipu- late that all appointments would remain provisional until each individual passed the appropriate qualifying examination in Great Britain or Halifax. For this reason Macdonald asked the governor general to persuade Luard to tone down his criticism and to do the best he could with those who had been selected for political reasons.[9]

Luard did as he was told, but he remained far from happy. Although he had always been reconciled to the fact that Canada's regular officers would be mediocre until they gained experience, he had not counted on individuals owing their position to the minister alone. That challenged the twin pillars of military discipline and subordination. More to the point, the GOC despaired of improvement in the future. Why should Canadian officers better themselves professionally, he wondered, when any promotions they received were likely to depend on their political connections? For that matter, why should they pay attention to the general officer commanding when his opinions obviously meant so little?

Luard was right. Patronage dominated the permanent force for the next thirty-five years as minister after minister proved all too ready to 'drive a coach and six through the Militia Act'[10] to play favourites. Able men, such as George Mutton (Otter's choice as quartermaster in Toronto) who supported the wrong political party, or who lived in a part of the country already well represented in the army, were ignored, while political friends were rewarded with preferential treatment and accelerated promotion. More pernicious still, the prevalence of such partisan behaviour enhanced the development of a self-serving ethos totally at odds with the corporate loyalties normally expected of a professional military organization. Judging from the experience of Colonel Otter, com- mander of Canada's Boer War contingent, this activity extended even to the battlefield. Time and again he felt compelled to look over his shoulder as his subordinates jockeyed for position to replace him. Pandering to the political system that had created them, Canadian officers routinely sought personal gain at the expense of their comrades-in-arms through direct appeals to friends in Parliament and party.[11]

Furthermore, the ethical decay of the permanent force became well known. The *Canadian Military Gazette*, self-styled 'Organ of the Canadian Army,' habitually published diatribes against the regulars, but nothing moved it to complain so loudly or for so long as the patronage connected with the permanent corps. Most officers were denounced as 'influential incompetents,' products of the 'political grab-bag' who had found a career without the least regard to 'qualification and merit.' How, the *Gazette* asked, could the militia look up to such men with confidence when they clearly knew so little about the army?[12] Bad publicity like this simply reinforced traditional Canadian antipathy to the standing army – a sentiment that was never far below the surface.

Although not quite so widespread in the early 1880s as it had been only a decade before, the hostility to the permanent force grew markedly in the 1890s when the militia budget had to be trimmed for the sake of economy. For the first time, it seemed, the regulars were actually beginning to usurp the role of the part-time citizen force as the nation's first line of defence, and this was a development that could not be tolerated. 'We have held, and always will hold,' the *Canadian Military Gazette* proclaimed, 'that our permanent corps owe their existence wholly to the educational requirements of the militia force, and what prouder or more honourable distinction could the officers and men of the permanent corps wish for?' But, the *Gazette* continued, the regulars had 'fallen short of their mission just so far as they have allowed their ambition to be considered a standing army or a separate fighting machine ... to get the better of their desire to provide the best instruction possible ...' to the militia. The *Gazette*'s editor promised that he would 'not cease to expose the absurdly false position taken by those ... who, like jackdaws in peacocks' plumes, want to be something they are not, and never cease bewailing the fate which "makes officers nothing but merely school masters." ' To have greater ambitions was ludicrous for members of a 'one-horse service.'[13]

Another perceptive and respected critic was Thomas Scoble, a long-time militia officer responsible for organizing the first volunteer company of engineers, who warned that the 'arrogant attempt to secure ... the position and reputation of a "permanent force" ... [was] subversive of its own best interests.'[14] The greater the pretensions of the regulars, the worse was their public image, and the louder the complaints made against them. An accommodation between the permanent corps' natural desire to be 'real soldiers' and the popular view that they were teachers first, administrators second, and fighting men perhaps a distant third, might have been possible had they been able to impress the militia with their knowledge and expertise. But as long as so little was required of the regular officer and so little was offered to him in the way of professional education and training, it was next to impossible for him to earn the genuine respect of his citizen force colleagues. Indeed, it would have taken a great deal of consistently high-calibre work for the regulars to overcome their tarnished image as second-rate political hacks.

The poor reputation of the permanent force was not helped by the conditions of service in the infantry and cavalry schools. These were scarcely conducive to attracting the best and brightest young Canadians to the army or, for that matter, to fostering a spirit of initiative and self-motivation among the officers who did join up. Pay was initially pegged at the comparable British rates without taking into account the higher cost of living in Canada, so that military service in the Dominion was both less exciting and more of a financial sacrifice than in the mother country.[15] By the 1890s the comparison was even less favourable. Canadian rates were now marginally lower than in the United Kingdom, but substantially below the salaries offered by the North West Mounted Police and the United States army.[16] Furthermore, no pension was offered for service in the permanent force. But perhaps more debilitating was the simple truth that no officer could be confident of promotion even if he performed his duties better than his colleagues. For one thing, the school companies were so small, and retirement ages so flexible, that vacancies in the more senior ranks were long in coming. For another, advancement increasingly depended upon ministerial whim, so that neither seniority nor merit eventually counted for much. In terms of promoting professional competence, therefore, there was no carrot – and no stick.

The physical amenities of military life were no more appealing. Many of the barrack blocks and officers' quarters had been built to British garrison standards many years before, and so provided less in the way of creature comforts than Canadians were accustomed to. The hutments at Winnipeg, for instance, occupied by the cavalry school in the 1890s, were legacies of the 1870 Manitoba Field Force, had not yet been winterized when they were taken over, and offered a miserable existence. This was an extreme case, of course, but there were problems even in established stations such as Toronto. In 1888, to take another example, Colonel Otter's wife found it necessary to petition the minister directly, asking him to delay long-overdue repairs to the other ranks' quarters in order that she and her husband might finally have a furnace.[17]

At least Colonel Otter had married quarters. Many others were not so lucky because, as in almost all late-Victorian armies, little provision had been made for officers with wives and families. Yet when they requested living-out allowances to help them find suitable accommodation in town, most were turned down coldly by the militia department. Indeed, in 1886 the deputy minister decreed that henceforth all available living space was to be divided equally among the officers at each station so that none could complain that they had no official place to stay, no matter how unsuitable and uncomfortable one room measuring fifteen feet square may have been for raising a family. Sons of wealthy parents were not bothered by such parsimony: they could afford town houses, country homes, and summer retreats. However, the number of applications for various forms of financial relief on the departmental files (as well as the biographical evidence available) strongly suggests that Canadian regular officers did not come from the monied or landed classes.[18]

Sam Hughes, a militia officer and future minister, put the case against them as bluntly as anyone. Failures at everything else they tried, he wrote, the regular officers looked upon the permanent force as their employer of last resort. Yet even then they could not succeed on their own merit, but required the assistance of a patron. As a result, he grumbled, it was 'no compliment to very many prominent ... Militia Officers to be compared with [the regular] officers as a class.'[19] In all fairness it must be said that Hughes went too far. The system which the Conservative government had instituted in 1883 and would not readily change was responsible for much of the permanent force's inadequacies. Still, neither Hughes nor his fellow critics were wrong to think that the conditions of service, the lack of opportunity to do real soldiering, the financial insecurity, and the continuing importance of party political considerations crimped the development of a self-disciplined, cohesive, and professional military force. A few good officers consistently stood out from the rest – T.D.B. Evans, Victor Williams, Henry Burstall, T.D.R. Hemming, George Maunsell, and W.D. Otter – but when so little happened to improve the public's image of the army as an institution there was no reason to expect a popular outcry for change.

That the permanent force did not stagnate altogether was due almost exclusively to the perseverance of the British officers sent to command the militia between 1883 and 1904, and to the three chiefs of the general staff who succeeded them. Indeed, what they were able to accomplish for the permanent force marked their only real achievement in this era. For, as we shall see, most of the GOCs had foreshortened careers in Canada, largely because they ran afoul of the political process in futile attempts to root out patronage in the militia and to forge closer military ties with the mother country. They also failed to train or equip the part-time militia to take the field. But almost all were able to improve the lot of the regular force in one way or another.

Luard's successor as GOC was Major-General Frederick Middleton, a portly man in his sixties who realized very quickly that it did not pay to criticize the militia strenuously or to interfere with Caron's designs for his department. This was true even during the Riel Rebellion of 1885 from which Middleton emerged victorious (but later tainted by a scandal involving allegedly stolen furs). For although the minister played an energetic role in Ottawa, making the best of a flawed military machine that had not been designed for so quick and sudden a mobilization, he had also been faithful to tradition by carefully employing political friends not only to command frontline battalions but also to purvey military supplies of all kinds. The lessons Middleton learned from this experience were evident in his post-rebellion reports, which treated the militia far more kindly than it deserved. Nevertheless, when it came to the permanent force the GOC was adamant that its career system must be based on merit. Although he failed to convince Caron to make all future appointments from among the graduates of the Royal Military College, he was at least able to dissuade the minister from permitting militia officers who transferred to the regular army to retain their militia rank.[20] As a result, the permanent corps were protected against an influx of unqualified part-time officers in relatively senior positions. At the same time Middleton was forcing the government to acknowledge, even if subtly, that there was a distinction to be made between the country's amateur militiamen and those who had made the army a career – a small, yet essential, step in improving the credibility of the permanent force.

But this was as much as Middleton could do during his years in Canada. In 1886, for example, his proposal to lead the infantry and cavalry school companies into the North West to manoeuvre over the ground where the field force had recently been in action was turned down. Lack of money, and fear of the popular reaction to any increase in the regulars' share of the defence budget, was one reason for this decision; but it also seems likely that the politicians wished to avoid giving any credence to the view that the permanent force might one day have a legitimate fighting role.[21] Three years later the government rejected a well-reasoned proposal to introduce a retirement and pension plan based on the British model and aimed at providing the regular officer with some reward for his services. Money again was a key consideration, but the fact that a similar scheme had recently been adopted for the North West Mounted Police made the rebuff all the more frustrating.[22]

The man who followed Middleton was made of sterner stuff. An officer of private means who had passed staff college, and who was known for his temper, Ivor Caradoc Herbert would not accept continuing decay in the militia without a struggle. But he also perceived that he could not improve the part-time force without first transforming the regular army into something that could win the respect of the country's citizen soldiers. The enormity of this task was apparent on his first tour of inspection. In British Columbia, for example, he found the drill of C Battery of artillery, formed at the Esquimalt fortress in 1887, well below the standard set for the British militia, while the school in Winnipeg was so badly organized and so poorly led that the mounted infantry were eventually amalgamated with the dragoons.[23] However, it was the state of the permanent force officer corps in general that disturbed him most. Few of those now holding senior appointments had qualified for their rank, while the majority of subalterns seemed to have been selected without regard for their 'natural fitness ... or educational qualifications.'[24] Most, indeed, had come to regard their jobs as sinecures and, prevented from undertaking realistic training, were satisfied with instructing their men to form fours and with making up regimental accounts. Lacking all 'higher sentiment of duty,' and oblivious to or ignorant of the responsibility to improve their knowledge and expertise, they exerted themselves only out of self-interest. Little wonder, Herbert concluded, that insubordination and disloyalty to superiors were so prevalent in the force.[25] When added to the stifling routine, low pay, and the high cost of buying out of the service, it was hardly surprising that the desertion rate among the other ranks sometimes approached 50 per cent.[26]

Moulded in particular by his experience in the Guards, where esprit de corps and a sense of noblesse oblige were everything, the GOC decided to transform the independent school companies into miniature regiments, in the hope that a family atmosphere might reduce petty bickering and jealous competition while fostering regimental spirit and pride in the greater whole. He also hoped that the change would permit a broadening-out of the army's training syllabus. For although the government could oppose field exercises for the scattered instructional cadres on the grounds that company-sized units did not fit conveniently into the active order of battle, it would be difficult to make the same case against complete regiments of infantry, cavalry, and artillery. Finally, Herbert reasoned that linking the dispersed and independent school companies by way of over-arching regimental headquarters would be the best way to produce uniformity in their approach to training, discipline, and administration.[27]

It was clear, however, that mere reorganization would not correct all the faults Herbert had discovered. The new regiments could easily slip back into their old routine unless something was done to reform an environment that tolerated, and even encouraged, indolence and indifference. The GOC acted quickly and decisively where he could. Concerned particularly about the under-employment of junior officers, Herbert directed that they take over the day-to-day administration of their units in order to gain experience in leadership and management. To ensure that this actually happened, he further ordered commanding officers to submit monthly reports on the progress their subordinates were making.[28] Finally, the GOC planned to use his hybrid regimental system to insist upon compulsory postings from one station to another. For he had discovered that there was a tendency to leave officers in one place, where all too often they neglected their military duties in order to make their mark in local business and social circles. Herbert eventually won his fight to create the Royal Canadian Dragoons and the Royal Regiment of Canadian Infantry (later the Royal Canadian Regiment), and he was able to institute some exchange of personnel, although never to the extent he desired.[29]

The GOC realized that these reforms would have little more than cosmetic value as long as the majority of officers remained unqualified for their appointments and yet were not forfeiting the possibility of promotion. Eager to raise standards, but aware that he dare not risk wholesale change which would threaten powerful vested interests, Herbert had struggled for some time to find an acceptable rationale for forcing these officers to qualify or retire. His solution was brilliant, and carefully couched in terms any Canadian politician would understand and respect. Having already secured a promise that all officers would eventually have to pass fitness tests, Herbert simply calculated the financial implications of waiting until they had moved up a step or two before sending them away (with the pay of their new rank) to take a course in Britain. He then posed an embarrassing question. Why should the government bear the additional expense involved if officers continued to be promoted before they were qualified when the extra funds could be used to increase drill pay for the part-time militia? The tactic worked. Although the government declared that it would not cease making provisional appointments altogether, or dispatch all unqualified officers to England immediately, those without any formal training were to attend the nine-month RMC long course as soon as possible or risk being retired.[30]

At the same time that he was demanding more of the regulars than any previous GOC, Herbert also strove to offer them more. It was only as a result of his efforts, for example, that permanent force rank was accorded a distinct place in the official table of Canadian precedence – an inconsequential achievement in practice, perhaps, but one that acknowledged further the separate status of regular army service.[31] Of more consequence was his success in convincing the government to be more generous in its provision of living allowances to married personnel for whom no suitable official quarters were available. Acting true to form, the minister rewarded political favourites first, but in time all benefited from the change.[32] Somewhat later, after having failed to persuade the government to underwrite pensions for the regulars, Herbert secured a gratuity of one year's pay for all permanent force officers upon their retirement.[33]

Herbert always justified his support for the regulars on the grounds that the permanent force had to be improved before it could serve the militia well. There were, however, many who doubted his motives. 'The latest move made by [General Hebert], viz the transformation of the School Corps into a Regiment of Regular Infantry, I confess, I do not understand,' wrote one rural militia officer, but there was definitely 'a suspicious look about them.' The new regiment appeared to be the first step toward creating a standing army which, the writer continued, was 'an evil thing ... born in sin and conceived in iniquity.'[34] Lieutenant-Colonel Davis's suspicions were undoubtedly correct. Explaining his purpose to the minister in April 1892, the GOC freely acknowledged that combining the infantry and cavalry companies into regiments would 'reflect more accurately their actual organization' because they were more than mere schools of instruction.[35] He had already intimated as much the summer before, when he brought the regular companies together under his personal command for field training at Lévis, Quebec, to show them 'what a regiment is.'[36] That this occurred in a year when militia training had been cancelled for lack of money enraged those who, like Colonel Davis, already feared the worst. But one brief manoeuvre, or even a succession of summer camps, could not produce real regiments ready for battle – there was no solid foundation upon which to build.

Herbert was also concerned that training the Canadian regulars in splendid isolation from the British army was not preparing them to defend the empire, which was the ultimate goal of the Colonial and War Offices. Accordingly, in May 1894 he proposed that the British garrison at Halifax should serve as the training centre for the permanent force just as the regulars were models for the militia. Canadian officers could 'go through the mill of regimental life' while they were still young and then proceed to the United Kingdom for courses, attachments, examinations, and manoeuvres, all of which would fit them to command Canadian forces in the field.[37] The government accepted all these recommendations, and in due course the British army once again became directly involved with training the Canadian military. More important, the Dominion had at last decreed that permanent force officers and men could legitimately aspire to be real soldiers as well as instructors to the militia.

Herbert had achieved much by the end of his tenure, but the reforms he had implemented were actually less well entrenched than he had imagined. In fact, they were products of a historical accident. The death throes of Macdonald's Liberal-Conservative coalition and the succession of administrations from

1891 had thrown up a series of militia ministers too weak or preoccupied to resist the GOC's initiatives, but such conditions would not last.[38] At the same time, so many of Herbert's reforms came at the expense of the militia that they produced an unusually hostile reaction against both the GOC and the permanent force. Led in Parliament by Sam Hughes, the newly elected member for Victoria, Ontario, the critics launched a concerted attack on the regulars, denouncing them as poor cousins of the British army that had been so badly mauled by the Boer commandos at Majuba Hill in 1881.[39]

The frailty of Herbert's program was clear within a year of his departure. Despite the threat of war with the United States over the Venezuela boundary dispute in 1896, the permanent force was reduced in strength from over 900 to 732 all ranks. At the same time the 'VRI clubs, sponsored in the regular regiments by Herbert to foster a sense of unit pride and identity, fell into disarray once his active support was withdrawn.[40] And sadder still, the interest shown by permanent force officers in attending training courses in Britain declined sharply. In short, within twelve months conditions and attitudes within the regular force were distressingly similar to what they had been before Herbert's arrival in Canada.

The irony, of course, is that such deterioration took place in an era that has been correctly identified as a period of major military reform in Canada.[41] Frederick Borden, the minister of militia in the new Liberal government, was the catalyst for this renaissance, but the ideas he brought to his portfolio did not bode well for the regulars. The Swiss concept of a national army involving the country's total male population was Borden's ideal; however, as this was far-fetched, the minister was determined at the least to see that militia training was more realistic and that the part-time force was better equipped. In this context he had no doubt about the role the permanent force should play. In total opposition to what Herbert was trying to achieve, Borden demanded that the regular regiments concentrate on providing instruction in the militia schools even if this interfered with their own training and threatened their aspirations to be 'real soldiers.' 'Let the permanent force understand that their office is to teach,' he declared; 'we have no standing army and do not need to have one.'[42]

Major-General William Gascoigne, who had replaced Herbert, believed that Borden's priorities were fundamentally wrong; an efficient militia would develop only after a strong and capable regular army had been created. But Gascoigne knew that to contest the minister on this matter so early in the game would be wholly counter-productive. Accordingly, he complied with the minister's directive without comment, and established a number of transient provisional schools across the country – schools which took men away from, and thereby weakened, the permanent force units to a greater extent than ever before. Still, Gascoigne had reason to hope. If the provisional schools persuaded militia officers of the importance of good instruction, and if the regulars did their job well, the image of the permanent force might improve. And in time Canadians might even be reconciled to the need to allow the permanent units to conduct their own training.[43] Meanwhile, the GOC found a way to exploit Borden's program to benefit the regulars. Arguing that they should work more closely with the British garrison at Halifax – ostensibly to become better teachers, but in fact so that they would obtain experience in the field – Gascoigne won approval for an exchange between the Canadian infantry at Fredericton and one company of the Berkshires. The results were gratifying. Lieutenant-Colonel George Maunsell, commanding the former, reported that the experience had been good for all concerned. Not only had the warm welcome by their British hosts raised the RCRI's sense of pride and self-esteem, but it had moved the Canadian company to greater efforts after returning to its home station. His officers and men were not only better teachers, Maunsell concluded; they were also better soldiers.[44]

Gascoigne's hopes were misplaced, however. There was only one such infantry exchange, while most of the other recommendations the GOC submitted to assist the regular force were either rejected or ignored. Borden could not be convinced to limit new officer appointments to graduates of the military college; political connections continued to influence promotions; and all requests to allow the permanent companies to conduct operational training on their own were denied. The edict that there would be no standing army was as strong as ever. Gascoigne had, in a sense, gambled and lost. He had failed to parlay his early efforts at co-operation with Borden into reforms that improved the permanent force; in fact, lacking Herbert's drive and energy, and unable to force them to believe in themselves, the GOC may have caused the regular regiments to deteriorate during his tenure.

All this was known to Major-General E.T. Hutton when he arrived to take over as general officer commanding in 1898. But where Gascoigne had blamed the Canadian political system for his lack of progress, Hutton placed responsibility squarely on the shoulders of the regular officers themselves. Despite Herbert's example, he pointed out, they had lapsed into easy-going indolence, whining about the lack of material comforts instead of getting on with the job. As a result, the new GOC made it clear that he would do nothing to improve conditions of service until the regulars accepted a 'higher standard of professional knowledge.'[45]

Hutton's ill-concealed attempt for the permanent force reflected his own military philosophy as much as it did frustration and anger with the regulars' self-induced shortcomings. For unlike both his predecessors, who aimed at building up the permanent force before anything was done for the militia, Hutton believed that a national army of citizen soldiers, well-trained, well-equipped, and well-led, was 'the true form for an army for an Anglo-Saxon state to possess.' By contrast, 'a considerable standing army was an unnecessary and unwarranted expense' and was of little use 'except for military instruction and the maintenance of law and order within the nation's domaine.'[46] Under Hutton, therefore, priority would go to the militia, while the regulars would concentrate on teaching.

It is plain to see that although their terminology differed, Borden and Hutton were saying almost the same thing, especially where the permanent force was concerned. But once the possibility arose of sending a Canadian contingent to fight the Boers in South Africa Hutton began to reconsider his position. Despite all that was wrong with them, the regulars were the most competent soldiers in his command. Accordingly, both before and after the Laurier government arrived at its painful decision to commit the Dominion to military intervention in South Africa, Hutton made every effort to ensure that, if troops were sent, the Royal Canadian Regiment, the Royal Canadian Dragoons, and the regular artillery would be among the first to see action. He also insisted that officers from these regiments receive all the senior appointments in the expeditionary force. Borden was less sure – he remained loyal to the militia as the country's first line of defence – but in the end he was persuaded despite the fierce opposition from the militia's supporters in Parliament.[47] Permanent force officers shouldered the burden of leadership in the early months of the fighting.

Not satisfied with this victory, Hutton remained convinced of the need to build a 'national army,' divorced from party politics, for the future, and it was here that he and Borden parted company. For although Borden championed reform, he still believed that politics and military service could be mixed in the militia. An open conflict with Borden over the officers selected for advanced militia training, coupled with rumours about the GOC's work behind the scenes to secure Canadian involvement in South Africa, eventually cut short Hutton's career in the Dominion, and he therefore had no opportunity to build upon the experience the regulars had gained in South Africa. However, his comments from the front after he was sent to South Africa suggest that he was pleasantly surprised by what he saw. Not only was the overall performance of the Canadian contingents more than acceptable, but the permanent force officers had done quite well indeed.[48] Accordingly, there is little doubt that had he returned to Canada and participated in the discussion of what had been learned from the war, he would have sided with those who saw the result as a victory for the

British regular army, rather than with Sam Hughes, who not only extolled the performance of the Boer commandos, but went so far as to argue that victory was possible only after the arrival of British and Dominion citizen soldiers.[49]

Borden had also become more sympathetic to the regulars after the Boer War perhaps because, following the death of his son on active service, he finally understood the ultimate risk of a military career. Victory – and the casualty lists – produced a similar reaction across the country, and the results of this conversion were soon apparent in Parliament. Where only three years before there had been outright hostility to the regulars, after 1901 there was a veritable stampede to pass legislation to improve their conditions of service. A pension scheme was introduced in 1901; rates of pay were increased the next year; and in 1903 all but the most junior officers became eligible for living allowances to offset the cost of housing when suitable government quarters were not available.[50] Even so implacable a foe as Sam Hughes was moved to support these measures, although he could not let the moment pass without reminding the Commons that the defence of Canada rested on the militia, not the permanent force.[51]

Yet if militia headquarters or the government believed that the new spirit of generosity had increased the attractiveness of a military career, they were sadly mistaken. When five vacancies in the officer corps opened up because of casualties suffered in South Africa, there was no rush to join. Not one RMC graduate was interested; and of the very few militia officers who expressed an interest most were unqualified.[52] Despite recent events, the regular force apparently still lacked the prestige and drawing power of continuous active service, army pay remained low enough to cause complaints, and the desertion rate among the other ranks was still high. The situation was likely to improve only when there was widespread acknowledgment of the regulars' claim to be Canada's military elite.

This was the goal of the next GOC, Major-General Lord Dundonald. Of much the same temperament as Hutton but more orthodox in his views, Dundonald quickly discovered the chimera in his predecessor's vision of a 'national army.' For although there was reasonable material among the militia officers and non-commissioned officers, the talent was not distributed evenly throughout the force; many units were too poorly led to even bother working with in the field. Accordingly, Dundonald chose to concentrate on leadership, on producing good officers and NCOs, and to worry about the men later.[53] The process would take longer than Hutton had forecast, but in time Dundonald was convinced that he could create a one-hundred-thousand-man army of which Canada would be proud.

Everything depended on the availability of a highly trained and motivated instructional staff and this, to Dundonald, meant a regular force trained and educated to British standards. It is Dundonald, therefore, who may be regarded as the father of Canada's first systematic – and lasting – program of officer education. As a first step he directed the commanding officers of the Royal Canadian Regiment and the Royal Canadian Dragoons to send all their unqualified subordinates to the next RMC long course without fail.[54] Then he worked out rigid criteria for future officer appointments in the regular army: graduates of the Royal Military College would have first priority, then those who had attended university and finished the militia long course, and finally those who had qualified for a commission in the militia. But anyone who had not attended RMC would be on probation for five years, and their performance would be judged by both the commandant of the military college and the GOC.[55] The intention was that ultimately no one 'not in every way eligible for a commission in Her Majesty's Army' would be accepted into Canadian service.[56]

That was the first step in Dundonald's master plan. To ensure that officers could not rest on their pre-commissioning laurels, he also insisted that they write the British army's examinations for promotion to captain and each step in rank thereafter, including a trip to the United Kingdom to take the 'Tactical Fitness for Command' test before their appointment at the lieutenant-colonel level. Furthermore, any officer still serving who had not earned an RMC diploma or a long course certificate would be ineligible for promotion beyond his current rank whether or not he had seen service in South Africa.[57] This was harsh, but the GOC was determined to set standards that prevented any deviation from the merit principle.

Borden accepted all of Dundonald's recommendations, adding at the same time that while he still considered the militia to be fertile and legitimate soil for patronage, he would not tolerate the same kind of behaviour from or attitude to the permanent force. At the Militia Council meeting of 27 April 1905, for example, he announced that he would henceforth invoke the War Office regulation which treated letters seeking favours for individual regular officers as if they had been written by the officer himself – and therefore as prejudicial to his career.[58] Subsequently he increased the size of the permanent force to three thousand, raised its pay schedule to bring it in line with that of the mounted police, and then promised the regulars time to conduct their own training.[59] These were important steps, and the fact that they reflected the minister's sincere and genuine interest in the well-being of the permanent force was proved three years later. Told by the finance minister that he must reduce defence expenditures by one million dollars, Borden accepted the advice of his military staff without complaint and slashed the militia's drill pay while leaving the regulars' training budget as it was.[60]

This was an act of political courage in return for which Borden demanded loyalty – to himself, and to the students at the country's military schools. Little wonder, therefore, that he was so bitter when he received complaints that the regulars were showing no interest whatsoever in instructing officers of the militia. In his view such apathy was a betrayal of the bargain he had struck with Dundonald to offer the permanent schools more scope to develop as a professional fighting force. His anger showed in the circular letter he caused to be read to all regular officers in February 1906. Reminded that their future was 'indissoluably bound up with the ... Active Militia,' they were warned against any tendency to regard their responsibilities to the citizen force as secondary to the interests of their own regiments. Instead they were to offer the best possible instruction to the volunteers, and to offer it gladly. As an inducement to do so, Borden announced that the annual evaluation of an officer's professional abilities would henceforth be determined primarily by his performance as a teacher.[61]

Dundonald had left Canada by this time, recalled to England because of an indiscreet public challenge to appointments within the militia,[62] but Major-General Percy Lake, his successor as head of the Canadian army, was no more prepared to sacrifice regular army routine for teaching. Accordingly, despite Borden's unambiguous instructions to the contrary, Lake directed the commander of the Western Ontario district, Colonel Otter, to experiment with the British army's new, incremental, training syllabus, which would keep his men busy in individual, platoon, and company drill from October to May, and culminate in a six-week tactical concentration in the field during the summer. Militia training would be fitted into this timetable, not the reverse, and at no time would the RCR interrupt its schedule to accommodate the needs of the volunteers.[63]

These instructions created the obvious impression that militia training was an unwanted intrusion into regular army routine that had to be tolerated for political reasons alone. They also seemed to reinforce the regulars' sense of superiority over the citizen army, an élitist sentiment with which the minister had little sympathy. The regulars were different, Borden admitted, but they should not boast about it. Lake therefore justified his action on the grounds that it was intended to make better teachers of the permanent corps, a dubious rationale at best, yet perhaps because he found the general so congenial and co-operative in other areas, Borden was charitable in this instance, and allowed Otter to proceed. But when he received another deluge of complaints about the way the regulars were shirking their responsibilities to the militia in 1911, his response was immediate and stern: there would be no second chance for officers found guilty of neglect this time.[64]

This episode illustrated the fact that despite the best of good will on both sides – and the most harmonious relationship ever to exist between a Canadian militia minister and his senior military adviser – a fundamental contradiction existed in the roles set out for the permanent force. So long as the regulars were prohibited from training for battle they were in a poor position to offer good training to the militia; yet whenever the regulars were granted permission to exercise in the field they inevitably began to think of themselves as an embryonic standing army that had better things to do than instruct part-time soldiers. Resentment was bound to grow, especially if the regulars continued to view militiamen as rank amateurs unworthy to command in the field or, like Colonel J. Wilson, complained that militia officers were 'not gentlemen, [had] no gentlemanly instincts, and never could be made to act and feel like gentlemen.'[65] For their part, militia officers persisted in exploiting their political power to thwart the ambitions of the regular force and to challenge its credibility in the classroom and in the field. Frustrated by this pressure, compelled by Borden's two warnings to give higher priority to teaching, and still yearning to soldier, the permanent force mastered no task well.

The answer to the conundrum was worked out, curiously enough, by Major-General Colin Mackenzie, a dour and somewhat unsympathetic Scot who spent the better part of his three years (1910–13) as Canada's senior soldier writing bitter denunciations to the governor general and the War Office about the treatment he was receiving. Seeing at once that the regulars would never improve as long as they maintained a dual identity, Mackenzie put forward the simplest of solutions: divide the permanent force into two parts, designating one as an instructional cadre whose sole duty would be to work with the militia, and allowing the other to adhere to Percy Lake's training regimen as an embryonic professional, standing army.[66] Borden agreed, and the positive effect was apparent within months. Morale in the militia schools improved dramatically, and with it the teaching, because the instructional staff knew that subsequent postings would eventually let them train as real soldiers. The regular companies, meanwhile, enjoyed the freedom to prepare for battle without the administrative and other distractions of running a school.[67]

The compromise worked out between Mackenzie and Borden survived as the basis of permanent force organization for thirty-five years. Of course, it was not a perfect solution. There were no guarantees that the 'combat' element of the standing army would be large or adequately equipped, that its training would be realistic, or that all regular force officers would make the most of their opportunities. And as we shall see, there was nothing to prevent individual ministers from reviving the practice of political favouritism in appointments and promotions, or from consciously setting the militia against the permanent force. Still, when combined with the pay increases, the pension plan, the strict qualification standards introduced during Dundonald's tenure, and the growing tendency to appoint junior officers from among the graduates of the Royal Military College – a group of young men who, in the old-fashioned sense, desired only to serve – these latest measures provided the diligent officer with a much better environment in which to learn his job. This was essential if a true profession of arms was ever to be realized in Canada.

PART II

MILITARY PLANNING AND CIVIL-MILITARY
RELATIONS, 1860–1914

3

Politics, planning, and the staff, 1860–1898

Colonel George Taylor Denison was anxious, impatient, and more than a little angry on 2 June 1866. He had waited for forty-eight hours to receive the call ordering his Toronto regiment of cavalry to join the Canadian infantry already on the move against the Irish-American Fenians who had established themselves on the north shore of Lake Erie the day before – the first step in their campaign to liberate British North America from imperial rule. When his unit finally left for the front, too late to participate in the battle of Ridgeway, it marched without adequate food, fodder, arms, or ammunition. Despite the fact that ten thousand men had been called out only a few months before and stationed along the American frontier to guard against just such an eventuality, by June neither the government nor the military authorities were ready to meet the sudden crisis with anything beyond improvised measures and hastily drawn-up plans. In fact, the militia could not even be furnished with accurate maps of their intended area of operations.[1]

Had the Fenians hesitated for a few months before launching their attack, or simply tried again, they would have faced a quite different opponent, for planning had just begun to place the colonial military forces on a sounder war footing. Colonel Patrick MacDougall, a British staff college graduate, had arrived at militia headquarters in Ottawa a few months before. Based on his experience as an observer during the American Civil War, he was convinced of the need for extensive mobilization planning if Canada ever hoped to overcome the very considerable advantages the United States would enjoy in the event of war.[2]

What MacDougall found upon taking up his appointment as adjutant general of the militia was scarcely inspiring. Although a headquarters staff had been established by the Militia Act of 1855, it amounted to very little. Operational planning, it was thought, was the responsibility of the commander of the

British garrison in North America, as were all measures for the supply of the field army, and as a result the handful of officers who served in Ottawa spent their time counting heads, weapons, and uniforms. They did not concern themselves with providing the militia with mobilization stores, victualling arrangements, transport, or maps so that it could move to the front quickly and efficiently.[3]

Fear of attack by the North during the American Civil War convinced John A. Macdonald that the Canadian military system was inadequate. Following the advice of Colonel Daniel Lysons, a British officer sent to Canada as a surrogate adjutant general in 1862, the government speeded up the process of forming volunteer battalions, but only a few steps had been taken to increase Canada's military potential before MacDougall's appointment. Of these perhaps the most important was the division of the country into a number of military districts and the posting of staff officers, many with British experience, to each of the district headquarters to assist the local regiments, to pass on Ottawa's mobilization instructions, and to administer the militia whenever it arrived in its concentration areas.

The creation of the military districts and their subordinate headquarters gave Canada the potential for a well-ordered and decentralized mobilization and command structure, but it was not used as such. The districts had, in fact, been designed primarily for geographic or demographic convenience, and so neglected to group the militia and volunteer units according to their likely wartime employment. It was not considered important, for example, that each district should have a reasonable mix of all the combat arms or that it be linked in any way to the British formation in the area. Furthermore, the district headquarters and staffs were given no command responsibilities. These were left to the senior British officer on the spot who, as a result, would have to sort out what colonial forces were available and how they should be grouped while he was managing the initial skirmish battles on the frontier. It was, in short, a cumbersome organization that did little to add to Canada's military preparedness and much to disgruntle the militia.[4]

MacDougall's appointment as adjutant general was made to meet British criticism that Canada was doing too little for its own defence, but the decision to pay the salary of one officer was not much of a commitment. Canada continued to maintain the skeleton, but not the body, of an army, and it would be stretching things to say that MacDougall's arrival added significant amounts of flesh. Still, in some respects MacDougall was fortunate to be working in such an amorphous environment. The militia department was as yet primitively organized, with only the smallest civilian bureaucracy, and no deputy minister stood between the adjutant general and his minister. MacDougall's access to the government was therefore direct and total. At the same time the military establishment at headquarters was small and inexperienced, and thus was in no position to challenge his advice from within. But the price of this freedom was high: a mountain of purely administrative work MacDougall had to tend to himself, at the expense of the concentrated and detailed strategic and tactical studies he insisted upon before any mobilization plans could be drafted. Moreover, the government soon gave notice that its commitment to improve Canada's military capabilities had indeed been limited at the time of MacDougall's appointment. When he asked for additional staff to ease his workload his requests were denied, while his warnings about American military might were dismissed by the premier. Since the Union army had been demobilized without marching on Canada, Macdonald explained, there would be several years of peace in North America, and because of that the colony could afford to be patient and to embark upon a 'gradual and systematic' improvement of its forces that would allow any additional expenses to be amortized over a number of years.[5]

Macdonald's optimistic forecast was upset when rumours of possible Fenian activity against Canada began to circulate late in 1865. Precautions had to be taken to reassure public opinion, and nine companies of militia were eventually called out for full-time service on the country's southern border. Amazed at the government's reaction to such a minor threat, MacDougall attempted to exploit the atmosphere of fear and doubt. Canada could never be considered entirely secure, he declared, until there was a mobilization plan specifying the militia's likely theatres of operations. Still somewhat jittery, the government agreed in January 1866 that such a defence scheme should be produced, but for the moment it offered to finance a smaller headquarters staff than MacDougall had requested to assist him in his work.[6]

The Fenian attack on Fort Erie and the subsequent action at Ridgeway occurred just as MacDougall began to organize his staff, but the lessons learned from this minor skirmish confirmed all that he had been saying about the importance of mobilization planning and stockpiling arms and ammunition. In addition, the problems encountered in co-ordinating the action of the several volunteer battalions involved and the local British troops gave ample evidence that units likely to serve together in battle should train together beforehand. The adjutant general built solidly and methodically. After further hastening the organization of volunteer battalions he directed that the best of them should be brought together with the British regiments in their region to form joint brigades, both for training and operational purposes, the idea being to stiffen the performance of the citizen militia if it ever faced the American army. Just as important, however, British officers would know long before they went into action what frustrations and uncertainties were likely to arise from working with colonial troops. Canadian units not allocated to the field army were organized into separate district brigades and given the task of protecting lines of communication and supply and guarding the province's vital points. Drafts of the plan were ready by the spring of 1867, but with proposals for the confederation of the British North American colonies under discussion this was an inopportune moment for the government to embark upon a large procurement program. MacDougall's advice to purchase weapons, ammunition, and other mobilization stores was, accordingly, never taken up.[7]

Confederation undercut the adjutant general's plans further. Convinced that the United States itself posed no threat, relieved by the apparent demise of the militant Fenian movement in the United States, and still hoping that the British would be persuaded to keep their troops in the Dominion, Macdonald's government adopted a rather loose military framework in its 1868 Militia Act. The new legislation shifted emphasis to the volunteer force (and away from the militia levée en masse upon which MacDougall had based his manpower calculations), but the government's first budget provided little in the way of weapons and equipment for the volunteers.[8] Nor was the headquarters staff enlarged sufficiently, in MacDougall's view, to meet the obligations of administering the country's larger territory. Disillusioned by the politicians' attitudes, and sure that he had achieved all that he could, MacDougall asked to be relieved of his appointment. He returned to England in 1869, where he promptly launched a campaign to reform the British army so that it would be better prepared for war.[9]

The small planning staff at headquarters did not survive MacDougall's departure. In the military districts, meanwhile, the officers appointed over the previous few years were left in place, but were charged now with purely administrative tasks. Without benefit of the former adjutant general's drive and direction, most failed to keep his contingency plan up to date, so that none of the schemes were modified to take into account the additional volunteer battalions then being raised. In addition, reconnaissance of likely battlefields, supply routes, and vital points – all regular activity in MacDougall's day – ceased completely, as did the tallying of stores that would be required in an emergency. In their place came ceremonial parades and rigid, overly theatrical sham battles on convenient fields and commons.

Beyond this, the 1868 legislation adopted a bureaucratic organization for the Department of Militia and Defence that not only threatened the professional independence MacDougall had enjoyed, but also created a potential rival power base. Adhering to standard practice, a civil branch was established under a deputy minister to look after all accounts, monitor expenditures, supervise contracts, and take custody of the departmental's real property and buildings. All this was essential to sound management and administration, but the powers of the deputy minister had been defined so broadly that he could also claim authority over military administration and the procurement of military stores of all kinds. This seemed wrong to thoughtful men in uniform, who believed that the selection, acquisition, and safe storage of arms and ammunition should belong to the military side of the department. Conflict between the deputy minister and the senior officers at headquarters was not inevitable because of this arrangement, but it was more likely. Similarly, the powers of the minister were extensive, particularly because the militia lacked a corporate head. The adjutant general was, by definition, an administrative officer, not a commander with executive authority. Confederation had removed the British garrison one step from the Dominion's chain of command so there was no one at headquarters other than the political head of the department to take charge in a crisis.

Still, it was the withdrawal of the last imperial garrisons from all North American stations except Halifax in 1871 that dealt the mortal blow to MacDougall's system. He had counted on the presence of regular troops, at least for the short term, to bolster the local militia, to provide effective military leadership, and above all to support his efforts to build an efficient headquarters organization against the day when Canada could become reasonably self-sufficient in matters of defence. But from 1871 there would be no British force in the interior, no supply service to fall back on, and no command structure ready to be superimposed on the skeletal militia framework in the event of war. Before they left, therefore, the British generals implored the Canadian government to appoint a regular officer to command the militia and to provide him and the several district headquarters with experienced officers who could formulate war plans. That would enable the adjutant general to concentrate on administration and to set about organizing a military supply system capable of supporting the Canadian army when it took the field. This was the single most important requirement for Canada to defend itself, the British officer commanding at Halifax told the secretary of state for war, and it was the one piece of advice the imperial government must repeat time and again.[10]

Major-General Lindsay's recommendations were ignored in Ottawa. Convinced that American intentions towards Canada were entirely peaceful, the government understood the Treaty of Washington, signed before the British garrisons left, to mean that Anglo-U.S. relations would remain good for the foreseeable future. The politicians were therefore reluctant to increase the country's defence expenditures, particularly if the money was to be used for something as hidden from public view and as poorly understood as a headquarters staff. Besides, far better political capital could be made by providing directly for the militia in the form of drill pay, uniforms, and rifles. Yet even such relatively popular expenses became too much of a burden when the economy fell into severe depression in the mid-1870s.[11]

One of the suggestions put forward by Lindsay and MacDougall was eventually taken up, however, when in 1874 the Canadian government finally realized that the militia required a general officer commanding to supplement the purely administrative branch of the staff headed by the adjutant general. The British had long maintained that their general at Halifax would best fill the new appointment because he would unite the Dominion and imperial commands in North America, but this was unacceptable in Ottawa. The government did not want to be bothered by overly 'exuberant' British officers who might ask too much of the Dominion; and, as Governor General Lord Lisgar reported, some Canadian politicians were unhappy with the prospect of an imperial soldier being named administrator of Canada during the governor general's absence from the country.[12]

As it was, the Canadian minister, Sir George Etienne Cartier, already had someone in mind when he raised the issue of appointing a GOC; Colonel P. Robertson-Ross, MacDougall's successor as adjutant general, had proved popular with the government because he accepted its way of doing things. Unfortunately, the War Office considered him to be far too mediocre for the appointment and quickly made its objections known to Ottawa. When Cartier persisted, the British simply stalled for time, all the while searching for alternatives, until the Canadian minister became so aggravated that he began to question the Dominion's need for a general officer commanding in the first place. At that point the governor general intervened on Robertson-Ross's behalf because, he explained, the Canadians had behaved well over the Treaty of Washington despite having to share their fisheries with the United States. Moreover, he declared, the British had no legitimate grounds for 'holding out' against Canadian wishes.[13] A mediocre GOC was apparently better than no GOC at all.

Lisgar's arguments failed to move the British government, but further embarrassment was saved by Robertson-Ross himself when he resigned following Cartier's death in 1873. Once the search to find a regular officer willing to replace him as adjutant general in Canada proved fruitless (word had spread that this was a thankless, and hopeless, job), all sides agreed that the next appointment should be as GOC. Sir Edward Selby Smyth was gazetted as such when he arrived in Canada in 1875.

The appointment of a general officer commanding was a change in both form and substance. For the first time Canada had its own fully formed chain of command extending from the governor general (as nominal commander-in-chief) through the minister, cabinet, and Parliament to the GOC and thence to the regiments and battalions of the militia. The British would be involved only in the event of war, when it was assumed that their general officer at Halifax would carry overall responsibility for co-ordinating the defence of the Dominion. Furthermore, for the first time the country's senior military officer would be freed from the day-to-day burden of administration in order to concentrate on improving the militia's readiness for war.

But this reorganization also carried with it the seeds of a fundamental clash between the army and its political masters that was already brewing in the United Kingdom. There the problem was with the Duke of Cambridge, who argued that because he had been appointed commander-in-chief of the British army by his cousin, the Queen, her exercise of the royal prerogative gave him absolute and exclusive jurisdiction over matters of purely professional, military concern. Taken to the extreme, this meant that no civilian, including the secretary of state for war, should interfere in the army's affairs once its budget had been passed by Parliament. Instead, it was up to the army's senior officers – those with the requisite knowledge, training, and experience – to decide such things.

The politicians, of course, preached a contrary doctrine. Parliament, not the monarch, was supreme, even over military affairs, they contended, and ministers carried ultimate responsibility for all military policies. This gave them the right and duty to speak to any issue concerning the army. To do as the Duke of Cambridge suggested would make the army a law unto itself, a development that did not fit British constitutional practice.

Both arguments had merit. The government had the legitimate right to make policy and ensure that the high command carried it out, while the soldiers were not being disloyal if they merely wanted to protect the army against unfortunate and harmful meddling by civilian amateurs. The problem was to find a way to integrate these different points of view; but intransigence from both quarters between 1870 and the early 1900s produced an atmosphere of distrust which poisoned the civil-military relationship, and impeded the implementation of much-needed army reform. Every time there was a call for the modernization of the British army along Prussian-German lines the politicians responded with alarm, warning that a 'war cult' would result if the soldiers were rewarded with anything like the independent status accorded the German general staff. Although these fears were exaggerated, the campaign for army reform was inexorably linked to a military assault on cherished constitutional principles. For their part, the soldiers seemed unable to understand that the German military system they admired so much was incompatible with parliamentary responsibility, and as a result mistook the politicians' cautious approach to military reform as signifying their desire to subordinate military policy to the less-than-honourable dictates of party politics.[14]

The potential for this kind of civil-military conflict existed in Canada before 1875 simply because the country adhered to the principle of ministerial responsibility to Parliament; but it was muted somewhat because the adjutant general had no justification for asserting that he should enjoy the panoply of rights and privileges claimed by the Duke of Cambridge. But once a GOC had been appointed, Lord Dufferin warned the Colonial Office, a case could be made that his status corresponded to that of the duke. When that happened, and the GOC acted independently of his minister, the civil-military relationship in Canada was sure to deteriorate.[15]

It did, largely because of the conflicting demands made on the GOC by the British and Canadian governments which divided his loyalties. The view from London was clear and consistent. The splendid isolation Britain had enjoyed earlier in the century was a thing of the past, not only because new technology had increased the United Kingdom's vulnerability to attack but also because strong rivals had emerged to threaten imperial interests around the world. Britain could no longer afford to subsidize the defence of the Dominion, and the GOCs were instructed to bring pressure on successive Canadian administrations to support a substantially larger military establishment, including a small regular army. Canadians, on the other hand, argued that Britain alone could bring war to North America. Accordingly, the imperial commitment to defend the Dominion remained as valid as ever, and British responsibility to pay for this defence was no less fixed. The volunteer militia was considered adequate to the country's requirements under these circumstances, while the concept of a standing army remained, for the time being, an anathema. From Ottawa, then, the GOCs were being directed to do what they could with the existing volunteer force without upsetting its fundamental organization and traditions, and without making excessive demands on the Canadian treasury.

Although the creation of a regular army was obviously out of the question, Selby Smyth saw that something might be done to improve the work of the district and headquarters staffs. These had long been one of the weakest links in Canada's military organization, not the least because they were convenient outlets for patronage at a level where, on a day-to-day basis, incompetence was not visible to the public eye. Even previous military experience was not required before men were appointed to these positions. Lieutenant-Colonel A.C. de Lotbinière Harwood, deputy adjutant general at Montreal, had not seen a day's service before taking up his post, and he was by no means an exception.[16] The result of such inexperience was predictable. Intelligence and administrative reports arrived late; mobilization plans drafted in the 1860s were left unrevised; and militia inspections were carried out half-heartedly and uncritically.[17]

Robertson-Ross was aware of all this, but chose to ignore it: one reason Cartier admired him so much.[18] Selby Smyth was less accommodating, however, and urged the government to rid itself of the incompetent staff officers before the Dominion had to rely on them to organize the defence of their districts. Sensitive to Canadian concerns, he asked that the government avail itself of a British offer to provide experienced staff officers, but only until the Dominion could train its own. To this end he advocated the creation of a higher military school to produce 'a scientific class of officers' fit for all senior militia appointments.[19] Alexander Mackenzie believed that he had done precisely that when he authorized the establishment of the Royal Military College of Canada at Kingston, but the prime minister was asking too much of an institution whose primary task was to graduate subalterns. Selby Smyth therefore continued to press for the creation of a genuine staff college and, in the meantime, to add to the experience of staff officers already on strength by giving them appropriate responsibilities during the militia's summer camps. The government agreed, but when these camps fell victim to the austerity program of 1875 this opportunity for staff training disappeared.

In the end, Selby Smyth's lasting achievement was to comb out the most useless district staff officers, yet even this victory was more than a little hollow. Most who were released were Tories, a fact that enabled Alexander Mackenzie's administration to boast about the way in which it was reducing expenditures while punishing its political opponents at the same time.[20] However, the prime minister had no intention of replacing those he let go with more qualified men – or even with Liberals. As a result, the country's military staff organization became too small to cope with routine administration, let alone to oversee the preparation of a comprehensive mobilization plan. The desire for economy, faith that Britain continued to be the ultimate guarantor of Canadian security, and the assumption that the existing militia framework was sufficient to hold off the Americans during the first crucial weeks of war convinced politicians from both sides of the House that military reform was a luxury.

This sense of complacency was undermined in 1878 by the threat of an Anglo-Russian war. With the steamer *Cimbria* rumoured to be just off the Atlantic coast, ready to disembark its Russian marines at a moment's notice, the Dominion seemed for the first time to face the threat of invasion from an overseas power. Concerned about the safety of Canadian ports, Alexander Mackenzie asked the Admiralty to station cruisers in the St Lawrence River and then, without fully comprehending the costs, undertook to set up coastal artillery batteries. 'We will not ask the Imperial government for anything,' he wrote to the governor general, 'as we think Canada should have, and does have, pride enough to be above shirking her duty in providing for the defence of her coasts.' One hundred and fifty thousand dollars were allocated to the project.[21]

As it turned out, the Russian crisis subsided before substantial sums were spent, and Selby Smyth extracted only a promise on the government's part to buy heavy artillery to defend the Maritimes. He then went home, his tour of duty over. Although little had been accomplished as a result of the recent scare, Selby Smyth's successor sensed that attitudes had changed, and that this change could be exploited. Applauding the government's efforts to protect the country's east coast harbours, General Luard nevertheless passed word to the adjutant general that plans to improve coastal defences would be incomplete without a broader survey of the Dominion's defences.[22] The preliminary report of a British fortifications expert sent to Canada at the same time arrived at conveniently similar conclusions and, with Luard's blessing, emphasized the importance of employing trained staff officers to undertake the studies upon which a thorough war plan would be based.[23] The GOC returned to this theme repeatedly over the ensuing months until there were rumours that a quartermaster general (QMG) – the officer responsible for military planning in those days – would be added to the headquarters staff. Indeed, in April 1883 the minister of militia went so far as to raise the issue in Parliament, explaining that the appointment of a QMG was under serious consideration because he was 'one of the most important staff officers required.'[24] Luard was ecstatic.

Yet within five months the way to the new appointment was blocked, apparently to punish Luard for challenging Caron's authority. The affair began innocently enough. Knowing that both he and the adjutant general would be away from headquarters at the same time during the summer, Luard made the customary arrangements for the next senior officer, Director of Artillery Lieutenant-Colonel de la T. Irwin, to exercise temporary command during their absence. Unknown to Luard, however, Caron had promised the job to the adjutant general's clerk, a civilian friend who was entirely outside the military chain of command. Having had no forewarning of Caron's intentions, Luard was astounded to discover, upon his return to Ottawa, that a clerk who was not even in the army, much less a senior officer, had been issuing orders to Colonel Irwin on a whole range of military matters the GOC believed to be beyond the competence of the minister himself.

Luard immediately went on the offensive, condemning this encroachment into the military sphere by a civilian bureaucrat. One such attack on Caron's lack of judgment and propriety was bad enough, but the GOC did not stop there. He continued to criticize the minister and, on one occasion, unwisely made reference to Caron's lamentable conduct as one of the major reasons justifying the appointment of a quartermaster general. For once this position had been filled, Luard pointed out, there would be no mistaking who should command the militia if the GOC and AG were again absent from headquarters at the same time: the QMG would be unmistakably third in line. Caron cooled to the idea of bringing in the new staff officer within days of receiving this memorandum, offering the excuse that it was impossible to overcome parliamentary opposition to the proposed appointment. This was less than honest, and Luard knew it. Caron had carried the day in the Commons' debate on the question some months before; the number of members opposed to it had not increased; and nothing stood in the minister's way if his desire to move ahead was genuine. As it was, the appointment of a QMG was postponed for thirteen years.[25] Luard, unrepentant and unforgiving, meanwhile lost what little political support he had with a foolish attack on Canadian parliamentary procedures, and resigned his appointment in March 1884.

A semblance of harmony returned to the militia department with the arrival of General Middleton the next year. Content to be a 'complacent placeman,'[26] Middleton did nothing when Caron ignored persistent requests from the War Office for the information required to allow the British army to plan for the defence of Canada. Any and all protest was left to the governor general.[27] Compliance of this sort made the GOC's life easier than it might otherwise have been, but Caron's insistence that he enjoyed a kind of ultramontane omnipotence as minister nevertheless rankled. So did the obvious incompetence of the Canadian staff. Lieutenant-Colonel John Gray, Otter's brigade major in Toronto, had been appointed to save him from bankruptcy, but was no better at soldiering than he had been in business.[28] Perhaps because he had proved cooperative in other areas, Middleton eventually won concessions on this touchy personal matter, and persuaded Caron to place several of the military districts under the commandant of the local military school. In this way a handful of older and generally useless officers were dismissed without running the risk that they would be replaced by still more of the minister's militia cronies.[29]

Whether Middleton could have achieved better results by pursuing a more forceful line with Caron is none the less doubtful. The rebellion in the Northwest rekindled interest in defence, it is true, but only for a while. Once Riel's forces had been defeated with such apparent ease the minister and cabinet reverted to form. From the evidence it seemed that the country's militia was adequate after all, and that further reform, especially as it related to the permanent force, was not required. This was, of course, a blow to whatever aspirations the War Office had for the Canadian army. Beyond that, however, Dominion politicians remained jealous of their position, and more than a little suspicious of imperial efforts to exercise centralized control over defence from London. As a result, any GOC who campaigned for too many changes in the Dominion's military organization and pushed too strongly the merits of the permanent force and headquarters planning staff was on dangerous ground, especially when such initiatives were regarded as serving imperial rather than Canadian interests.

Some modification of this self-satisfied and complacent attitude was probably inevitable over time, but left to its own devices – and as long as the Americans posed no direct threat – Canada might have taken decades to acquire the trappings of a modern military establishment. However, Britain's continuing concern about the state of Canada's defences, the Colonial Office's desire to co-ordinate a common imperial foreign policy, and the struggle for army reform and professional independence within the British army, all influenced the pace of change in Canada. Motivated by developments at home, the generals sent to command the militia in the 1890s could not be satisfied with a series of small, symbolic victories, or place great faith in vague promises about the future. For them it was already time for action.

Major-General Ivor Caradoc Herbert arrived in Canada in November 1890 bristling with ideas on how to improve the Canadian militia. Having studied the Franco-Prussian War, he had learned the importance of mobilization planning and was determined that, by the end of his term, the Dominion would have an army capable of going to war at short notice, and in good order. Herbert was also intensely loyal to Sir Garnet Wolseley's campaign to establish a professional army enjoying considerable independence from political control, and so believed that there were times when soldiers must stand up to their political masters. Finally, he embraced wholeheartedly the Colonial Office's goal of knitting the armed forces of the Dominion so securely into the fabric of imperial defence that Canadian soldiers could be counted upon to come to the aid of the empire wherever and whenever it was threatened.[30] All of these programs were certain to upset Canadian authorities, but in 1890 one of them had unmistakable priority. Arriving in Ottawa just as Sir Henry Campbell-Bannerman, the British secretary of state for war, was attempting to curtail the authority of the British commander-in-chief, Herbert decided that he must win the parallel civil-military battle in Canada. For if he emerged victorious, and secured general recognition of the army's professional independence, the GOC was convinced that all else would fall in place.

The assault began soon after Herbert took up his appointment. In concert with the governor general, Lord Stanley, he attacked 'the custom which has grown up without written authority'[31] that required the GOC to seek out ministerial approval for every decision or action he wanted to take, no matter how minor or technical. This so encumbered the minister in petty detail and day-to-day administration, Herbert claimed, that he was unable to give appropriate care and attention to more substantive questions, or even to implement policies already approved by Parliament. Of course, Herbert was really concerned with the minister's intimate involvement in militia affairs and the way it prolonged the problem of political interference in areas which were more properly of purely professional interest; however neither Herbert nor Lord Stanley was foolish enough to admit this so early in the game. Matters of high policy were being neglected inadvertently, they said, and that was what worried them most.

Caron, who was no fool and who also enjoyed the support of his colleagues in cabinet, rejected these arguments out of hand, holding fast to a definition of ministerial prerogative that gave him the right to be heard and to issue orders as he saw fit on any or all matters coming before him. Under normal circumstances Caron's response should have called a halt to Herbert's efforts. The minister was so obviously upset that nothing was to be gained from proceeding further. But fate intervened to offer Herbert a second opportunity to speak and, moreover, to do so outside the confines of the minister's office.

In January 1892 the general officer commanding was called upon in his capacity as a senior departmental official to testify before a royal commission investigating administration in the public service as a whole. There, at least, he could seek a wider audience for his point of view, and perhaps generate external pressures that might force Caron to relent. Then, two days before he was scheduled to take the stand, Herbert received even better news. Caron had been transferred to the post office portfolio, leaving the GOC in the enviable and lucky position of making his case to a new minister, Mackenzie Bowell, in a public forum practically the moment the latter took up his appointment.

Following much the same line as he had with Caron, Herbert complained about the 'most complete ... centralization' in the militia department, and singled out for special comment the unnecessary exercise of '*personal ministerial authority*' when, in fact, '*parliamentary authority*' and 'standing regulations' already approved were sufficient to allow the general officer commanding to act in his own right. He added, albeit less than honestly, that no such authority was ever demanded by the secretary of state for war in Great Britain, yet no one could argue that civilian authority over the military was not 'rigorously maintained' there. Herbert then turned to the powers of the deputy minister and to the way they encroached upon the military realm through his control of mobilization stores, munitions, and the engineering branch – all of which, Herbert contended, belonged in the GOC's chain of command.[32] To be sure that Bowell missed nothing, Lord Stanley followed with similar advice three weeks later. There was no response.[33]

Mackenzie Bowell left the militia department that December, handing over to J.C. Patterson, a lazy man generally content to leave most of the work in Herbert's hands. This was a glorious opportunity to establish a new 'custom' in the militia giving more control to the GOC, but cold, hard political reality soon upset Herbert's calculations. Having had some difficulty controlling Colonel Walker Powell, still adjutant general, because of his long tenure and his brief interlude as acting GOC following Middleton's departure, Herbert seized upon a slight indiscretion on the old colonel's part – he had dealt directly with the minister – and dismissed him as being of no further use to the service.[34]

He should have known better. Walker Powell fought back tenaciously, employing every weapon available to retrieve his position. He appealed first to his Tory friends, and they came to his defence in droves, no doubt in part because they feared Powell would make good his threat to expose Adolphe Caron's plundering of the 1891 militia budget to finance that year's general election.[35] This was probably sufficient for the specific problem at hand, but looking to the future Powell also complained about Herbert's efforts to define the limits of the adjutant general's authority, a timely argument now that the adjutant general in England had recently been awarded additional rights and responsibilities at the expense of the commander-in-chief. Among these was the right of direct access to the army's political head, the very 'crime' for which Walker Powell was being punished.[36]

The GOC responded articulately enough, and easily dismissed the recent change in British practice as something that would not last; but lacking friends and influence the outcome was inevitable. Colonel Powell was reinstated, and his freedom to deal with the minister on his own was confirmed. Prepared to quit at once, Herbert in the end chose to remain to complete his term and protect the progress he had made. But, like Luard, he too forfeited what influence he had when, taking advantage of Patterson's ineptness, he committed Canada to reinforcing Britain's garrison at Hong Kong. Although the Dominion's offer was refused, the government's disenchantment with Herbert was complete, and he spent the last months of his term in England, convinced that friction within the department would stifle all further reform unless the general officer commanding's authority was clearly defined and broadly based.[37] He was right. For the next few years an officer at headquarters, Colonel Percy Lake, was routinely protesting the fact that political interference and lack of co-operation amongst the staff had reached the stage where little planning could be undertaken, and no plan was likely to be accepted.[38]

As it was, the fact that Colonel Lake was in Canada to voice these complaints in the first place was Herbert's greatest triumph. Although he had always maintained that settling the civil-military problem in the country was an essential precondition before a satisfactory environment for strategic planning could ever exist, he had not ignored the planning issue. When he discovered that Caron had merely suspended the deliberations of the Canadian Defence Committee in 1888 – formed to gather military information for the War Office – instead of cancelling them altogether, Herbert asked when the forum would be reopened and whether the revived CDC might be given specific terms of reference so that it could draft a comprehensive defence scheme for the country.[39] Caron, as might be expected, did nothing, but Herbert pursued the matter with Bowell and Patterson, asking that the defence committee be reconvened at the earliest moment possible.

His memoranda included a request for additional staff officers, to be brought over from Britain, to support the work of the defence committee; experience with Colonel Walker Powell and others had convinced him that he could not trust Canadians to do the job effectively or loyally. Still, Herbert had grown more sensitive. Although his private correspondence is full of adjectives like 'useless,' 'obstructive,' and 'worse than nothing'[40] to describe those working for him, his briefs to Bowell and Patterson carefully avoided all such characterizations. Instead, the GOC explained that public disinterest in defence had simply led the Canadian staff to perform its duties 'in a perfunctory manner.' No blame could be attached to any individual, he continued, but 'if the serious ... responsibilities' which were 'the primary reason for the staff's existence' were to be taken up in earnest, a capable British officer would have to be imported, especially to work with the defence committee, at least until Canadians had been trained to do the job.[41]

Herbert then played his master stroke. When he saw that the Canadian government had been convinced of the military requirement for a capable QMG to lead the general staff planning section, and was hesitant only about the prospect of employing yet another British officer at militia headquarters, he put forward the name of Percy Lake without delay as the officer best qualified for the position in the view of both the GOC and the War Office. What the Canadian government did not yet know, however, was that Lake also had close ties to the Dominion. Not only had his father served with the 100th Foot (a British regiment originally raised in Canada for general imperial service) and settled in Quebec upon his retirement, but his mother was from an old Loyalist family. Indeed, the War Office identified Lake as a Canadian despite his having been born in India. Herbert's method was obvious. Instead of playing up

Lake's professional qualifications, when the government asked for more information, he made the most of his pedigree in the hope that this would neutralize the politicians' concerns about additional imperial influence in Ottawa.

The gambit succeeded. With Lake's availability secretly and skilfully pre-arranged with the War Office, Herbert persuaded the government to put in a request for this 'native son' on the chance that he might be free to come to Ottawa as quartermaster general. The War Office (naturally) agreed, much to the delight of the Canadian government, and all that remained was to bring Lake to Canada without raising a fuss in Parliament. This proved easy. Expenditures already voted on but buried in the defence estimates were applied to an order-in-council appointment that was not made until the conclusion of the parliamentary session – a standard ploy used whenever the government preferred to hide a specific appointment. For once a GOC had outmanoeuvred the politicians, and as a result Herbert had his competent and loyal subordinate.[42] When Lake discovered that his administrative duties as QMG left little time for the mobilization planning he was supposed to do, Herbert approached the minister to ask that another experienced intelligence officer be added to the staff. It seems clear that he intended to employ the same tactic he had with Lake's nomination, as once again the preferred choice, the Dublin-born Major F.W. Stopford of the Grenadier Guards, was referred to in official correspondence as a Canadian. But Herbert had left Canada before anything more could be done, and the QMG was left on his own.[43]

Colonel Lake was not at all impressed by his new chief when he met Major-General William Gascoigne in September 1895. It seemed that the GOC intended to be entirely uncritical of the militia and that he did not care 'two pence' about defence schemes.[44] In fact Lake's initial assessment was unduly harsh. Gascoigne was aware of all the faults in Canada's military organization, but he feared that he would prejudice his position by acting too quickly and displaying too much initiative before the Dominion and imperial governments had settled the outstanding questions about their respective roles in empire defence. His moment would come after there was an accord. Until then, he would rather 'encourage' than 'pitch into' the volunteer force.[45]

Gascoigne's annual reports to Parliament nevertheless sounded all the familiar warnings about Canada's unpreparedness. He also made clear his feelings about the inadequate planning staff and his determination to see improvement in this quarter. When, for example, the Conservatives hinted that Lieutenant-Colonel Osborne Smith, long a party favourite, might replace Walker Powell as adjutant general, Gascoigne objected vigorously. Not only was Smith's administrative record demonstrably bad, he explained, but he was also a well-known Tory campaigner and this, declared the GOC, was 'most objectionable conduct in any military officer.'[46] The government did not force the issue, and Gascoigne was not saddled with an undesirable subordinate. Since it was clear, however, that Ottawa would continue to nominate Canadians to fill important staff positions at headquarters despite its refusal to provide them with a proper training course, Gascoigne turned to Britain for help and eventually won support for his proposal to send officers from the Dominion to the Staff College at Camberley. Bureaucratic fumbling on both sides of the ocean prevented Major Septimus Denison from attending, but with Gascoigne's persistent backing Captain D.V. Eaton of the Royal Canadian Regiment found himself among the commander-in-chief's nominees in 1897.[47]

Although Gascoigne's patient approach had paid some dividends by the time he returned home in 1898, much more would be accomplished in the next two years than he had ever imagined possible. Events simply overtook his steady campaign. On the domestic side, the Liberal victory in the 1896 general election brought Dr Frederick Borden into the defence portfolio, and after a slow start he proved to be surprisingly innovative and co-operative in his efforts to improve the militia. At about the same time the movement for imperial solidarity in Britain was strengthened as Joseph Chamberlain became colonial secretary and Field-Marshal Lord Wolseley assumed the office of commander-in-chief of the army. Wolseley was the leading proponent of army reform in Britain and, like Chamberlain, was not afraid to express his concern about the lack of defence planning in Canada to Dominion authorities.

Still, the most dramatic influence on Canadian attitudes to and perceptions of national security was the sudden deterioration in Anglo-American relations over the question of the Venezuelan boundary in 1895-96. Though the dispute originated in South America, it was obvious that Canada would be the main battleground should it come to war. Confronted by the worst case it had ignored for so long, the Canadian government could not remain inactive: Colonel Lake was sent to England to buy modern rifles for the militia. Gascoigne, meanwhile, transferred Captain Arthur Lee of the Royal Artillery from his border survey duties to headquarters, where he was told to draft a defence scheme for the immediate operational deployment of the militia. Basing his appreciation on the traditional invasion routes to Canada from the United States – Montreal, Quebec, and Niagara – Lee proposed to send 'flying columns' of militia south across the border to cover these strategic crossing points and so delay the American advance. In the mean time other Canadian forces would be mobilized in the major towns and cities to serve as defensive garrisons whose task was to hold out until help arrived from overseas. This was expecting a lot of a citizen army, but under the circumstances Lee could do little else.[48]

It was now Gascoigne's turn to engage in subtle manoeuvre. Lee's plan, he knew, was not perfect, and would benefit from close scrutiny by senior officers at the War Office. But if the Canadian government saw the plan first – as it deserved to, particularly when there was a crisis – and made revisions which it believed solved the problems in the original draft, then either the plan would not be forwarded to London, or any criticisms originating there would be construed as imperial interference in local affairs, and very likely disregarded. Accordingly, for the duration of the crisis Gascoigne did not reveal the existence of the plan to the minister or to his Canadian subordinates at militia headquarters. When, fortunately, relations with the United States improved, and there was no cause to implement Lee's plan, Gascoigne reasoned that it would be a mistake to disclose a flawed scheme to the Canadian government. But it was sent, secretly, to the War Office on the understanding that any amendments made there should be forwarded, again in secret, to Gascoigne so that they could be incorporated into a revised memorandum which would subsequently be presented to the minister as the original, made-in-Canada contingency plan prepared for the recent crisis. If the ruse worked, Canada would have a comprehensive review of its military requirements without realizing the extent to which imperial authorities had been involved.[49]

As might be expected, the War Office did not accept Lee's draft as a long-term option for the defence of Canada. The haste with which he had attempted to meet an unexpected crisis had led him to seriously over-estimate the militia's capabilities, particularly when he argued that it should advance into American territory alone. Enough was wrong with Lee's plan, in fact, that the War Office wanted to undertake a comprehensive study of its own rather than amend what had been produced so far. Making no reference to the draft plan, therefore, but also leaving no doubt that the militia's deficiencies had been cause for concern during the recent period of tension, on 14 May 1896 and again in July 1897 the Colonial Office approached the Canadian government with this in view, warning that only a massive military reorganization and the completion of a practical defence scheme would offer any hope of countering an American assault in the future.[50]

This message from London was followed in the fall of 1897 by similar advice from Major-General Sir Alexander Montgomery-Moore, commanding the imperial garrison at Halifax. Taking advantage of an informal meeting with Frederick Borden, and drawing close parallels to the experience of Ridgeway in 1866, Montgomery-Moore described in detail how ragged and futile Canada's mobilization in 1895 would have been.[51] It is doubtful whether this appreciation shocked Borden, who was sufficiently aware of the militia's shortcomings not to be fooled by the positive tone of official reports or articles appearing in the press. But Montgomery-Moore's comparison could nevertheless be of use, Borden decided, if it allowed him to remind cabinet of the widespread fear that had existed in 1895, and thereby gain support for his own package of military reform. Borden was also aware of Wilfrid Laurier's heady experience at the Diamond Jubilee and colonial conference of 1897, where the prime minister had seemingly embraced the idea of closer empire co-operation with a sense of joy and exhilaration. Aiming to capitalize on this mood, Borden told Montgomery-Moore to write to Laurier direct, promising to support whatever he said when it was discussed by cabinet. Taking no chances, Montgomery-Moore also sent a copy of his brief to General Gascoigne, who in turn forwarded it to Borden. Better than his word, the minister used this document to initiate discussion of Montgomery-Moore's ideas. Moreover, when the cabinet decided that it lacked the technical and professional expertise to assess the merits of the report, Borden's hand could be seen in its decision to seek imperial assistance through the Colonial Office. Chamberlain responded with the suggestion that a commission of four British experts working under Gascoigne launch a thorough investigation to determine the country's defence requirements. Although this would entail substantial imperial involvement in what had been customarily (and jealously) guarded as a matter of purely domestic concern, Laurier's government agreed.[52]

Consequently, just when Anglo-American and Canada–U.S. relations seemed to be improving, the Dominion began to undertake the most serious and comprehensive review of her defences since the commission established by John A. Macdonald in 1862. What neither Borden, Gascoigne, nor the British government could know for sure was whether this was a delayed, but in the long run insignificant, reaction to the 1895 crisis, or whether it heralded a radical break with the past and the start of a policy of genuine military preparedness on Laurier's part. If it were the latter, and if it meant that the need for a peacetime planning staff was acknowledged, then the chances for military reform along the lines of recent developments in Britain were good.

4

Politics, planning, and the staff, 1898–1911

The Leach Commission, to use the popular title of the 1898 defence inquiry, was an instrument of British policy aimed at serving imperial, not Canadian, interests. Its object was to persuade Canada to build up its armed forces, in part for home defence, but primarily to promote Dominion participation in a highly structured and closely integrated scheme of empire defence directed from London. Gascoigne was to have been its chairman, but when he resigned before any work had begun, the British government proposed that Major-General E.P. Leach, a fortifications expert familiar with Canadian conditions, take his place. Surprisingly, this was acceptable in Ottawa, where it was assumed that the GOC-designate, Major-General Edward Hutton, knew too little about Canada to offer useful advice.[1]

This was not true. Previous experience in Australia meant that Hutton was not only conversant with the problems of colonial defence but also had definite ideas about what kinds of military reforms were required in the Dominion. Foremost among these was a redefinition of the limits of military and civil authority in the militia department to increase the power of the GOC, after which, he believed, all else would fall into place.[2] As a matter of tactics, however, it was best that he not show his hand too early, and Hutton was therefore content that Leach should head the inquiry and provide 'independent' corroboration of the advice Hutton already had in mind. In fact the jury was rigged, Hutton and Leach having worked out before hand what the latter should say so that it would not contradict Hutton's recommendations.[3]

The imperial bias and focus of the Leach report was muted, at least so far as Canadian liabilities abroad were concerned. But as a catalogue of the Dominion's persistent neglect of its defences, particularly as they related to war with the United States, Leach drafted a frank, uncompromising, and powerful indictment. The Canadian militia was so deficient, he declared, that it could offer little more than token resistance to an American invasion force before the British army was in a position to intervene. Indeed, Leach was convinced that no matter how quickly the British formations crossed the Atlantic they would arrive too late, long after Canada had fallen.

The single most important reason for this sorry state of affairs, the report explained, was the excessive influence wielded by the civil side of the militia department. It was bad enough that the deputy minister should control the procurement and allocation of war matériel and mobilization stores, but the long-standing reluctance of the civilian officers at headquarters to co-ordinate their activities with the military staff was worse still, and had made a complete mockery of all attempts at defence planning in the past. Beyond that, the habit of every minister since Confederation of ignoring merit when it came to making promotions and appointments had negated efforts to place the militia and permanent force on a sound and efficient footing. What's more, Leach had evidence that ministers had sometimes withheld information vital to the War Office's planning in order to preserve and protect the practice of patronage and partisanship in personnel policies.[4]

Hutton found much to agree with in Leach's report, but despite the collusion between the two generals before the exercise began, the GOC was not entirely satisfied with the commission's conclusions and recommendations as they related to the future defence of Canada. The report assumed, for example, that because the Dominion would inevitably play a subordinate role in dealing with a major emergency, Canadian troops must inevitably come under British command even before imperial reinforcements arrived in North America. Maintaining Canada's dependence on the British army to this extent was a mistake, in Hutton's view, because it offered no inducement to Canada to improve its militia and firm up its national command structure. After all, what did it matter if senior Canadian officers were incompetent if they were not going to lead their troops in battle?

Leach had also ignored the problem of defending the west, having decided that the decisive battles in a war with the United States would be fought along the St Lawrence River–Lower Great Lakes frontier. This was madness, Hutton declared, if the goal was to create a 'national army' enjoying widespread popular support: a national army without nation-wide responsibilities for defence was really a contradiction in terms. Hutton therefore drafted his own defence plan, which envisaged the creation of a distinctively Canadian field army, commanded by the Dominion GOC, and having an operational role on the prairies and in British Columbia as well as in the east. In so doing he expected not only to secure support for subsequent, more extensive, military reforms, but also to persuade Canadians to embrace his ultimate goal: the organization of an expeditionary force able to reinforce the British army outside North America when circumstances required. This last step, as he knew, was revolutionary. Despite the limited assistance proffered by the Dominion during the Sudan expedition of 1885, the idea that Canada's military forces should form part of an empire reserve carried the concept of imperial defence far beyond what many Canadians were willing to accept, particularly if they were expected to foot the bill.[5]

The fact that within the year Canadian troops were waging war against the Boers in South Africa in no way signalled the realization of Hutton's dream. Caught between French-Canadian opposition to the war and the jingoism displayed in much of English Canada, Sir Wilfrid Laurier resisted pressures to participate in the conflict until he was ultimately forced to accede to the demands of the anglophone community that Canada fulfil her obligations to the empire. It was clear, however, that the prime minister did not believe that the dispatch of Canadian contingents to South Africa had set a precedent or that Canada would henceforth be an automatic belligerent in every imperial adventure.[6]

Hutton was inclined to think differently but, as we have seen, he was compelled to leave the country before the Canadian contingents returned from South Africa and so was unable to capitalize on their success to further the twin causes of imperial solidarity and military reform. Rumours about the GOC's involvement in the campaign to force the government's hand with respect to participation in the Boer War undoubtedly contributed to his fall, but by then he had also forfeited the support of Frederick Borden through his constant hectoring of the minister about the need to reorganize militia headquarters. Six times at least he pointed to recent changes in Britain, where the authority of the commander-in-chief had been strengthened vis-à-vis the adjutant general and secretary of state for war, and six times Borden refused to do the same for the GOC, each time a little more coldly than before.[7] Then, in November 1898, he attacked the minister's role in deciding upon promotions in the permanent force. Borden was willing to compromise – Hutton could promote officers he considered deserving as long as the minister remained freed to help his friends – but the GOC refused on the grounds that this was no way to inculcate professional values among the regulars.[8] The tension increased on both sides.

Tempers rose again a few months later when Hutton demanded the resignation of Lord Aylmer, the adjutant general, for incompetence and disloyalty to the GOC. Borden refused, but instead of accepting the minister's decision Hutton resorted to a complex subterfuge to rid himself of his unwanted subordinate. The adjutant general would be posted away from Ottawa, supposedly to broaden his experience, but before he took up his new appointment he would be asked to write the British army's colonel qualifying examination at Aldershot. Of course he would fail (Hutton's private arrangement with Major-General Sir Evelyn Wood, commanding at Aldershot, would see to that) and thereby disqualify himself for the proposed posting. Although Borden agreed that Aylmer should go to England, he would not hear of his permanent transfer away from headquarters, a decision Hutton took as a denigration of his professional judgment. Relations between the two became even more strained.[9] Subsequent disagreements over who should decide appointments to the South African contingents made matters worse still.[10]

The irrevocable break came in January 1900, when Borden rejected two of Hutton's nominees to the second militia staff course because they were senior Tory party workers. Consistent with his disdain for political soldiers, the GOC acknowledged the validity of the minister's objections and had the officers concerned so informed. The truth embarrassed Borden, however, and he directed Hutton to rectify the situation by explaining that the advanced age of the two candidates was the only reason for removing them from the course. Despite this direct and unambiguous order, the GOC continued to insist that the shameless partisanship of the officers involved was sufficient and legitimate justification for rejecting their applications.[11]

It is doubtful that Hutton's intransigence in this specific case was reason enough for the Canadian government to seek his recall and for Parliament to agree to it. He had survived similar battles before, once when he secured the removal of Colonel James Donville, a Liberal MP with many friends, from command of the 8th Hussars, and again when he resisted pressure from all sides of the House of Commons to make room for Sam Hughes as a combatant officer in South Africa.[12] But each of these victories had cost him valuable capital, as had his upbraiding of Hughes for launching a personal campaign to raise an expeditionary force for service in South Africa; as a result he had few supporters left when the minister decided, in February 1900, that he must go.

Moreover, the evidence against Hutton was compelling. Although Borden had repeatedly denied the GOC's request to redistribute authority at headquarters in the winter of 1899, Hutton had proceeded anyway, secretly ordering the adjutant general and quartermaster general not to communicate directly with the minister without the GOC's permission. They obeyed, and Borden was none the wiser until he tried to see the QMG to discover the source of the embarrassing exchange of letters dealing with nominations to the militia staff course. Once the truth was known, the request for Hutton's recall followed within a week. The GOC's order may have reflected the situation in Britain accurately enough, Borden admitted, for Lord Lansdowne had agreed to subordinate the

AG and QMG to the commander-in-chief; but Hutton's loyalty was to the Canadian minister, not the British secretary of state. Having failed to do as Borden directed, therefore, the GOC was guilty of gross insubordination.[13]

London's response to the Canadian demand was to rebuke Laurier for his government's meddling in purely military affairs, but the prime minister stood firm: Hutton's conduct had been inexcusable.[14] In the face of such strong resolve, the British government could do little else but recall Hutton, saving what face it could by offering him immediate employment in South Africa. But the potential impact of the circumstances surrounding the GOC's departure was seen to be enormous. Although the South African war and the need to prepare for the upcoming legal battle over the Alaska boundary were good reasons for the Canadian government to have done nothing about his report so far, Major-General Leach was convinced that, because of Hutton, it would never be brought before cabinet.[15] Similarly, Governor General Lord Minto, who had worked closely with the GOC and who had tried to save his Canadian career, also recognized that Hutton's dismissal would have far-reaching consequences. The military profession had lost a decisive confrontation with the civil power, and as a result 'political party influence' would continue to dominate defence policy 'regardless of the cost to discipline and efficiency.' Furthermore, Borden's victory had so enfeebled the office of GOC that good officers were likely to shy away from the appointment.[16]

Laurier confirmed this forecast when, in conversation with Lord Minto about Hutton's successor, he reminded the governor general of the absurdity of thinking that the status of the Canadian GOC and the British commander-in-chief were in any way parallel. The Dominion's political traditions had always allowed the minister of the militia more freedom than his counterpart in London, the prime minister explained, and this was not going to change. Canadians recognized that, he seemed to be saying, but would British officers in the future?[17] Minto was devastated. Here, in a few choice words, was the rationale for naming a Canadian officer to replace Hutton. Lord Aylmer, a Canadian, was already acting GOC; Borden had alluded to the possibility of appointing a Canadian as GOC in the House of Commons;[18] and it could be argued, if Aylmer's nomination was opposed in London, that William Otter's experience of command in South Africa made him perfectly suitable for the appointment.

Minto soon learned that the Dominion government would not demand that a Canadian officer be named GOC, but he was worried nevertheless. The War Office was experiencing great difficulty in finding competent officers willing to serve in Canada under the prevailing terms of reference.[19] But when he asked whether these could be changed, Laurier either raged on about Hutton or chortled 'with selfish pleasure' at the trouble Lord Lansdowne was having in London with Field Marshal Lord Roberts now that the commander-in-chief had increased power.[20] The Canadian prime minister was not about to saddle himself, or his government, with the same problems.

Under these circumstances the War Office decided against sending another strong officer to Canada and dispatched an inferior replacement for Hutton. Major-General Richard O'Grady-Haly was a mistake, Minto was soon protesting, because he lacked the will to challenge anything Borden did and would not prod his Canadian staff to produce even passably acceptable work.[21] Recognizing their error, the home authorities immediately cast about to find a suitable substitute, eventually choosing Lord Dundonald, a cavalry officer who had had some success leading Dominion troops in South Africa. (Joseph Chamberlain, still fuelled by the dream of closer imperial federation, thought it better to place the Canadian militia under the British GOC at Halifax.)[22] By then, however, Borden had developed a distinct liking for O'Grady-Haly's quiet compliance, and twice asked that his tenure be extended. The War Office reluctantly agreed, but when the time finally came for O'Grady-Haly to leave, Borden surprised everyone by indicating his willingness to accept Dundonald as the next GOC.[23]

Having learned from experience, the Canadian government asked Dundonald to read its 'Hutton file' as his first assignment: the new GOC was to be under no delusions regarding Borden's power as minister. Dundonald was also told that the Militia Act would soon be amended to permit Canadian officers to serve as GOC. With such evidence of local feelings before him, Dundonald would have been well advised to proceed cautiously, but that was not his way. Nothing Canadian authorities said or did could deter him from his course; he had an army to mould, and he believed it was essential to enhance the power, prestige, and status of his office in order to carry out the task. If the government refused to co-operate, or simply ignored his advice, he had already decided to go over its head and seek the approval of what he anticipated would be a thoroughly sympathetic public opinion.[24]

The opportunity to do so was not long in coming. Dundonald's first official report to the governor general and Parliament on the state of the Canadian militia was singularly blunt and uncompromising. Where his predecessors had carefully found a positive remark to offset every criticism, Dundonald listed fault after fault, failure after failure, laying the burden of guilt squarely and unequivocally at the feet of successive Canadian political administrations. Then, making it clear that the United States was the enemy in mind, he outlined his own plan for military reorganization, referring constantly to the unfulfilled recommendations of the Leach inquiry. There was no room for half-measures. Either the government followed the GOC's advice, or it would shoulder the blame for the country's complete and utter lack of preparation.[25]

Dundonald's candour incensed Borden, as did the criticism of his own efforts to improve the militia. Accordingly, he prohibited publication of those parts of the report in which the GOC's language was strongest. It was soon widely known that the report had been censored, and Minto reported grimly that he doubted whether Dundonald would last out the spring, at which time Borden was certain to ask for the appointment of a Canadian as GOC.[26] Despite Borden's denial of this possibility only a week before Dundonald's report was issued, London now feared the worst and Minto was asked to persuade the minister to travel to England for discussions before making his final decision.[27] Meanwhile, Chamberlain and other officials met to determine what they should do about Canada.

The British deliberations were an accurate reflection of the unhappy state of civil-military relations in both countries. 'Amateur criticism in the South African war has minimized ... the value of professional advice ... in the eyes of the Colonials,' remarked Lieutenant-Colonel E.A. Altham, assistant QMG at the War Office, and Canadian politicians in particular thought they knew more about military affairs than the professionals. On this account they were almost always ready to condone excessive civilian control of the army. What was called for, he concluded, was a forceful declaration of professional independence by the Dominion's military hierarchy.[28]

Sir John Anderson, the civilian permanent under-secretary of state at the Colonial Office, disagreed completely. He found only one example of the abuse of power, and that was Whitehall's assertion of its right to define the nature of the civil-military relationship in Canada. In particular he objected to all attempts to force or persuade Ottawa to give the GOC a freer hand. The doctrine of 'a Commander-in-Chief independent of the Secretary of State for War' was a 'constitutional absurdity' already rejected in Britain, and London therefore had no business trying to impose the concept elsewhere. Indeed, as far as he was concerned the Canadians were guilty of nothing more than 'putting their feet down' and rightly insisting upon 'ministerial responsibility and control.'[29] That was the British way.

Neither the War Office nor Dundonald understood Anderson. To the men in uniform the issue was a matter of convincing the Canadian government of Britain's moral right to make certain demands on the Dominion by virtue of the mother country's ultimate responsibility for its security. Were the Canadian militia efficient no one would question Canada's controlling its own military affairs, but the problem, as Major F.S. Maude, military secretary to the governor general, explained, was that Canadian ministers, unlike their

British counterparts, had acted irresponsibly in the past. They had exploited their portfolios to further partisan ends, destroying the army in the process, and could be expected to act in the same way again. The point, therefore, was not whether the civil power should be paramount in the Dominion, but whether the Canadians had forfeited the authority their constitution gave them.[30]

Correct or not, Maude's analysis offered no easy solution. Either Whitehall became involved in the internal affairs of a self-governing Dominion, a constitutional contradiction, or the GOCs would continue to suffer. Even the Colonial Defence Committee, asked by Chamberlain to find a way around the impasse, was so bewildered by the facts presented that it could not agree on the best course of action to follow. Instead, the committee circulated a memorandum outlining five options reflecting the broad spectrum of opinion that existed in London and Ottawa.[31]

Case A was the status quo. The GOC was a British officer responsible to the Canadian government but at liberty to report privately to London on the efficiency of the militia. Whether he was able to influence the Dominion's military policies depended almost entirely on who happened to be minister, and whether the GOC could work with him. Case B looked to the appointment of a Canadian as GOC. Although this would presumably please Ottawa (and help the career prospects of Canada's professional officers) it was the worst possible solution for the maintenance of strong imperial ties. Case C revived the idea of amalgamating the Canadian and Halifax commands under the British GOC at Halifax, Chamberlain's preference, but the committee cautioned that Ottawa was traditionally hostile to this proposal. Canada had looked after its own defences for too long to accept an officer as GOC who was also directly responsible to London for the maintenance of an imperial fortress. Case D was a compromise. The British lieutenant-general at Halifax would undertake Canada's strategic planning and command all empire forces in North America in wartime, while the Canadian GOC would supervise training and ensure that local organization and administration complemented imperial defence schemes. However, there was bound to be trouble, the committee warned, if either officer had the right to publish reports critical of Canadian authorities. The final option, Case E, foresaw the possibility of a Canadian serving as GOC and exercising full command over the militia, as long as a British general could make periodic and independent inspections of the Dominion's forces.

Of the five alternatives the Colonial Defence Committee preferred Case D for the obvious reason that defence plans would at least be written. As compensation for the small surrender of sovereignty involved, the committee recommended that Canadians should be offered vacancies at the British Army Staff College and that successful graduates be given command of British units and formations.[32] St John Brodrick, secretary of state for war, thought Case E would best avoid friction,[33] while Lord Dundonald picked Case C, but only if the GOC had his headquarters in Ottawa, and only if suitable Canadian officers were invited to command British units and sub-units.[34] All agreed that Borden and Laurier were bound to press for Case B.

London was understandably cheered when, during these deliberations, word was received from Government House in Ottawa that Borden had recently provided Dundonald with a resumé of his responsibilities which expanded the authority of the GOC and reduced that of the adjutant general. In addition, Dundonald had been told to make a start on strategic and operational plans. Indeed, Major Maude went on, the War Office would probably find Borden 'very agreeable' when he arrived in London. The minister's heart 'was in the right place,' but he was worried about appearances, particularly as they related to imperial control. Consequently, although Borden would probably accept a British officer as GOC for the foreseeable future, he was also likely to demand access for Canadians to the Staff College and other professional courses so that in due course they would be ready to take over the other senior staff positions at militia headquarters.[35]

Armed with this advice, the secretaries of war and the colonies met on 3 December 1903 to plan their strategy. Ultimately they decided that while they would not insist upon the appointment of British officers as GOCs in perpetuity, Borden would be told that employing a Canadian at the moment would be detrimental to both the Dominion's and imperial interests. Specifically they would emphasize the inevitable isolation of the militia from professional developments in the British army should a Canadian take command. If Borden was adamant, however, and a Canadian had to be named, care must be taken to persuade him that all other senior staff positions should be filled by qualified British officers. The Canadian minister accepted these terms during his meetings with Joseph Chamberlain, and it seemed that a mutually acceptable compromise had been arrived at.[36]

Events in Britain undermined this careful Anglo-Canadian agreement almost immediately. Having suffered through three decades of tense and unhappy relations with successive commanders-in-chief and profoundly disturbed by failures in military administration and leadership during the Boer War, in 1902 the British government concluded that it had no recourse but to re-examine the country's higher military organization. The first of the far-reaching reforms proposed by Lord Esher's War Office (Reconstitution) Committee began to be made public during Borden's visit, but it was in the spring of 1904 that he learned that the traditional military hierarchy would be replaced by a general staff system in which the office of commander-in-chief would disappear, to be replaced by a chief of the general staff as the senior military appointment. But responsibility for the army was not the purview of the CGS alone. Rather, policy and administration was to be vested in an Army Council that included not only the secretary of state and the chief of the general staff but also the adjutant general and quartermaster general sitting as equals. In short, Lord Esher expected a committee, operating according to principles of collegiality, to bring an end to civil-military confrontation.[37]

Whether Borden initially understood that this was the way to rid Canada of GOCs who sought too much power, or whether he simply believed that it was illogical for the Dominion to cling to a military organization declared obsolete in the mother country, is not clear. Whatever the case, on 29 March 1904 he broached the subject of implementing Esher's reforms in Canada.[38] His question was unwelcome in London, for professional and imperial reasons alike. Esher's plan had been designed to promote efficiency in a large army having world-wide commitments in which commands and field formations all had their own general officers commanding. While policy and planning was the responsibility of the general staff and the Army Council, its implementation would be left to the GOCs, who also gave the army its command structure in peace and war. Despite the Dominion's freedom to develop policies and procedures, Lieutenant-Colonel Altham pointed out, Canada had always been considered as one of the subordinate commands that was supposed to look to London for guidance. As a result, the creation of a separate Canadian staff distinct from and not linked directly to its British counterpart was tantamount to a declaration of military independence.

In short, Altham explained, the new British organization was neither needed nor wanted in the Dominion. Moreover, if Canada did adopt Esher's outline it would still have to appoint a GOC to lead the force in war since it was never intended that the general staff, CGS, or Army Council would take on that task. Accordingly, blind adherence to British practice was pointless for a small military establishment such as existed in the Dominion. Should Borden nevertheless insist upon creating an organ to perform the general staff's planning function, Altham thought he could be told that it would be easy to attach such a body to the GOC's office without incorporating any of the other measures put forward in Esher's study.[39]

Altham's paper conveniently overlooked the fact that Canada could copy the British model completely by increasing the status of the existing military districts – in effect by making them 'commands,' each with its own general officer commanding – a simple structural change that would have presented no difficulty to Canadian authorities. His silence on this point probably reflected the British view that Canada's adoption of the Esher reforms would dangerously weaken the imperial tie, and that was the crucial problem. How could a British officer serving as the Canadian chief of staff ensure that the militia adhered to a set of uniform standards established in London when he could be outvoted in the Dominion's version of the Army Council? For he would be facing not only the minister but also those officers whom the minister had selected for the other senior staff appointments. Experience with Colonel Walker Powell and Lord Aylmer had already shown that, in Canada at least, a soldier's loyalty to his military commander could be extremely fragile, and much less important than his sense of personal obligation to the political man who chose him for his job. The implications were obvious. Since it was the minister, not the GOC, who made senior appointments, introducing the general staff/army council organization in the Dominion would give the minister a virtual stranglehold over all aspects of military affairs. Better to say very little, then, than to point out how the status quo could be altered.[40]

Once again Borden surprised everyone. Having toyed with change, he did not follow through with the project. The War Office was informed that Dundonald would remain as GOC; there would be no Canadian Army Council; and both the adjutant general and quartermaster general would continue to be regarded as subordinate officers on the GOC's staff with precisely defined and limited fields of responsibility.[41] London's worst fears had not materialized.

They did later that summer. Apparently learning nothing from Hutton's experience, Dundonald was foolish enough to complain to the Conservatives about his Liberal minister's persistent meddling in militia appointments. When this became known an outraged Borden demanded Dundonald's immediate dismissal. This time Lord Minto was in no position to argue – even he characterized the GOC's behaviour as inexcusable -- and the governor general forwarded the Canadian request to London without delay.[42] Then, on 1 July, Borden wrote to Percy Lake, the former quartermaster general, and to the War Office asking that Lake be posted to Canada as chief of the general staff. London could not object, and with the signing of an order-in-council in November Canada had a new military regime embracing most of Esher's reforms; henceforth all orders would be made and signed by the Militia Council as a collective entity, whether they dealt with purely professional, service matters or had wider departmental implications.[43]

Frederick Borden always justified this reorganization on the grounds that he had brought modern British practices to Canada. Like the Army Council, the Militia Council would afford the minister day-to-day contact with all the senior staff while providing more continuity in the army's upper echelons than was the case when GOCs replaced each other every two or three years. This meant that everyone on the council, but especially the minister, would have a better chance of 'knowing exactly what is going on.' Moreover, the division of responsibilities between the CGS, AG, and QMG would be precisely the same as in Britain. Each would be supreme within his own sphere when it came to administering agreed policy, but all would have to obtain the approval of the Militia Council as a whole on anything new. When Sam Hughes questioned the competence of Canadian officers to undertake such tasks, Borden replied that here too he would adhere to British regulations. Although it would take time, eventually all officers on the headquarters staff would be Staff College graduates, and in due course there would be a definite career progression taking officers from their regular force units through the district staffs to regimental command and thence to the most senior appointments in Ottawa.[44]

In fact, Borden had not followed the British precedent exactly, and he knew it. Although any three members of the Army Council could exercise that body's executive authority whether the secretary of state was present or not, in Canada the Militia Council was little more than an advisory body. 'There was no question of withdrawing power from the minister,' Borden noted, and no question that the military members could not determine policy on their own. Borden's approval was required for everything, no matter how minor, and he was to have the last word on all appointments and promotions.[45] Having surrendered nothing, he actually had a veto to use as he wished. That was not how Esher's system was meant to work.

Borden's cautious and careful draft regulations did not frighten Percy Lake. He had maintained an interest in Canadian affairs after he left the country for the first time in 1898, and he had kept up a correspondence with Frederick Borden which cemented their already warm friendship. It was therefore no surprise for Borden to ask for Lake as CGS, or for the War Office to promote Lake ahead of two hundred colleagues in order to make him available. Both sides realized that the essential factor in improving the Canadian militia was not Borden's program of reform but that the minister and his chief military adviser had a harmonious working relationship. Since Borden and Lake obviously understood each other, it was hoped that they would achieve a great deal together.[46]

Lake's specialty since the mid-1890s had been mobilization planning, and with Borden's blessing it was to this that he turned first. To begin he set up the major branches of the Dominion's general staff, asking that a British officer, Lieutenant-Colonel Willoughby Gwatkin, serve as head of the most important, that is, operational planning. And because militia headquarters no longer exercised direct command, he recommended that the officers in charge of the military districts assume this responsibility as well as that for developing local defence schemes. Next he insisted that officers on the district staffs be paid more because of these additional duties. Finally, he advised that for operational reasons the military districts along the St Lawrence–Great Lakes frontier should be transformed into embryonic field divisions to make it easier to mobilize frontline formations in the region on short notice. Borden approved all these suggestions.[47] Patrick MacDougall's plan had finally taken shape, forty years later.

Lake's initial string of successes was a remarkable achievement, but there was better yet to come. Despite the fact that both Hutton and Dundonald had been recalled following their criticism of politically motivated appointments, the CGS none the less asked Borden to be more judicious in rewarding his friends. Much to Lake's relief, when political acquaintances of permanent force officers began to lobby on the latters' behalf to secure some of the new, and higher paid, district staff positions, Borden announced that he would no longer tolerate such influence-peddling.[48]

Once the immediate problems of district organization and appointments had been settled, Lake moved on to examine Dundonald's plan to create a one-hundred-thousand man 'national army.' Noting every unit on the proposed order of battle not yet established and the severe deficiencies in equipment required for total mobilization, he informed Borden that no less than seven million dollars would have to be spent to outfit the frontline divisions and a further eleven million for the strategic reserve. With the four million currently expended in the annual militia budget already under attack, the CGS was understating things when he remarked that there was 'much to do,' but he was nevertheless determined to find the extra money and forge ahead.[49]

At a meeting of the Militia Council which Borden did not attend, the other military members applauded Lake's efforts to bring Dundonald's scheme to fruition, but advised him to proceed slowly and cautiously. Radical change, they warned, would undoubtedly 'disturb vested interests,' by which they meant the volunteer militia units who continued to assert their precedence over the regular force. The adjutant general and quartermaster general nevertheless agreed that, since Parliament had passed Dundonald's plan in principle, some of the eighteen million dollars would have to be made available to give effect to its recommendations. The regular force would have to grow, and a much larger staff would have to be authorized to train and administer the force under consideration. The advice was forwarded, probably with some diffidence, but Borden not only accepted it, he also permitted its publication despite having prohibited Dundonald from doing the same.[50]

This took courage. Of all the items in the militia budget the size of the permanent staff came under criticism more often than any other. Sam Hughes repeatedly accused the government of adopting 'the old fossilized systems of

Europe,' while George Foster, a future Tory trade minister, brooded about the amounts being spent on 'useless fubelous [sic] "staff management." '[51] Borden was nevertheless prepared to ignore the inevitable hostility in the Commons, and made a strong case to cabinet: the number of staff officers must be increased immediately, and British officers employed until qualified Canadians were available. The minister failed to win any sizeable increase in the defence estimates, but this did not stop him from moving ahead. British officers were appointed to the new vacancies on the staff, and plans were approved to expand the permanent force. Moreover, this was achieved at the expense of the volunteer militia, whose share of the departmental budget was reduced.[52]

London was elated at the Dominion's military renaissance. Intelligence reports from Canada began to arrive regularly at the War Office, while Colonel Gwatkin was finally able to undertake comprehensive mobilization planning. By August 1906 the district staffs had received the details of his home defence scheme and in June the following year the officers commanding most of the country's militia battalions knew how their units would fit into the field army.[53] The British nevertheless discovered that they could not push Borden too far, despite his eagerness for reform. Still seeking to find a substitute for the service chain of command that had existed between the Canadian GOC and the British commander-in-chief, the War Office and Colonial Office together decided to take advantage of the anticipated presence of Canadian Staff College graduates in London and British officers serving in Canada to create an imperial general staff linking the forces of Britain and all the self-governing Dominions. The natural assumption was that such cross-fertilization (and in particular the provisions allowing Canada, Britain, Australia, and New Zealand to participate in each other's policy-making process) would generate a common school of military thought throughout the empire without challenging an individual government's right to control its own armed forces.

Borden was less positive. Concerned that the proposed imperial staff would eventually presume to dictate to his department, at first he rejected the idea outright; however, once reassured that London had no intention of challenging the current constitutional relationship between Britain and Canada, he relented. The British were again jubilant but, as we shall see, technical and political difficulties delayed the formation of the Canadian section of the imperial staff until 1911, and even then it did not take the shape that had been agreed upon in 1907. In the interim both Borden and Lake hoped that the good intentions of recent British and Canadian governments would produce substantive results, and that the improvement in Canada's military posture would not cease altogether.

As part of the process of regeneration as well as to strengthen his arguments to cabinet, Borden told the CGS to revise the memorandum he had submitted two years before outlining the militia's shortcomings. This Lake did, noting that the Dominion's lack of preparation since 1905 '[had] not escaped the notice of the one enemy Canada had most to fear – the United States.'[54] Borden again pressed Laurier to support a larger militia budget on account of the American military revival, but the prime minister refused, stating that both he and the rest of cabinet remained in opposition to any substantial increase in defence spending.[55] Even the Department of Marine, which might have been expected to share the army's concern about the security of Canada's coastline, turned down Borden's offer to have the two departments co-ordinate their efforts in this area.[56]

Although they could not accomplish all they set out to, Borden and Lake made a good team. Indeed, only one incident seems to have threatened the mutual respect they had for each other. Speaking before the Courtney Commission investigating the civil service, Lake repeated Herbert's assertion that too much power was concentrated in the hands of the minister. This testimony annoyed Borden, but probably because of the CGS's otherwise exemplary conduct, there was no serious break between the two.[57] Consequently, when the scheduled date for Lake's departure drew near Borden asked that his friend remain in Canada as inspector general. The rest of the cabinet also respected Lake and readily accepted the terms and conditions he set down before he would take up the new appointment: a salary of $7,500 a year and a seat on the Militia Council.[58] The latter demand was particularly significant because it was entirely contrary to contemporary practice in Britain, where it was felt that the inspector general should be divorced from the management and direction of the organization whose policies and operations he was meant to criticize. But Lake knew that he had to be a member of the Militia Council if he was to have day-to-day influence, while the Canadian government did not want to lose his helpful advice. Accordingly, the principle of imperial uniformity could be dispensed with.

The War Office undoubtedly had plans for Lake – there was talk of his becoming chief of the general staff in India – but it offered no opposition when Canada asked that he remain in the Dominion. After all, he had been the most successful of all the British officers sent to Ottawa. At the same time, however, London was concerned by Canada's decision to appoint a Canadian officer, Colonel William Otter, as the new CGS. For one thing, the War Office considered Otter unqualified for the job, despite his experience commanding the Canadian infantry in South Africa, and for this reason alone there was good reason for Lake to remain. Beyond that, there was doubt about Otter's commitment to the idea of imperial military centralization, which was a better reason for Lake to stay where he was: as long as he served under terms of reference he had made for himself, imperial requirements would not be entirely ignored while the steadying influence of the British army would remain strong.[59]

British concerns about Otter's supposedly nationalist sentiments were unduly exaggerated. Although his dedication to the Canadian military profession never required slavish adherence to the British model, his sympathies were at least transatlantic if not entirely anglophile. Proud of the Dominion's efforts in South Africa, and resentful of that smug sense of superiority displayed by some imperial officers, he was nevertheless moved by the Canadian militia's familiar association with the British army.[60] Unfortunately, the subtleties of the mix in Otter's character and beliefs were missed in London, where imperial authorities frequently misunderstood his motives. For example, when the War Office asked when Canada would form its section of the imperial staff and the Canadian reply of 28 May 1909 cited Otter's advice that a domestic general staff should be functioning first, he was roundly condemned as a 'separatist.' It seemed in London that a local, less competent, staff would usurp the role allocated to the imperial staff by the 1907 agreement, and provide the Canadian government with strategic analysis and advice which did not reflect the view from London.[61] What the British failed to perceive, however, was that Otter understood the political environment in which he worked. Imperial centralization had always been a contentious issue in Canada, but so had the professionalization of the Dominion's armed forces. And since military reform at home was Otter's paramount concern – it was the rock upon which any future strengthening of the empire's war potential was based – he was not prepared to sacrifice material progress in this area at the altar of imperial co-ordination no matter how this affected British aspirations in the immediate future. Closer ties with the British army would have to come later.

Confirmation of Otter's longer-range objectives came in June 1910 when, with the development of the Canadian staff progressing satisfactorily, he informed Borden that it was now appropriate for the Dominion to create its section of the imperial staff as called for by the imperial conference of 1907.[62] Borden refused, however, and London's hopes for an easy and uncomplicated melding of empire strategic planning were dashed. The blame, so London thought, lay with Otter, and particularly with his refusal to support the creation of the Canadian section of the imperial staff only a year before. But had he badgered Borden about it then, as the British wanted him to, when the Canadian minister was not clearly sympathetic to an imperial staff, he might actually have jeopardized the development of the Dominion's own general staff as well any expended imperial co-operation in the future. Instead, relying upon his own judgment, Otter had at least secured the formation of a head-quarters staff in Ottawa and a promise from Borden that all staff officers would be Staff College graduates. This, in itself, would serve to disseminate the 'imperial idea,' and therefore represented a considerable achievement.

Other initiatives taken by Otter in 1910–11 should also have shown the British that he supported the goals of imperial defence. Shortly after his return from England in 1910, for example, he formed a mobilization committee at headquarters to study the problems of home defence and the measures to be taken if elements of the Canadian militia were again sent overseas to assist the British army. Although the protection of Canadian territory was consistent with traditional government policies, the latter contingency went so far beyond the commitments made in peacetime by any previous administration in Ottawa that the CGS risked being disciplined for trespassing on territory belonging entirely to the civil power. Moreover, the terms of reference he provided to the committee practically pre-ordained its conclusion that Canada should adopt the war establishments of the British territorial army (the counterpart of Canada's militia) for a conflict in North America, and those of the proposed British Expeditionary Force for an overseas war. In either case the adoption of British standards would simplify the process of incorporating Dominion units and formations into a larger imperial army.[63]

Similarly, had they looked closely enough, the British would have seen that Otter's appointment as CGS had no appreciable effect on the nature and extent of the British army's influence over the Canadian militia. Adhering to the provisions of the 1907 imperial conference, and with Otter's full concurrence, the Canadian government asked that the inspector general in Britain, General Sir John French, tour the country and issue a public report on the efficiency of the Dominion's armed forces. Despite Percy Lake's subsequent challenge to criticisms made of the Canadian staff system, most of French's recommendations were implemented without interference or complaint. The militia was reorganized into the six divisions French had estimated were necessary for home and empire defence, and Ottawa agreed to pay the salaries of five additional British staff officers who would fill vacancies in the new divisional staffs.[64] Yet the War Office could not forgive Otter for what they saw as his original sin, and so ignored him when unilaterally making appointments to the Canadian branch of the imperial general staff in 1911.

Ever mindful of the anti-imperial sentiments that still existed in the country, and worried by the attitudes of some of his own cabinet colleagues, Borden chose to concentrate on the contributions French's plan would make to home defence when the matter was discussed in Parliament.[65] But his private concerns were by now beginning to extend as far beyond North America as

Otter's. How he handled the distribution of Gwatkin's revised mobilization scheme to the six divisional commanders was a case in point. Despite a foreword warning that 'knowledge of [the plan's] existence might lead to false inferences and cause much mischief,' it was obvious to all who received the documents that headquarters and the minister had decided that a Canadian infantry division and cavalry brigade might one day be called upon to serve abroad against 'a civilized country in a temperate climate.' Given the direction of British policy at that time, this indicated that preparations were under way in Ottawa to ready Canadian forces to fight alongside the British army in Europe against Germany.[66] There was no separatism here, in thought, word, or deed.

The progress made in Canada during Borden's term as minister and Lake's and Otter's tenures as chief of the general staff thus witnessed the realization of much of what Patrick MacDougall had advocated before he left Canada in 1866. With sufficient numbers of professionally qualified staff officers increasingly available at all levels, mobilization planning had organized the militia on a concrete footing of six field divisions, with units, commanders, and staffs allocated to each. Equipment shortages remained a severe handicap, and some of the smaller support and service elements could not be included in peacetime establishments. But these deficiencies were at least known, so that the funds necessary to arm the militia and bring it up to strength in an emergency could easily be brought before Parliament.

The fundamental premises of Canadian defence policy had also changed dramatically since MacDougall's day. Total reliance on an ad hoc call to arms when a crisis appeared had been superseded by a systematic plan geared as much to the defence of the empire as it was to the defence of Canada. To be sure, the Dominion had been forced to borrow a number of British staff officers for the time being, but it was understood that they would eventually be replaced by Canadians who had passed the British army's staff course. The process had begun in 1898, when Captain Eaton was nominated to Camberley, and it was resumed in 1904. This was an important step because the British had to depart if officers in Canada's permanent force were to enjoy a complete career and if the country was (and was seen) to be served competently by its own army.

Even the volunteer militia was caught up in the enthusiasm for professional reform. Although primitive staff courses for the citizen force had been introduced at the Royal Military College in the 1880s, it was not until General Hutton developed his four-month militia staff course that the country had even a watered-down version of Camberley. For the first time militia officers were afforded the opportunity to learn operational as well as administrative staff duties and to test the practical application of what they had been taught in field exercises and staff rides. Unhappily, Hutton's course lost credibility following his battle with Borden over the selection of students, and it died a natural death in 1903, the victim of indifference and a certain amount of dismay at the heavy demands being placed on part-time officers when there were few tangible rewards for successful graduation.[67]

The idea of militia staff education was not revived until 1908, when Colonel Otter decided that part-time officers must again have the means to prepare for the staff and command appointments that would be theirs upon mobilization. Anxious to avoid a failure, he instructed his staff not to discourage students by asking too much of them and to see to it that those who did well received good appointments afterwards.[68] Such considerations caused the new staff course to flourish; 124 officers graduated between 1908 and August 1914.[69] As things turned out, however, the staff training made available to both permanent force and militia officers in the years leading up to the First World War played only a marginal role in the Canadian Corps' later success. Rather, its significance lay in the increased emphasis on professionalism and professional qualifications within both 'branches' of the army – a radical departure from what had been the Dominion's traditionally amateur military ethos.

An equally momentous change had occurred in the civil-military relationship during the Borden-Lake-Otter years. The management of the Dominion's military affairs was no longer a source of confrontation, acrimony, and distrust between the country's senior professional soldier on the one hand, and the minister and his militia cronies on the other. Instead there emerged a more collegial and co-operative spirit in which professional knowledge and political power were more equitably shared.

Of course, these developments did not occur in a vacuum. The Boer War had established a major precedent despite Laurier's injunction to the contrary. Never again could Canadians ignore the possibility that they might be called upon by the mother country for military assistance. Britain was also the source of the impulse to modernize, to build an efficient, professional force, in no small way because the War Office had to face the prospect of fighting a major continental power – first France, then Germany. Borden, meanwhile, had brought an open mind to the militia portfolio in 1896 and had the moral courage to hold to his convictions, and to the recommendations of his staff, despite strong political opposition, once he knew that he had the trust, support, and loyalty of his military advisers. For their part, both Lake and Otter were wise enough to choose their ground with great care and forethought. Both knew that Borden favoured reform, but not in all areas at once. The permanent force, he had said, must become a professional army in which only merit, ability, and knowledge counted, but the same was not the case for the militia. There politics would remain important, if decreasingly so. The two generals also knew that Borden was relatively powerless in determining the course of Canada's relations with the empire. They therefore skirted around these issues, avoiding the tensions they were sure to create, until the way seemed clear.

This useful partnership ended abruptly. Percy Lake returned to England in 1911, and that same year the Liberal government of Wilfrid Laurier was defeated at the polls for reasons only vaguely connected with its military policies. For the first time in fifteen years the army would be dealing with a Conservative administration, and its minister would be Sam Hughes, a long-serving militia colonel who was never known for his tact – or for his failure to have an opinion on any matter of military interest.

5

Politics, planning, and the staff, 1911–1914

Sam Hughes notwithstanding, a more helpful attitude to defence questions on the part of the government seemed certain with the election of Robert Borden's Conservatives in 1911. The new prime minister was known to be more sympathetic to the idea of empire co-operation than his predecessor, and although he did nothing to improve the small Canadian navy formed during Laurier's regime, he was clearly aware of the threat to Britain posed by the recent (and remarkable) growth of German naval power. Eventually his government would offer thirty-five million dollars to the United Kingdom to build battleships – an unprecedented commitment on the part of Canada to imperial defence, particularly in peacetime.[1]

The army was also relatively content in the summer of 1911. Plans were ready for the permanent force to hold its first all-arms manoeuvres at Camp Petawawa, the large training area recently acquired on the banks of the Ottawa River one hundred miles upstream from the national capital. In addition, regular officers were travelling to Britain in ever-increasing numbers for periods of training and regimental duty with the British army or for higher-level staff and command courses. At militia headquarters, meanwhile, Colonel Willoughby Gwatkin was busy refining the defence scheme prepared the year before. Revisions to the section dealing with Canadian participation in an overseas war were completed in 1913 and were forwarded to the minister's office in the normal way. When no objections were forthcoming Gwatkin assumed that his plan for mobilizing an expeditionary force had been embraced as government policy.[2] Whether General Sir Ian Hamilton, who replaced General French as Britain's inspector general and toured Canada in 1913, knew the details of Gwatkin's work is not known, but he would have been happy to learn that Canada evidently shared his conviction that the self-governing Dominions must be prepared to organize their armies for service abroad.[3]

Planning for war with the United States was, however, a much more difficult problem, both for the United Kingdom and Canada. As far back as 1908 the Committee of Imperial Defence had decided that Britain should no longer contemplate defending Canada against the Americans. This conclusion was based on the Royal Navy's contention that the emergence of the U.S. navy as a major force and Britain's need to protect its home waters against Germany together precluded successful British operations on the Atlantic coast of North America. Winning naval supremacy on lakes Ontario and Erie – a necessary precondition for holding Ontario and Quebec – was altogether impossible.[4] As a result, the Admiralty reasoned, Britain was by and large 'committed ... to friendship with the United States' and must, through diplomacy, avoid war with the Americans at all costs.[5]

The War Office did not agree. The defence of Canada remained of concern to the imperial general staff until 1913 at least, although it must be said that it was never a preoccupation: Germany was the enemy to be feared most. Still, British staff officers studied the likely conduct of operations in North America until the outbreak of the Great War, and the forms and scales of attack established for the Halifax defence scheme of 1914 continued to be set at the levels anticipated in a major war with the United States.[6] It was assumed, for example, that coastal fortification was not enough, and that some force must be available to meet an overland attack.

It is doubtful whether very many Canadians would have identified the United States as a potential enemy in the years immediately preceding the First World War. Those who believed in or hoped for the eventual unity of the English-speaking peoples considered the Americans as cousins, perhaps slightly wayward, but none the less members of the same family. For them, war between the dispersed branches of Anglo-Saxondom was unthinkable. Others may have acknowledged the futility of any such racially based political union, but even so this did not make the Americans enemies. In fact, it is unlikely that many of those who were hostile to Sir Wilfrid Laurier's 1911 election program calling for free trade with the Americans went so far as to regard the United States as a military threat to the Dominion.[7]

Colonel Gwatkin agreed that the possibility of armed conflict with the United States was 'very remote'; but as the militia's director of mobilization he could not ignore the contingency altogether. He would, he believed, be abrogating his professional responsibilities were he to prepare nothing and the improbable actually occurred. Moreover, the Liberal government had previously signalled its approval of his home defence plans on at least two occasions: once when Frederick Borden had authorized distribution of the 1906 version of his scheme, and again in 1910–11, when the militia was reorganized along the lines recommended by General French.[8]

Assuming that there would be continuity between the Liberal and Conservative administrations on an issue of such fundamental importance (and which was also so inherently technical or professional in nature), headquarters did not stop work on its defence plans simply because the Conservatives came into office. Accordingly, the district staffs continued to compile intelligence summaries of military developments in the United States and to pass on information about topographical features likely to be of tactical importance in halting an American advance. On the basis of these reports, as well as its own studies, headquarters allocated militia units to specific brigades and divisions. It tried wherever possible to achieve a balance of all arms in the field formations while remaining faithful to the traditional principle of territorial affiliation: Toronto units, for example, would be brigaded together for service in southern Ontario. Citizen soldiers fought best, it was felt, the closer they were to their own hearths and homes.[9]

Gwatkin's staff was also busily engaged in anticipating the Americans' likely course of action in the event of war. In January 1912 Lieutenant-Colonel George Paley, on loan from the Rifle Brigade, declared that American forces would not be able to take Canada in a walk-over despite their many advantages. In the decisive St Lawrence–Great Lakes theatre, for example, the United States would have to concentrate an army of at least one hundred thousand men, half of them reservists, to accomplish its mission. The resources were available, Paley explained, but the process of mobilizing so many troops would take from two to four weeks, and that was ample time for Canada to prepare its forces to hold out until help arrived from overseas.[10]

Paley was wildly, even foolishly, optimistic. As his successor, Lieutenant-Colonel Gordon-Hall, discerned immediately, the psychological and physical impact of an American thrust into the prairies, where there was only a narrow ribbon of population hugging the frontier, had been ignored completely by Paley, just as it had by the Leach Commission. With Canada's major rail links west of Lake Superior within easy reach, American forces could cut the country in two in the first day or two of hostilities, and roll through the rest of the region before the week was out, defeating the scattered prairie battalions piecemeal as they entered the fray one by one. In Gordon-Hall's view, such a calamity would probably break eastern Canada's will to resist long before the militia divisions there had been committed to battle. He therefore urged his superiors to strengthen the volunteer units in the west so that they would not be destroyed before the army in central Canada had the opportunity to exploit its favourable strategic position to check the Americans' momentum. Reorganization of the prairie commands into field brigades to meet Gordon-Hall's objections began that year.[11]

Gwatkin and Gordon-Hall had reason to be pleased with these developments, but both were concerned that continuing to work in isolation would do little to interest and then actively involve other branches of government and the cabinet in bringing the militia up to strength. Accordingly, they sought the creation of an interdepartmental committee to prepare Canada's War Book – a guide to all the administrative arrangements and procedures necessary for co-ordinating government activities on the outbreak of hostilities. They also advocated the creation of a Canadian counterpart of Britain's Committee of Imperial Defence, preferably under the chairmanship of the prime minister, to produce a national strategy approved by the head of government before being submitted to cabinet.[12]

As Gwatkin later recalled, all such efforts to promote greater efficiency within the Militia Department were 'useless' because the minister, Sam Hughes, evinced no interest in them whatsoever. Indeed, it was only after the direct intervention of the Duke of Connaught, governor general in 1914, that a War Book Committee was struck that year. Satisfied that preparations for war with the United States were well in hand, its chairman, Joseph Pope, chose to concentrate instead on an imperial struggle against a European power. His draft regulations were ready just in time for the outbreak of hostilities in August. The proposal to establish a Canadian defence committee patterned after the Committee of Imperial Defence was, however, still-born. As a result, when war was declared the general staff had developed few contacts outside the Militia Department when it came time to put its mobilization plan before the minister.[13]

Colonel – later General – the Honourable Sam Hughes was a product of mid-Victorian Canada. A long-time militia officer, he could not bring himself to embrace the view that the permanent force and its professional ethos should be the foundation of Canada's national defence. 'The days of standing armies are gone,' he announced in the House of Commons soon after taking up his portfolio: 'The old Saxon days have returned, when the whole nation must be armed.' This was a popular notion in many western countries; but where most translated it into a requirement for compulsory peacetime military service to produce a well-trained nation-in-arms, that concept was anathema to Hughes, the great proponent of amateurism and voluntarism. Instead, he wanted to teach Canada's male population to ride and to shoot, adding only enough military drill, order, and discipline to raise his soldiers above the level of a mob or rabble.[14]

The origins of Hughes's ideas were complex.[15] On the one hand they clearly derived from his experience as a volunteer officer and from his profound acceptance of Canada's militia myth – the belief that the free-born, independent men of Upper Canada, and not the regular soldiers of the British army, had saved the colony in 1812 and were good enough to do so again. By implication, this myth also propagated the belief that, when taught to shoot, the yeomen of Canada were inherently superior to any regular formation because they had not become stultified and overly regimented by the parade-square mentality of the standing army. By contrast, Canadian militiamen remained innovative and creative individuals who knew when to forget 'the book' and all its foolish rules in order to adapt to changing conditions.[16]

Yet Hughes's views were by no means atypical or idiosyncratic. We have already seen how the tiny permanent force had to struggle against antipathy and outright hostility to become more than a corps of school teachers, and how even then its aspirations to find an operational role were the subject of dissent and disapprobation. Indeed, Hughes had led the fight to keep the regulars in their place, and to safeguard the image of the militiaman as the Dominion's only true warrior. But the vehemence with which he denounced the regular soldier, whether British or Canadian, was unique. It stemmed not only from his own fiery personality but also from the disgust he had for the way he had been treated by Ottawa and London at the time of the South African War.

Sam Hughes believed in the empire and the British connection (even if he did not admire Britons in regular army uniforms) and as a soldier he was sworn to its defence. He was not being inconsistent, therefore, when he wrote directly to the Colonial Office in 1899 offering to lead a Canadian contingent to help put down the Boers. But instead of praise for his efforts to further imperial solidarity, Hughes soon discovered that he was the odd man out, a figure to be disavowed in both Canada and Britain, because (although he did not know it) his offer threatened to provide the Canadian government with an excuse not to make a formal commitment to contribute men to the war in South Africa. With no explanation forthcoming, however, Hughes concluded that the rejection of his offer by Hutton was but another in a long series of insults to the part-time militia and its good intentions.[17] He complained, only to find that he was subsequently left off the roster of the Dominion's official contingent. Incensed at this, and at the fact that so many permanent force officers had been chosen, Hughes lost his temper. The regulars about to depart for South Africa were '*failures*,' he told the GOC, and they could in no way compare with

'Militia Officers as a class.' As for his own case, he noted that Hutton had intimated that Hughes would be 'incapable to serve [*sic*] alongside British regulars.' Why, he asked contemptuously, had the GOC made such a remark? 'Could I not retreat or surrender quick enough to the Boers?'[18]

Sam Hughes eventually reached South Africa, having manufactured a place for himself on the railway lines of communication staff. But once again he ran afoul of imperial officialdom, and was finally sent home by Field-Marshal Lord Roberts just when the future minister himself expected to be awarded the Victoria Cross.[19] Together with the shockingly lacklustre performance of the British army, particularly in the early months of the war, this experience confirmed all of Hughes's prejudices against the character and value of professional soldiers and the 'old fossilized [military] systems of Europe.'[20]

Hughes's understanding of his role as minister was also a throwback to earlier times. Devoutly partisan, he was anxious to help his friends wherever and whenever possible. When combined with his belief in his own soldierly expertise, and more especially in his ability to judge good military talent when he saw it, this led him to ride roughshod over militia regulations and the protests of his professional advisers to reward those he considered deserving. Certainly the last thing that concerned him was the effect of his actions on permanent force morale or the career development system introduced by Frederick Borden and Percy Lake. Accordingly, he saw nothing wrong in appointing Colonel E.W.B. Morrison, a journalist friend and part-time militiaman, as director of artillery – in other words as professional head of that branch – in place of several more highly qualified permanent force officers. Because of initiatives such as these, the relationship between Hughes, who wanted to be commander-in-chief, and the chief of the general staff, the strict and very proper Major-General Colin Mackenzie, soon deteriorated.

The trouble between the two began innocuously enough. When Hughes directed the Militia Council to extend the network of week-long provisional schools to as many towns as possible in order to make qualifying more convenient, Mackenzie was only too willing to ease the training burden for militia officers who lived at some distance from regular force stations. But he objected to the wholesale proliferation of provisional schools, whose standards were predictably low, because he was convinced that large numbers of men would choose this relatively easy path to a commission or promotion instead of the more demanding three-month attachment to a permanent force company. Further, the extra duties imposed upon the regulars to supervise instruction at additional provisional schools would interfere with the teaching program at the regular schools as well as with the permanent force's own training. Mackenzie was by no means alone in his opposition to Hughes's directive, but after several futile attempts to persuade the minister to reconsider his proposal the CGS acted on his own to kill it. Since he was the officer charged by the Militia Act with the responsibility for training, Mackenzie argued, he had the undeniable right to protect professional standards.[21]

Hughes was outraged, and in a stinging rebuke ordered the CGS never again to decide such matters on his own initiative. For it was Hughes, Mackenzie must remember, who carried ultimate responsibility for all the Militia Department did. The CGS responded in kind. If the minister continued to ignore professional advice, Mackenzie would resign at once, but not before informing both the prime minister and the governor general of the situation.[22]

In fact, Hughes was quicker off the mark. In a detailed account to Borden he noted that Mackenzie was behaving as if the minister's authority was limited to directing the civil branch of the department, while the CGS exercised complete and independent control over the military side. In addition, Mackenzie seemed to believe that his membership on the imperial general staff – an appointment made by London on its own – meant that he was superior to the minister in areas of general policy. Because of this, Hughes continued, Mackenzie had been warned against becoming 'autocratic in the management of the service,' particularly as he was serving under the first militia minister ever to know completely the needs of the army. But since Mackenzie had agreed with this assessment, it was likely that the matter had been resolved.[23]

Robert Borden was familiar with Sam Hughes's characteristic immodesty, and probably did not believe that the CGS had come around to the minister's point of view. He was right. For when Mackenzie forwarded his own letter to Borden he offered no apology for the decision to ignore Hughes's order respecting the provisional schools, and refused to retreat even one step from his denunciation of the minister's behaviour. By failing to listen to his professional advisers, the CGS complained, Hughes had become de facto commander-in-chief – an absurdity in British constitutional practice. Worse still, the minister grossly over-estimated the capabilities of the militia (which Mackenzie himself judged to be 'ill-trained and badly officered') to such an extent that he was actually placing the country at risk.[24]

For the moment Borden did nothing, hoping that time would heal these wounds. Indeed, there were two months of relative calm in the Hughes-Mackenzie relationship until April 1912, when the other military members of the Militia Council finally sided with Mackenzie against Hughes on the question of opening still more provisional schools.[25] Despite this setback Hughes ordered compliance with his directive, whereupon Mackenzie resorted to a complex of delaying tactics. However, the issue had to be faced again in July, when Hughes discovered that large numbers of militia officers still had not qualified for their appointments. This time he issued unambiguous orders to open provisional schools all across the country.

Mackenzie was no less concerned than Hughes with the number of unqualified officers in the militia, but he was convinced that to follow the minister's plan would court disaster. The army would simply promote underqualified officers who did not recognize their own limitations. Still, given Hughes's personal interest in the matter and the tenor of his last order, Mackenzie's reply to the minister was anything but diplomatic. Hughes must realize, the CGS warned, that despite his acknowledged lack of esteem for the regulars, a system of new schools lacking rigorous instruction would be little more than a 'farce.' Furthermore, the minister had failed to understand that the real culprits in the officer corps' lack of competence were the many militia battalion commanders who failed to train their subordinates. The obvious solution was to replace these individuals but, Mackenzie charged, Hughes 'did not care to do this' for reasons that had nothing to do with military efficiency. The guilty parties were, after all, his friends and compatriots – men who shared the minister's conviction that citizen soldiers were superior fighting men only so long as they remained untarnished by regular force training.

Moving to broader issues, Mackenzie then repeated his assertion that Hughes constantly over-reached himself by authorizing changes in policy without consulting the general staff. Although he stated that he would 'not presume to comment further' on this charge, the CGS did, in fact, dig deeper, and his concluding paragraph amounted to a complete indictment of the way in which Hughes was destroying the army's morale by discounting the principle of professional merit. In addition, the minister was undermining service discipline by inviting officers to use 'political influence' to secure their promotions.[26]

Remarkably, the files contain no reply to Mackenzie's memorandum, and in fact the record suggests that there were no further confrontations between Hughes and the CGS for the rest of the year. It must be said, however, that by late 1912 the minister was in complete control of his department and so had no reason to engage the virtually impotent chief of staff in a war of words. The Militia Council met rarely, and when it did, questions of high policy were simply not discussed. General Mackenzie coped with this situation until January 1913, when he finally unburdened himself in a long letter to the governor general, who was himself an old soldier. Since the Militia Council no longer dealt with policy, Mackenzie explained, co-ordination of departmental activities except by Hughes had all but ceased.

More disheartening still, the CGS's colleagues at headquarters were proving all too happy to limit themselves to administering their individual branches of the staff, and none would take any step, no matter how small, without first receiving 'the customary "o.k. s.h." ' from Hughes.[27] Indeed, the other members of the council were so cowed by the minister that, despite having previously agreed that any reduction in the size of the permanent force would jeopardize militia training as well as the regulars' ability to perform garrison duty in the initial stages of mobilization, they said nothing when he told them to pare the permanent force establishment from twenty-seven hundred to twenty-two hundred. In Mackenzie's opinion this was the first step in the inevitable dissolution of Canada's standing army; next would come an order prohibiting the regulars from conducting their own field training exercises.[28]

The situation became intolerable later that month when Hughes announced that he would promote himself to major-general, for the dubious reason that he was a militia colonel who also happened to be minister. Since this would give Hughes virtually unassailable authority both as minister and in the military chain of command, Mackenzie decided to resign.[29] Hughes had won, but he made a tactical error when he accepted the cGs's letter of resignation without allowing him the customary leave with pay granted to officers whose performance was not at issue. Such ungracious conduct was too much for Borden, who not only ensured that Mackenzie received his leave but also asked the chief of the general staff what had gone wrong.[30]

With Borden apparently disenchanted with Hughes, Mackenzie had good reason to expect a sympathetic hearing for himself, and perhaps even to prepare the way for his successor to work in a friendlier environment. Insisting that he had never ignored or defied the minister, Mackenzie none the less admitted that he had pressed Hughes very strongly whenever he believed that matters of principle or operational efficiency were at stake. Of these the most crucial was 'Major-General' Hughes's desire to act as his own commander-in-chief, which (Mackenzie hastened to add) was contrary to the spirit and the terms of the Militia Act. The 'unfortunate accident' that Hughes was a militia officer and minister at the same time was irrelevant, as possession of army rank had no bearing on his political authority. Yet Hughes was making his own policy, overlooking his staff and the permanent force in the process, and because of this was endangering the country through his exaggerated estimates of what the part-time militia could do to defend it. If Hughes's power remained what it was, Mackenzie concluded, no self-respecting British officer would ever again consent to serve in Canada.[31]

Hughes also wrote Borden. In his view it was Mackenzie's 'frigid demeanour' that had prevented the cGs from accepting the 'free and easy manner' in which Hughes preferred to run the department. The cGs also had difficulty coping with the minister's pluralistic approach to seeking advice and as a result had been entirely negative, particularly when it came to policies aimed at promoting the interests of the citizen militia. This reflected the 'irreconcilable conflict spirit' that separated regulars and militias the world over, Hughes declared, and it confirmed the suspicion that Mackenzie was wedded to the 'old Permanent Force idea' whose goal was to create a 'Small Standing Army' against the wishes of right-thinking Canadians. Hughes took pains to point out that he did not disapprove of all British officers, but emphasized that he wanted nothing to do with those who, like Mackenzie, acted 'ignorantly, illegally, unconstitutionally, tyrannically, and contemptuously.' As if this were not enough, he added, Mackenzie was also incompetent, the mobilization plans drafted under his supervision being singularly 'devoid of all military merit.'[32]

Not satisfied with striking at the former CGS through Borden alone, Sam Hughes arranged to give his attack the widest possible distribution in England as well. Copies were sent to both the War Office and the Colonial Office, where they could ruin Mackenzie's career, and to the press.[33] This offended the prime minister, who asked Sir John French not to take Hughes's diatribe seriously, but despite this gesture Borden was actually admitting that he would not (or dared not) challenge his minister: nothing in the letter to French suggested that Hughes shared any of the blame, while Mackenzie was credited with little more than trying to do his duty 'as he understood it' – lukewarm praise at best.[34] Borden's reluctance to control Hughes was confirmed a short time later when the Duke of Connaught objected strongly to the minister's widely publicized denunciation of the regulars as 'bar-room loafers.' Not only was the statement untrue, the governor general complained, but it had also caused several of the British officers on loan to Canada to return home in disgust. Borden promised to speak to Hughes at once, but cautioned at the same time that his performance as minister had brought 'warm commendation ... in important quarters.'[35] Those British officers who remained in the Dominion in anticipation that Hughes might fall because of his outbursts found to their dismay that he had survived, and was perhaps stronger than ever.[36]

As word of these incidents spread through London, Sir John French found that no officer was willing to move to Ottawa as Mackenzie's successor.[37] Perhaps it was just as well, however, because instead of asking the War Office for assistance Hughes forged ahead on his own, naming the director of mobilization, Colonel Willoughby Gwatkin, as the new CGS. The Army Council in London deplored his appointment for all the obvious reasons – Gwatkin was young, junior, and inexperienced – but Hughes brushed these criticisms aside. It was more important, he told the governor general, to select an officer who not only knew general staff work but had also been 'specially trained to observe [the appropriate] rights and functions under responsible government than it was to satisfy the War Office.'[38] And with Gwatkin, Hughes was confident that he had raised a cipher, a yes-man who would not over-step authority, to the top.

Yet even this was not margin of safety enough. Accordingly, when it came time to consider replacing the British officers who had left with Mackenzie, Hughes demanded access to the personnel files of all the War Office's nominees so that he could veto those who, in his view, were unsuited for service in Canada. It was not their professional competence he was questioning, Hughes pointed out, but rather Britain's habit of saddling the Dominion with officers having a history of 'objectionable' political conduct at home. The charge was a gross distortion, as Borden well knew, but when confronted by the Duke of Connaught with a request for some sort of clarification or correction, the prime minister said that no rejoinder would be made.[39]

Sam Hughes garnered this kind of support because he was a valuable political asset, not because Borden or his cabinet agreed with everything he said or did. Still, the effect was the same. The minister was free to pillory the permanent force almost at will, and given sufficient time was quite capable of robbing the regulars of all aspirations to become 'real soldiers.' The co-operative civil-military relationship that had emerged over the previous decade was also being eroded as Hughes effectively stripped the headquarters staff of their professional ethos, expertise, and reputation. In 1913, for example, he dismissed the defence schemes drafted by Gwatkin and his staff because, he declared, they too were 'devoid of all military merit.'[40] His opinion had changed not at all when the German army marched into Belgium on 3 August 1914.

Few Canadians expected war when it came. Far removed from Europe, they knew nothing of the process which saw consultations become commitments to mobilize and fight following the assassination of the Austrian Archduke Ferdinand on 28 June. This was no less true of the Dominion cabinet, whose members enjoyed their summer recess with scarcely a thought about the possibility of conflict in the near future. One group of Canadians, Sir Joseph Pope's committee, was hard at work preparing for war in general, but even they had no idea that they were faced by an actual deadline. As a result, it was pure coincidence that the first draft of the country's war regulations appeared the very day that telegrams warning of the imminence of hostilities began to arrive from London on 29 July.

It was time to put the precautionary stages of Pope's War Book into effect, and preparations were therefore made to detain enemy shipping in Canadian ports and to protect all imperial cable facilities. A day later, on 30 July, the Royal Canadian Regiment was told to be ready for an immediate move to the fortress of Halifax, and on 1 August the Garrison Artillery was ordered to man coastal defence installations around Quebec City. On 3 August a number of militia battalions were called out to guard vulnerable points like grain elevators, hydro-electric stations, and the Great Lakes canal system. Canada was at war with Germany the next day. Civil preparations had gone remarkably well, in the main because of the preparatory work practically forced on the government by its military advisers and the governor general.[41]

Military mobilization was far less orderly. On 8 August Lord Kitchener, Britain's secretary of state for war, informed Canada that he would welcome a Canadian infantry division overseas, but by then there were two contradictory plans for raising an expeditionary force of that size in the files of the general staff. One was the 1911 scheme prepared by Gwatkin and Mackenzie which called for the formation of composite battalions drawn from the various regions of the country according to population. The other, drafted in the spring of 1914 by Colonel Gordon-Hall, director of mobilization following Gwatkin's promotion, recommended that the government use existing militia units as the basis of the infantry division.

Whether this new plan was a response to Hughes's rejection of Gwatkin's proposal, or simply reflected Gordon-Hall's own preference, is not clear, but in the event each plan had its advantages and disadvantages. To Gwatkin, the merit of forming composite battalions was twofold: headquarters would be saved the invidious problem of selecting a few of the country's militia units for overseas service and telling the rest to stay home, and it would not be committed to employing a particular regiment's slate of officers on active service – the calibre of personnel was dangerously uneven for that. Moreover, the formation of composite battalions would make it easier to fix a particular region's manpower contribution to its population base, and thereby ensure that no part of the country was over- or under-represented at the front. All else being equal, casualties would be evenly distributed across the Dominion, and there should be little difficulty in maintaining the principle of territorial affiliation when replacements were required.

Composite units had their drawbacks, of course, the main one being the confusion inevitable in organizing completely new formations during a time of crisis. But Gwatkin hoped to minimize this by insisting upon decentralized command and control during the first weeks or months of mobilization. Regiments would be held in their local recruiting areas, where they could rely upon friends, families, and local suppliers for some of their necessaries until the central procurement system was in order, and remain under the supervision of local staffs and permanent force instructors until they had completed basic training. Only at this point would the entire expeditionary force move to Camp Petawawa for final training and outfitting with the arms and equipment obtained since the outbreak of war. Concentration of the division any earlier than this, Gwatkin believed, would produce chaos: the untried Canadian staff was quite capable of maintaining order in, and providing instruction for, scattered battalions of one thousand men, but to manage a division of fifteen thousand from the outset was a problem of a different magnitude and beyond their competence.

Decentralization was also intended to help in the selection of good officers for the overseas contingent. Although it was understood that the Militia Council would have the ultimate authority to accept or reject officers for the expeditionary force, Gwatkin hoped that the minister would take notice of the recommendations made by the district commanders, who knew the officer corps best by virtue of their work with the militia during the summer camps, and who would also be closely involved in supervising the expeditionary force's initial training. Their evaluations would be current and, it was hoped, unaffected by the political considerations that so often influenced personnel decisions made in Ottawa.[42]

Gordon-Hall was not persuaded by Gwatkin's reasoning. A firm believer in the importance of esprit de corps as a foundation for tenacity and efficiency on the battlefield, he did not see how such an intangible quality could be built into essentially artificial, composite battalions as easily or as thoroughly as it could in militia regiments that already had strong traditions, a sense of history, and in a few cases, battle honours. He was even more worried that resorting to composite battalions – in effect, bypassing the country's well-established military system the moment there was a crisis – would put the lie to the notion that the militia was the heart, soul, and backbone of Canadian defence and eventually cause it to wither and die.

The problems involved in culling out incompetent officers from the militia units chosen for the expeditionary force concerned Gordon-Hall less than Gwatkin, as did the complaints certain to arise from regiments that were not selected for active service. Better to disappoint a few, he thought, than to upset them all with composite battalions. Moreover, the momentum of the war might actually sort things out. If, as was possible, Canada decided to increase its commitment beyond one division, additional militia regiments would be dispatched abroad, their feelings of resentment muted. But Gordon-Hall's efforts were for nought. Sam Hughes brushed aside his plan just as he had Gwatkin's, and informed the CGS that he would be charting his own course.[43]

The story of Canada's mobilization in August 1914 is well known, and the details do not need retelling here. Suffice it to say that the minister bypassed militia headquarters and the district staffs, sent telegrams direct to every militia battalion, and invited the hundred or so commanding officers to bring as many men as they could to an as yet unbuilt camp at Valcartier, Quebec.

Selection for the overseas contingent would take place there, and a division formed of composite units based loosely on region. No limits were set on the number of men the colonels were to bring with them, and no provision was made for training and equipping them before they left for Quebec. Gwatkin's first fears were realized. Many more men than required turned up and as they milled about, awaiting their call or, once chosen, their equipment, they simply added to the confusion and disarray caused by the rush to complete the camp's construction. Battalions and brigades were formed, disbanded, and formed again; officers were appointed, relieved, and reappointed; equipment dribbled in; training was confused; but somehow, by mid-October 1914, the Canadian division was on its way to England.[44]

To most Canadians, the early dispatch of the expeditionary force was a remarkable achievement confirming the military genius of their defence minister and justifying his faith in the country's ability and willingness to respond quickly to a crisis. The Canadian Expeditionary Force volunteers themselves were no less pleased. Major Walter Bapty, British Columbia Mounted Rifles, admitted that there had been considerable confusion at Valcartier, but on balance he applauded Hughes for ignoring 'the restraining hand [of] the old Permanent Force,' which, he declared, 'was still living in the past, doing nothing except on direct instruction, and then taking their time.'[45] Lieutenant-Colonel Frederic Curry felt the same way. In his view, Hughes's sacrifice of 'many of the elements dear to the military heart' (but which were major obstructions in the way of 'an army that wants to mobilize itself in a hurry') had given the expeditionary force a psychological boost of incalculable value. That, of course, was Hughes's argument.[46]

A minority was considerably less impressed – and also less charitable in describing the chaos that prevailed at Valcartier.[47] By far the most severe of the minister's contemporary critics was Major James Sutherland Brown, who served at headquarters during the period of mobilization and was then posted to the staff of the first division. Recently returned from the Staff College at Camberley, where he had studied the British army's mobilization plan, he was both amazed and disgusted by the antics of the 'foolish and irritable minister [and] his crowd of sycophants.' It was incredible, for example, that Hughes had ignored a perfectly good training area with more than adequate facilities at Petawawa and selected instead the wilderness site at Valcartier for no other reason than to serve the business interests of Sir William Mackenzie and Donald Mann, two friends who also happened to own the only railway link to the mobilization camp. Their venality, and that of the minister, was directly responsible for the confusion which Brown believed had delayed the training of the expeditionary force. Hughes had also posted the adjutant general, Colonel

Victor Williams, to Valcartier, a thoroughly illogical step considering that the AG was supposed to administer and co-ordinate mobilization from headquarters. Subordinate staff officers did their best to fill the vacuum left by Williams's departure, but with information flowing independently to them and to Quebec it proved impossible to maintain accurate records or to manage affairs effectively.

The legacy of confusion left in Hughes's wake could be corrected in time, of course, and the paperwork straightened out afterward. Even Sutherland Brown admitted as much. However, he maintained that the minister's interference in military mobilization had serious operational consequences that were much more difficult to rectify. The long delay in forming the composite battalions and brigades of the expeditionary force while Hughes listened to the hundreds of claims for preference left the men assembled at Valcartier to wander about at will when they should have been training. Similarly, the minister's preoccupation with personnel problems meant that only the vaguest provision had been made to equip the Canadian contingents with warlike stores and supply them with everyday necessaries once they reached England. As a result they were more or less dumped on Salisbury Plain in November 1914 and left to fend for themselves until better arrangements could be made. Finally, the minister had ignored the advice of his movements staff when the CEF was about to embark at Quebec City and allowed his battalion commanders to take so much into their own hands that most units crossed the Atlantic separated from what stores and equipment they were able to bring with them. This produced further unnecessary confusion upon their arrival at Devonport.[48]

Brown's criticisms were to some extent gratuitous, given the lack of proof that anyone could have done better than Hughes. And to be fair to the latter, it must be noted that the militia was not ready for war in July 1914, and probably could not have been completely prepared for active service between August and October, when the first contingent set sail, by any military authority. No one could have avoided a scramble to find food, fodder, arms, ammunition, uniforms, and other supplies; and since the permanent force was so small, no one could have avoided having to employ at least some militia officers who did not know their jobs as battalion, company, and platoon commanders.

From this perspective, the specific advantages and disadvantages of Gordon-Hall's plan to mobilize twelve existing militia battalions, about which Brown had no substantial complaint, become clearer. It is likely that there would have been less confusion at Valcartier if the expeditionary force comprised only previously formed units, but the pool of talent for the overseas officers corps would presumably have been limited to those on strength when war was declared. As might be expected, however (and as the Second World War would later illustrate), most militia battalions did not have a complete complement of competent officers in peacetime, and it would undoubtedly have become necessary to replace many who held more senior regimental appointments at the time of mobilization. The continuity Gordon-Hall was aiming for would therefore have been largely undermined, and Sam Hughes may have been correct in dismissing his plan.

The differences between Hughes's policy and Gwatkin's plan were less marked. Both relied on composite battalions, and both left the permanent force regiments out of the first contingent so that the regulars could train the rest. But the similarities ended there, and any comparison between the two alternatives leaves little doubt that Gwatkin's was more carefully thought out. We have already seen that he favoured decentralized command and administration in the early weeks, and localized kitting out and training before the expeditionary force as a whole assembled for its final moulding into a fighting formation. Furthermore, Hughes's unstructured recruiting campaign filled Valcartier with so many excess officers and men that the bickering and manoeuvring to find a place in the overseas force actually impeded its progress, interfered with training, and threatened morale. Everyone, Arthur Currie recalled, was at everybody's throat.[49]

This, in itself, had no lasting effect on the overseas force's fighting capabilities, but the experience was unsettling. The general staff was certainly appalled by what it had seen, and Robert Borden's files filled with complaints about Hughes's misadventure.[50] As a result, on 10 August militia headquarters enlisted the support of the district staffs to control the flow of volunteers to Valcartier. Then, in October, Gwatkin persuaded the prime minister and J.D. Hazen, minister of marine, who together were looking after the CEF's affairs during Hughes's absence in England, to follow the procedures of the 1911 mobilization scheme when the second division was being raised.[51] Borden agreed, despite Hughes's firm instructions to the contrary, because he finally recognized the inefficiency of his minister's methods. The Duke of Connaught remarked upon the difference. 'Everything has been running smoothly with no friction anywhere,' he told the prime minister after witnessing the mobilization of the second contingent, and it was essential to forbid Hughes from turning things around when he came back to Canada.[52]

Hughes was incensed when he discovered that he had been disobeyed. Borden tried to reason with his minister, advising him to be less hasty in rejecting the professional advice made available, but to no avail.[53] Hughes countered that he invariably accepted 'sensible' suggestions from the Militia Council and general staff, but he felt duty-bound to reject the army's arrangements for the second contingent; produced by 'limited minds,' they were 'unparalleled for inefficiency, intrigue, and weakness.' Despite having authorized the substitution of the 1911 scheme for Hughes's just a few weeks before, the prime minister capitulated, and gave his minister a free hand to do as he pleased. The second contingent was therefore raised like the first, with Hughes involved in practically every detail of its organization, including the appointment of officers at all levels.[54]

It was the minister's constant preoccupation with and participation in personnel matters that ultimately produced the harshest criticism of his actions. Today the popular impression is that he chose officers for the CEF for reasons other than military merit, passing over good men because they were Liberals, members of the permanent force, or simply not his friends.[55] This was hinted at the time. When the first contingent arrived at Devonport, J.F.C. Fuller, a founding father of the Royal Tank Corps and no conventionally minded soldier, remarked that the Dominion's contingent would be fine only 'if the officers could be all shot.'[56] The first commander of the division, Major-General E.A. Alderson, another British officer, agreed wholeheartedly that the officer corps in the overseas force left something to be desired. Far too many were 'very weak' and had 'no power or habit of command.'[57] Even some of Hughes's appointees shared this assessment. J.C. Creelman, commanding an artillery brigade, noted with dismay that many of the lieutenant-colonels finally selected for the second contingent had been rejected as captains by first contingent units because of their lack of experience.[58] Much earlier, Arthur Currie described to a friend how 'every squirt of a politician' had been actively trying to court Hughes's favour at Valcartier.[59]

Knowing the ways of Canadian politics, Gwatkin offered the Militia Council (that is, the minister) the authority to approve expeditionary force appointments in his 1911 scheme rather than leave the choice to a professionally constituted selection board – something he knew would be refused. At the same time, however, he sought to limit Hughes's influence by asking the district staffs to compile short lists from which to make the final selection. Gwatkin could do nothing when Hughes pre-empted this at Valcartier, where he made and unmade appointments almost whimsically during his tours of the mobilization site. But once the minister was safely in England the CGS directed the district staffs to nominate all officers in the second contingent. This could not be hidden, however, and once Hughes returned he moved very quickly to end the practice. Borden was told that the regulars were putting forward second-rate men who did not deserve commissions, let alone senior rank. Still unwilling to interfere, the prime minister accepted Hughes's complaint at face value and allowed him to replace the officers selected by the district staffs with a list of his own. This was the group that so upset Colonel Creelman.[60]

Was Hughes's record of appointments that bad, or did contemporary criticism reflect personal animus against the minister on the part of the regular and reserve officers who expected more than they received? Would the general staff have done any better? And did the officer corps Hughes sent overseas adversely affect the operations of the CEF? Ultimately, this last question was the only crucial one and, as we will see, senior officers at the front gradually came to the conclusion that the minister's policies were detrimental to the Canadian army's performance in the field. But if professionalization is seen as a cumulative process in which an ethos demanding merit and competence develops as a result of incremental steps, then the importance of Sam Hughes's actions from August to October 1914 cannot easily be dismissed.

Unhappily, the list of officers Gwatkin and his staff might have considered for overseas employment cannot be found, if indeed it ever existed. It is therefore impossible to draw definite conclusions as to how Canada's professional soldiers would have tackled the problem of finding suitable candidates for the CEF. It is possible, however, to compare the experience and qualifications of the militia officer corps as a whole with those of the officers chosen for the first and second contingents, and when that is done the extent to which Hughes ignored practical experience becomes abundantly clear. For example, of the nearly sixty officers holding senior command and staff appointments in the military districts at home, only four were accepted in the CEF, and of these only one was slated to command a brigade. The rest of the overseas brigadiers were promoted from militia lieutenant-colonel, except for one militia brigadier who dropped one rank to command an overseas battalion. Although nine of the forty-four battalion and brigade commands abroad were given to permanent force officers – a reasonable number given the permanent force's small size and its other responsibilities – it still seems unlikely that the general staff would have accepted so many officers for overseas commands who had not held similar appointments in Canada.[61]

Even more startling was Hughes's disregard for professional qualifications, a fact which has so far gone largely unnoticed. Indeed, Colonel A.F. Duguid, the CEF's first official historian, claims that 'practically all' the officers in the first two divisions had not only received pre-war militia training, but also had qualified for their overseas rank.[62] This statement is misleading at best, since Duguid fails to distinguish between certificates of qualification obtained after three months of study at a regular school of instruction and the seven-day diploma gained at one of Hughes's provisional schools. In fact, upon closer examination it becomes evident that the reverse of Duguid's assertion is true. At least one-third of all the officers in the first two contingents had not yet met the militia training standard for their rank. In the combat arms alone, 204 of 1,114 officers lacked the appropriate qualification, and another 186 were offered promotion above their level of training, some by as many as three grades. Of these 186, 27 became majors or lieutenant-colonels. By comparison, only one-fifth of the pre-war militia officer corps was reported as being unqualified, and most of these were junior officers. This statement may have been inaccurate, but even so it seems doubtful again that the general staff would have ignored so many officers who had completed the required militia course of training, or that it would have made quite so many double promotions.[63]

Beyond this, and against all professional advice, Hughes went further to help his friends by creating positions for them in a supernumerary officer establishment added to each of the first two divisions. Gwatkin objected to this because he knew that these hangers-on, who had no real responsibilities, would eventually cause trouble.[64] When they did, both the divisional commander and John Carson, Hughes's personal representative overseas, pleaded with Ottawa to return them to Canada and to prevent any more from sailing.[65] Fifty-five officers were shipped home by the end of December 1914, but in the months to follow many more than that were dispatched overseas on personal instructions from Hughes, where they again got in the way while constituting an unnecessary expense to the Canadian government.

The most destructive aspect of Hughes's personnel policies is more difficult to document. Still, it seems reasonable to suggest that there was little justification for doubting the fundamental loyalty to the military chain of command of an officer selected on the basis of professional merit by a general staff selection board. Hughes's methods, by comparison, threatened the principle of military subordination because they encouraged personal appeals to the political head of the department. Why would an officer who had pulled political strings to obtain his initial appointment to the CEF fail to do so again in order to gain promotion, whether he deserved it or not? Just as important, was there anything in the minister's character to suggest that he would begin to ignore the special pleading of his friends? One thing was certain. The army that Sam Hughes called forth in 1914, and the way he had called it out, gave concrete expression to his desire to return to the old Saxon days when there was no such thing as a regular soldier. Accordingly, there were no grounds for anyone to believe that he would suddenly insist that the CEF adopt the policies, practices, and principles of a professional army.

PART III

THE GREAT WAR AND THE EMERGENCE OF A PROFESSIONAL ARMY

6

Sam Hughes and the Canadian Expeditionary Force, 1914–1916

The policies of Sam Hughes provoked little criticism on the part of expedition-ary force officers during the first months of the war. Having benefited directly from the minister's decision to take personal charge of the country's military effort, few had any reason or desire to turn against their patron. Furthermore, nothing had shaken their faith in his vision of what the Canadian army should be and how it should function – a vision they largely shared. It was only when casualties began to mount, and when the support provided by the Canadian Expeditionary Force's London-based administrative headquarters seemed less than helpful, that doubts emerged about Hughes's continuing close control over the CEF. No matter how well-intentioned he might be (and for the first time there was disagreement on this score) it appeared that the minister was too far removed from England and the front to impose his will on the army, especially if his initiatives were likely to have an impact on the conduct of operations in the field.

In time, as we shall see, a number of very senior officers at the front, all former militiamen originally favoured and nurtured by Hughes, came to ac-cept Major-General Gwatkin's judgment that the minister was meddling too much in the army's affairs. And in time these former citizen soldiers, amateurs at heart, began to think like professionals. They remained uncomfortable with the 'bull' associated with the British regular army and the Canadian permanent force; but they no longer assumed that Canadians had an innate talent to wage war and therefore needed neither professional military education nor experi-ence on the modern battlefield in order to display their prowess.

This was a signal shift in outlook for a group of men who, before the war, applauded both Hughes's ideas and the way they were implemented. When their complaints to the minister about his interference went unanswered, their support for him turned to resentment, and then to hostility. But change did not come quickly in the Hughes era, particularly if it threatened his power. This was in part because he enjoyed considerable support both in his party and the electorate at large, which even the prime minister could not ignore. Beyond that, however, Hughes's exercise of authority happened to fit nicely with Robert Borden's desire to protect his government's right to manage Canadian affairs to serve Canada's national interests first.

The status Canada sought and deserved as a participant in the empire's cause was not well articulated in August 1914. It was clear that the Dominion had not entered the conflict in its own right – Canada was at war because Britain was at war – and Borden readily agreed that strategy and the conduct of operations were matters for London, not Ottawa, to decide. Accordingly, the CEF was more or less placed at the disposal of the War Office for the purpose of fighting the German army, and it was part of the imperial chain of command stretching from the field marshal commanding the British Expeditionary Force to London. Yet close as this relationship was, it did not signify that the Canadian contingent had been integrated completely with the British army along the lines advocated by Lord Kitchener, Britain's secretary of state for war, and by Canada's chief of the general staff. Instead, both Borden and Hughes insisted from the outset that the expeditionary force remained part of Canada's 'national army,' and that responsibility for its administration lay properly with the Canadian government. The Dominion's financial commitment to maintain an expeditionary force in the field was reason enough for Ottawa not to surrender total control over the CEF to the War Office, but there was also a feeling that Canada's national identity and interests were no longer congruent with those of the mother country. Absolute imperial control over the CEF was, accordingly, unacceptable.[1]

Canada's position on this question was strengthened considerably by the precedent established during the Boer War, when the British accepted a measure of Canadian autonomy in the administrative care, custody, and control over the Dominion's forces in South Africa. The terms of service and rates of pay applicable to the Canadian contingents differed substantially from corresponding British regulations, for example, while Canadian commanders were expected to report independently to Ottawa on the course of the fighting despite being subordinates within a larger imperial army. Kitchener and Gwatkin were fooling themselves if they thought Ottawa would accept less than this, and they wisely put aside their objections once Canada declared its opposition to a total integration of the CEF into the imperial war effort. That Sam Hughes also claimed certain rights to control appointments and promotions within the expeditionary force and to outfit it with unique items of equipment such as the Ross rifle gave greater cause for concern because both could have an impact on operations. But as long as reason prevailed Canadian and imperial policies were not predestined to work against each other.[2]

Nevertheless, it was easier to think about the importance of maintaining Canadian autonomy while preserving the cohesiveness and coherence of the imperial military effort than it was to set down on paper clear and unambiguous terms of reference for all the parties concerned. Inevitably, the task of implementing (and interpreting) the measures required fell to the commander of the CEF as the one officer subordinate to the British high command and yet responsible to the Canadian governments. This was a thankless task. For although his freedom (if not duty) to refer questions of a non-operational nature directly to Ottawa, bypassing the normal rules and protocols of the military chain of command, elevated General Alderson's status in comparison with officers holding corresponding appointments in the British army, the burden he carried was also greater. He had to determine whether orders issued to him by his military superiors in France impinged upon Canadian autonomy (and so required adjudication in Ottawa); but equally he had to take care that the administrative rules and regulations set in Ottawa were not going to interfere with the operational effectiveness of the CEF or of the British army as a whole. In short, he was a watch-dog serving two masters whose interests did not necessarily coincide.

Military officers are rarely trained to operate in a civil military environment of such delicacy, and the British generals who commanded the CEF were no exception. Both Alderson and his successor, Sir Julian Byng, had a difficult time adjusting to the requirement to refer routine military instructions to a 'foreign' government thousands of miles away, and to adhere to policies established by that government when they conflicted with regulations in force in the rest of the British army at the front. Friction between the soldiers and politicians was therefore inevitable, even forgetting for the moment that a minister so self-assured as Sam Hughes held sway in Ottawa.

This degree of civil-military disharmony was not a uniquely Canadian phenomenon, of course, as the question of who should run the war, ministers or their generals, was asked in all the belligerent capitals. Indeed, it could be argued that the requirement to satisfy the government in Ottawa simply added another dimension to a pre-existing and uneasy relationship between the 'frock coats' and 'brass hats' in England. From this perspective, the tensions created by Canada's insistence upon keeping administrative control over the CEF fell within the boundaries of what was known and experienced before. They also did not demand any fundamental systematic change or adjustment in the Dominion or British military efforts.

In fact, the positive aspects of Borden's determination to maintain a national contingent under national control far outweighed the negative. All the available evidence suggests that the Canadian contingents developed an esprit de corps significantly stronger that would have been the case had they been dispersed throughout the British army, and once it was formed the Canadian Corps was widely regarded as an entity greater than the sum of its parts. To some extent this was because the permanence of the corps' organization gave it a constancy and stability unknown in comparable British formations, which comprised divisions temporarily grouped together to meet specific military problems. As a result, the Canadian commanders and staffs had the opportunity to work together over a relatively prolonged period which furthered a special spirit of co-operation and community, and by the end of the war produced a cohesive and well-oiled military machine. But the boost to morale resulting from the rule that Canadians would serve together was probably the most important factor in developing the corps' sense of destiny about which Canadian veterans talked so much after the war; and there were many who believed that their success at Vimy Ridge on Easter Monday, 1917, gave birth to Canada as a separate nation.[3]

Sam Hughes applauded every step designed to further the Canadianization of the country's war effort, and he shares much of the credit for insisting upon the conditions and circumstances that allowed a proud, self-confident, and effective Canadian Corps to emerge by 1918. But his motives were not entirely altruistic; from the beginning he understood that his personal ambitions, if cast in the proper light, would be well served by Borden's policies. Promoting an image of himself as the personification of the Canadian army, therefore, he easily fended off critics of the way he was managing the expeditionary force by accusing them of participating in a concerted effort to restore imperial influence over the Dominion. Why, he asked, would a true Canadian want to replace Canadian-made rules with British regulations when the Dominion was struggling to assert national control over the CEF? Once his version of events was accepted – and it was believable even if untrue – the task of winning the support of cabinet colleagues was a relatively simple matter. Disruptive or dysfunctional as it might be, Hughes had cloaked his program in a mantle of respectability that blocked most attempts to challenge the soundness of his ideas.

Hughes's credibility may even have been strengthened somewhat by the fact that his chief critic in the first months of the war was Willoughby Gwatkin, a British officer chosen by Hughes as chief of the general staff despite his imperial background on the assumption that he would do precisely as he was told. Hughes underestimated Gwatkin's professional integrity. For his part, Gwatkin misunderstood the nature of Hughes's power and miscalculated the reception the general staff's professional advice would receive. We have already seen how he tried to confound Hughes's plan for raising the second division, only to be let down by Borden's lack of resolve. Later, Gwatkin protested bitterly when deserving permanent force officers such as F.L. Lessard and S.J.A. Denison were passed over for brigade commands; and once the first division had reached the front, he argued forcefully that his association with and knowledge of the pre-war militia should count for something when it came to choosing individuals for promotions and appointments in the field army.[4]

Whether Gwatkin was jealous of Alderson, afraid that the divisional commander might fall under Hughes's influence, or simply exploiting the arrival of the CEF in France to strengthen his own position is not clear, but the CGS soon discovered he was not being consulted before overseas appointments were settled, or informed after they had been made. This was nonsense if the CEF remained part of one national army under the authority of a single minister who had Gwatkin as his chief military adviser. Gwatkin complained unsuccessfully to Hughes until February 1916, when he finally approached the deputy minister with the revelation that, despite being the professional head of the army, the CGS had no idea who was commanding the several brigades and divisions overseas. Yet Major-General Fiset did no better than Gwatkin in persuading Hughes to co-operate, and for the next few months the staff at militia headquarters had to rely on newspaper accounts to obtain this kind of information. Not even telegrams addressed to the commander of the CEF seemed to work.[5]

The failure to consult with or even inform the CGS about overseas appointments before they became public knowledge was discourteous in the extreme. It was also a blunt and gratuitous insult to Gwatkin, who was supposed to be co-ordinating army organization and training at home to meet the needs of the expeditionary force. In fact, the dearth of information on personnel matters was symptomatic of a far more serious lack of communications on all aspects of the fighting in France. Labouring in a vacuum, Gwatkin was unaware of any special requirements for teaching the techniques of trench warfare, for example, and so could not incorporate lessons from the front into the home army's training syllabus. This became more than just a theoretical problem when, in December 1915, the government chose to double the country's commitment of men from two hundred and fifty thousand to five hundred thousand and to send more divisions to France. Units could not be given up-to-date training before they left for overseas.

Whether Canada could in fact support a larger army in the field was an entirely separate question. Militia headquarters had reasonably accurate data on the country's manpower resources – a product of Gwatkin's 1911 planning –

and conducted a study on the availability of volunteers as early as the spring of 1915, long before the final size of the CEF had been decided. Based on these findings, in June the CGS warned Loring Christie, Borden's legal adviser on external affairs, that the expeditionary force was nearing the maximum strength which could be maintained by voluntary enlistments. Indeed, he cautioned, given the casualty statistics he had seen, a commitment of more than three divisions to the fighting would eventually force the government to adopt some form of compulsory service.[6] For legitimate reasons of national policy the government chose to send more troops to France 'as a dramatic gesture to symbolize Canada's devotion to the Empire and to the cause for which the Dominion was fighting.'[7] Four, and perhaps five, divisions would serve under Canadian colours. That Gwatkin's prediction subsequently came true and the government had to impose conscription in 1917, nearly tearing the country apart in the process, is not our concern here; this was a political decision for the government to make and accept the consequences. When the manpower crisis came the CGS derived little satisfaction from the knowledge that had his advice been heeded two years before that trouble could have been avoided.

There were other examples of wastefulness about which Gwatkin was equally forthright, and equally powerless to correct. Home defence was one such problem. Since Canada faced the threat of serious attack at no time during the war, there was never any justification for retaining large home defence forces in the Dominion, a fact the CGS alluded to time and again. For a number of reasons, however, his advice to limit the army's commitment to guarding the few vital points that actually stood at some risk was not followed, with the result that at times as many as forty thousand soldiers were uselessly employed in Canada when they could have improved the CEF's manpower situation overseas.[8]

Reinforcement policy was a second area which cried out for improvement. Two options, both of which were advanced in the general staff's pre-war submissions, stood out as logical and workable in the Canadian context. One was to send replacement drafts to overseas battalions drawn from the same geographic region, thereby maintaining the original territorial affiliations and identities of the expeditionary force. The second was to create an anonymous, general service reinforcement pool from which individuals could be sent to wherever they were needed most. There were advantages to each plan. The British army had traditionally maintained that protecting the territorial integrity of its units provided a substantive boost to morale and regimental cohesion. On the other hand, the general service approach guarded against the possibility of certain regions running out of reinforcements – in which case geographic continuity would be undermined anyway. The requirements of the

CEF stood squarely between these alternatives. The composite battalions had, indeed, been raised on a firm geographic basis, suggesting that territoriality was the key. But little account had been taken of demographics, which meant that there was a risk that individual cities or counties had been overcommitted at the outset and would not be able to provide a steady flow of replacements to 'their' battalions at the front.

Perhaps because neither was ideal, Sam Hughes avoided both these options. Calling on leading notables who could motivate their local communities, he instead asked these men to raise entirely new, fully manned and staffed battalions for overseas service.[10] This may have been an effective means of expanding the CEF from two to five divisions, but it was not an efficient way to provide reinforcements for already existing units. For one thing, each of the new battalions came complete with its own staff, distinguishing badges, and other accoutrements of absolutely no use for replacing individual battle casualties. Worse still, it was not made clear to these battalions that, unlike Lord Kitchener's 'New Armies,' they would not be going into battle as formed units, but would probably be broken up as soon as they reached England. As Gwatkin predicted, the process of disbanding the one hundred and fifty battalions mobilized in excess of the CEF's actual war establishment proved to be a slow, awkward, inefficient, and sometimes ugly process. Although many of the officers participating in the reinforcement scheme suspected the worst, they were all told that their battalions might be lucky enough to survive disbandment and make it to the front with their identity intact. Similarly, promises were made that, even if units disappeared, the officers would be looked after and could expect to serve at the front keeping their rank. Of course, when it was learned that this or that battalion was about to be broken up, the commanding officers fought long and hard against their fate, and because they were Sir Sam's friends, many succeeded in postponing the inevitable for as much as a year. The result was a reinforcement stream in which thousands of replacement soldiers remained untouchable and were not sent to the front when they were needed, while officers of field rank with no experience expected to keep their grade if they were posted to battalions in France.[11]

The inevitable difficulties arose when the reinforcing battalions were finally broken up. Although it was a relatively simple matter to fit the other ranks into units in France – cannon fodder was cannon fodder, particularly in trench warfare – there was no place for the captains, majors, and lieutenant-colonels who had arrived directly from Canada and who, therefore, lacked the experience necessary to command companies and battalions in battle. The situation might have been eased if these officers had been willing to step back in rank to serve an apprenticeship as platoon commanders; but most would not, taking

Hughes at his word that he would guarantee their appointments and seniority. He did. No officer was compelled to revert, and no one was forced to return to Canada. Accordingly, the majority were left in England for the moment and, together with the supernumeraries still crossing the ocean, added to that group in the United Kingdom with little to do except complain and make incessant demands to see action. Unhappily, when these officers were employed, too often it was in training positions that would have been better filled by experienced veterans recently returned from France who had something concrete and useful to teach.[12]

Gwatkin mentioned this problem many times but Hughes refused to act because, in his view, nothing was wrong. The prime minister also ignored the CGS's warnings, apparently satisfied that if a mistake had been made it was not serious enough to warrant immediate correction. Borden was not altogether to blame for this reading, however, because the implications of Hughes's policy were not clear enough early in the war to generate widespread opposition, even from soldiers at the front. But the main thing saving the minister for the moment was the fact that casualties in France had not reached the point where frontline units had to depend upon replacement officers arriving from Canada with little or no training. At the same time, the general awareness that the expeditionary force was still expanding to an as yet undetermined size provided some justification for the continued mobilization of fully staffed battalions in Canada and their dispatch, as units, to England. Only Gwatkin, with all his professional experience and training, seems to have foreseen the long-term consequences of Hughes's reinforcement program.[13] Still, there were hints of trouble ahead, perceived in London, Ottawa, and France as early as 1915, over the arrangements Hughes had made for that part of the CEF stationed in England.

That Canada would maintain its own, semi-autonomous military presence in the United Kingdom was pre-ordained by the Borden government's insistence upon retaining administrative control over the expeditionary force. Serving as both the staging area and advanced training base for Canadian troops on their way to France, the CEF organization in Britain was the logical place to co-ordinate the needs of the Canadian army in the field and the efforts of militia headquarters to meet them. It was, for example, the obvious channel through which the British high command, the chief of the imperial general staff, or Major-General Alderson should communicate with General Gwatkin about training standards, manpower requirements, and changes to war establishments affecting the organization and preparation for war of CEF units still in Canada. It was equally well placed to monitor the progress of troop training in England, to teach the most recent lessons learned from the fighting, and to make known and implement the administrative policies set down by the Canadian government in those areas agreed to be under its control.

Given these complex relationships and dealings, it might have been wise to have created an overseas branch of militia headquarters in London, or at least an administrative office responsible to it, in which all the branches of the staff were represented in order to facilitate the exchange of information among 'opposite numbers' in France, Britain, and Canada. If there was concern that a purely military organization would not adequately protect the legitimate political interests of the Canadian government, the overseas headquarters or office could have been placed under the authority of Canada's resident high commissioner in London, an associate minister, or for that matter any other official enjoying the trust and confidence of the cabinet in Ottawa. In fact, the precise shape and form of Canada's military-political organization in Britain mattered little as long as it was an efficient and responsive medium for transmitting information, advice, and orders in both directions across the Atlantic.

Sam Hughes's priorities were different. To him, the essential thing was to enhance his own control over the CEF, at home and abroad. An intermediary headquarters or an administrative office was a potential rival to his authority; therefore no formal organization was put in place in England to link the commands and staffs overseas with those at home. Instead, he chose Colonel John Carson, a close friend, as his personal representative in London, and gave him the job of overseeing the administrative arrangements for the arrival and training of the first division between its arrival in Britain in October 1914 and its eventual departure for France.

This arrangement was not unreasonable in the war's early stages. Command of the first division, the only Canadian formation in England, was clearly vested in Major-General Alderson, who was also responsible for its training. And since the division was merely staging through the United Kingdom, neither Alderson nor Carson needed to worry about long-term measures for its supply. But once the first division had left for France and other follow-on units took its place, a permanent over-arching military organization was required to monitor training and to free Alderson from the distraction of administrative problems in England while he was trying to win battles in France. Colonel J.C. MacDougall, one of the few regular officers on good terms with Hughes, asked for and received the appointment of general officer commanding the Canadians in Britain, and was subsequently named GOC of the Canadian training division at Shorncliffe. At about the same time Colonel Carson appropriated for himself the unofficial title of 'Vice-Minister of Militia,' suggesting that his authority had been extended beyond the immediate concerns of the first division.[14]

At first sight these were useful and helpful moves. Command and administration of all Canadian units and formations in England seemed to be centralized in MacDougall's hands, while Carson was available to protect Canadian interests at the political level. The War Office was certainly satisfied, and began to use Carson as its point of departure for official discussions with Canada on civil-military matters. Unhappily, Hughes had not actually delegated plenary authority to Carson, and continued to insist that all but the most minor matters be referred to him for a decision. Confusion ensued until the limited nature of Carson's responsibilities were understood, at which point the War Office objected to the delays that would be caused by having to place all business before Hughes; but since the Canadian minister was adamant, his declaration had to be accepted.

Rather more upsetting was the way in which MacDougall's position as GOC Canadians (in England) was eventually undercut after the second division left for France. Major-General Sam Steele was its first commander, but upon the recommendation of the British, who felt he was too old to withstand the rigours of an operational command, he did not accompany his units across the Channel. However, he was too popular in Canada to be dumped unceremoniously on a ship returning to Halifax. Accordingly, Hughes found a place for him commanding a second training division at Bramshott, a formation that paralleled MacDougall's Shorncliffe command. MacDougall quickly realized the potential for trouble (and the threat to his own authority) if his status as GOC of all Canadians in England, including Steele's troops, was not confirmed. But despite many modifications in their terms of reference, Steele and MacDougall were left on their own, independent of each other and subordinate to no common officer, British or Canadian, in the United Kingdom. Both communicated directly with Carson, Hughes, and the War Office, and both ignored Gwatkin's efforts to co-ordinate CEF training in Canada with what the two generals were doing in England. MacDougall and Steele also ignored each other, so that in time the two Canadian training divisions, supposedly parts of the same supporting organization, developed different standards for promotion and followed distinct training syllabuses. Somewhat later, Steele and MacDougall began to treat their commands as permanently organized formations – as reserve divisions-in-being, in fact – and as such placed more emphasis on administration and interior economy than on preparing replacements to fight in France. Alderson complained frequently about their lack of support, but to little effect.[15] Loyalty to friends was a precious thing in Sam Hughes's eyes, and he was not about to side with a British officer against them.

The situation worsened when the commanders of the third and fourth divisions also asserted their independence of MacDougall, Steele, and the Canadian Corps. It made no sense whatsoever, for example, that Major-General David Watson, Hughes's choice to lead the fourth division, was able to work through Carson and the minister to hold on to his best troops (who would not see action for months) and to send instead inadequately trained soldiers to France at a time when the Corps was crying out for casualty replacements. Similarly, both Watson and Major-General Mercer, commanding the third division, jealously guarded their right to train their units as they saw fit.[16] Annoying as this was to the hard-pressed commanders at the front, however, when the decisive clash with Hughes came, it was over a prolonged argument about who should control appointments and promotions in France.

Initially the problem was limited to the question of how to make use of the supernumeraries in the first division and the senior officers who had brought reinforcement battalions to England. Officer casualties were beginning to rise now that the Canadians were fighting. Early in 1915, therefore, as the country's commitment seemed likely to grow, there was room for these majors and lieutenant-colonels at the front. As Gwatkin predicted, however, commanding officers in France generally preferred to promote junior officers who had seen action than to import majors and lieutenant-colonels from England who had done little more than raise their battalion and supervise its transatlantic crossing. Carson and MacDougall agreed with Alderson, and in March 1915 asked Hughes to recall all supernumerary personnel and senior reinforcement officers to Canada.[17] A month later the War Office added its own, more strongly worded, plea for the return of all the 'decayed and useless' officers then in Britain.[18]

Hughes would have none of this, and refused outright. Moreover, by the late spring of 1915 he was more concerned with criticizing Alderson for what he believed were excessive losses in the first division's recent battle (the German gas attack at Ypres) and was not about to increase the authority of a general suspected of faulty leadership. Vexed by Hughes's indiscreet attack on Alderson, and having heard of the complaints made about supernumerary and surplus officers being posted to France, the prime minister took advantage of one of Hughes's frequent trips overseas to change department policy. At Borden's request, in September 1915 cabinet approved an order-in-council giving Alderson and his brigade commanders authority to make promotions and appointments in the field without reference to Ottawa and to return to Canada any officer they judged unfit for further employment at the front. Personnel surplus to establishment in England were also ordered home.[20]

All might have been well had this policy been maintained.[21] The expeditionary force sent overseas in 1914 and 1915 could scarcely be described as a professional army: its officers and men had by and large come from the part-time militia, or had no military background whatsoever. Appointments and promotions, therefore, could not be made on the basis of an individual's proven ability to lead his men successfully, intelligently, and efficiently in battle, at least in the beginning. This had made it very easy for Hughes to employ non-military criteria when he chose his officers, clearly expecting that the talents or traits he admired in peacetime could be transferred to the battlefield or to the organization and administration of the Canadian Expeditionary Force behind the lines. He did not anticipate that they would fail. Once the Canadians had fought their first battles, however, it was clear that some of Hughes's men had done well while others had not, and probably would not. Moreover, the army's experience at the front, and the opportunity afforded senior commanders to see their junior officers under fire, meant that there were now solidly military criteria for judging their performance. Commonly accepted soldierly qualities like leadership ability and tactical competence could be measured, and individuals ranked by merit. Clearly, those in France were in the best position to see this evidence and make decisions of this sort, and the revised order-in-council gave them the professional independence to do so and to ignore all that was irrelevant.

Unhappily, what was irrelevant to officers at the front was important to Sam Hughes. He had made promises which had to be fulfilled, whether or not they could be justified by an individual's military experience or his performance in battle. Moreover, the new policy raised a chorus of complaints from the supernumeraries still in England, all of whom had benefited from the minister's largesse in some form or other. Arguing, with some validity, that they would be kept from France now that the new regulations allowed the Canadian formations there to look after their own, the supernumeraries claimed that they were being categorized, unfairly, as incompetents before they had an opportunity to prove themselves. Mindful of Hughes's temper, Generals Steele and MacDougall capitulated, enjoining Carson to find a way to send these officers to France.[22] Carson too succumbed, warning Alderson that if the supernumeraries continued to be neglected there would be strong and 'warrantable' dissatisfaction in Canada that would surely reflect badly on his leadership of the CEF.[23]

Alderson knew when to compromise. The minister had been defended by his friends in England even when they knew better and notwithstanding the new order-in-council, and further opposition would be seen as obstruction. Informing Carson that his main concern was that the frontline units should not suffer, Alderson therefore agreed to postpone further commissioning from the ranks in France until all the lieutenants and captains waiting in England had found appointments at the front. He drew the line there, however, because he still insisted that majors and lieutenant-colonels were not fit to lead men into battle.[24] Carson accepted Alderson's offer and followed his instructions until June 1916, when he found to his horror that the number of surplus junior officers in Britain had been so exaggerated by MacDougall that there was actually a potential shortage of casualty replacements in these ranks. Accusing MacDougall of living in a 'fool's paradise,' Carson immediately advised Alderson to recommence commissioning from the ranks as soon as and to whatever extent he wished. Junior officer appointments were once again in the hands of a professional.[25]

What is particularly interesting about this episode, however, is the way in which Major-Generals Arthur Currie and Richard Turner, militia lieutenant-colonels who had advanced to divisional command now that Alderson had taken over the Corps, were less willing than he to help Hughes, despite owing their appointments to the minister. Currie, for example, argued that junior officers then in England should train for six weeks in France just to determine their fitness to serve in the trenches.[26] Turner took a somewhat broader view. Anxious to protect his right to select subordinates for promotion, eager to extend the influence of the Corps to Bramshott and Shorncliffe, yet thoroughly familiar with Hughes's temperament, he drafted a scheme to amalgamate the officer lists in England and France to permit surplus lieutenants and captains in Britain to proceed to frontline battalions as a matter of course. That should satisfy Hughes. On the other hand, he wanted them to be replaced in England by non-commissioned officers and men commissioned from the ranks of the Corps who, after some months supervising training in England, would return to France as junior officers. Training in Britain would improve, Turner reasoned, because experienced personnel would be in charge. More important, once the original surplus had been reduced, all junior officers at the front would reflect the Corps' own preference.[27] Neither Currie nor Turner wanted anything to do with surplus majors and colonels.

Hughes was hostile to Turner's plan and the Carson-Alderson compromise for the obvious reason that they did nothing for these majors and colonels. Carson, MacDougall, and Steele were just as unhappy with Turner's scheme (and similar advice coming from the War Office) because their positions would be weakened if the Corps captured control of the CEF organization in Britain. Finally, Colonel Frank Reid, overseas director of organization, spoke for all who knew Sir Sam when he pointed out that Turner left no room for the minister's 'special promotions.'[28] It was up to Hughes to act, however, and he did so by asking his cabinet colleagues to revoke or amend the order-in-council signed at the prime minister's behest in September 1915 which had given Alderson independent authority over personnel matters in the first place.

Borden's policy had been wrong-headed, said Hughes, because Alderson's responsibility to superiors in the chain of command in France meant that authority to approve promotions and appointments in the Canadian Corps was left in the hands of British officers who themselves were ultimately responsible to the War Office, not the Canadian Department of Militia and Defence. Since British officers were, above all, loyal to each other, it was likely that the claims of Canadian officers would be neglected. Hughes therefore asked that the power to judge the competence of the Corps officers be returned to him so that the assertion of Canadian control over the CEF could be guaranteed.

The minister had made much the same point only a month before, when he charged that British 'Staff College theorists' had secured all the senior staff appointments in the Canadian third division because of 'Staff College paternalism' and the War Office's inclination to favour the 'pets' of British society.[30] This accusation did not sit well with the prime minister, who scolded Hughes for his intemperate language.[31] Nevertheless, in February 1916 a new order-in-council re-establishing Hughes's control over Canadian Corps appointments was approved without comment. The minister's appeal to nationalism had apparently succeeded despite the lingering fear that giving him a freer hand might lead only to more embarrassment.[32]

Hughes lost no time in righting the wrongs he had seen since the summer of 1915. Although he did not go so far as to dismiss anyone already serving at the front, all future appointments bore his mark. Regular officers were once again persona non grata and it was clear that those who had made it to France were unlikely to be promoted further, a development which angered both Gwatkin and Alderson. Carson was also upset, but for an entirely different reason. Despite looking after his close friends, Hughes had turned his back on many of the supernumeraries clamouring at Carson's door for employment in the Corps. No good reason can be found for the minister's quixotic failure to support individuals for whom he had campaigned so hard only a few months before, but the result was not surprising: Carson remained under fire from scores of already frustrated officers all the more disgruntled now that they had been betrayed (as they saw it) by Sir Sam himself. Without realizing it, Gwatkin and Alderson were beginning to gain allies from a most unlikely source.[33]

The War Office was no less upset. While admitting that the most recent Canadian order-in-council reflected their interpretation of ministerial responsibility better than its predecessor, British authorities feared that Hughes would inevitably involve himself in the day-to-day affairs of the Corps to a far greater extent than he should.[34] Hughes responded to such criticism in his typical emotional style. When British officers were responsible for approving Canadian appointments, he cried, their 'first hand cognizance' of officers' capabilities had too often hinged 'on influences other than military.' They preferred gentlemen, and British gentlemen at that. Hughes, by comparison, wanted to trust his knowledge of the officer corps and to take 'full advantage ... [of] the many authentic reports' he was receiving 'from officers, non-commissioned officers, and men in narratives to their friends ... as well as to the minister direct.'[35] Baldly, and without equivocation, he was justifying the practice Frederick Borden had disposed of years before, when officers regularly sought advancement through influence-peddling. Two months after this outburst Hughes told the new commander of the Canadian Corps, Lieutenant-General Sir Julian Byng, that he had never made a mistake in recommending or refusing an appointment or promotion, and Byng was warned to make no personnel moves without first discussing them with Hughes.[36]

There was little new in these charges or in Hughes's actions. The prime minister had heard or seen it all before and, when pressed, had never yet failed to give in to Hughes's demands. It was Alderson, for example, who paid for the sloppy battle for the St Eloi craters rather than Turner or Brigadier-General H.D.B. Ketchen, the two commanders most directly involved.[37] But as the summer of 1916 wore on, Borden became increasingly dissatisfied with the conduct of his minister. Already there had been a royal commission investigating corrupt practices in Hughes's supervision of munitions contracts; the overseas pay office, filled with Hughes's men, was said to be rife with venality; the Canadian medical service in England had been condemned in public; Steele and MacDougall were known to be at loggerheads, with Hughes doing nothing to solve the problem; and Sir John Carson's influence in Britain continued to grow without any formal approval by cabinet. Sir Sam had also caused delays in the dispatch of the fourth division to France, withholding authority for the move until his nominees for command of its brigades had been accepted. Finally, he was beginning to talk about sending a fifth division to the continent under his son, Garnet.[38]

All this was reason enough for Borden to ponder Hughes's future. His doubts increased, however, as he became more aware of the rising tide of complaints against the minister from formerly loyal and supportive officers in the CEF. Arthur Currie, for example, became so exasperated when he was sent a number of majors and colonels who, during their two-week tour of the front, behaved as if they were 'on vacation' and learned nothing, that he asked Carson when the Canadian government would 'stop playing and realize that we at least are serious.'[39] Soon after Victor Odlum, a Victoria newspaper proprietor and friend of Garnet Hughes, questioned the wisdom of allowing so distant a figure as Sir Sam to impose his appointments on the corps.[40] Even David Watson, selected by Hughes to command the fourth division over the highly regarded regular Henry Burstall, objected to the minister's all-pervading influence. Experience at St Eloi, he told Carson, had convinced him that divisional commanders must be free to choose their own subordinate commanders and staff officers.[41]

Much the same response greeted Hughes's subsequent proposal to replace the British staff officers in the Corps with Canadians who had no formal staff training. To a man the senior officers in France rallied to Alderson's support as he tried to block any such wholesale shuffle.[42] Currie, for one, protested that he knew of no Canadian qualified to serve on his staff, adding that he feared for his division's future should the minister get his way.[43] Major-General Mercer, soon to command the third division, agreed that only highly trained regulars should serve as senior staff officers in his brigades, and for the moment this excluded Canadians.[44] And Turner, who had joined in the criticism of Alderson and his staff a few months before, now admitted that he would prefer to keep British officers on his staff until Canadians could be properly trained.[45] Yet this was an unlikely prospect. Hughes's well-known bias against the Staff College had by and large prevented Canadian officers from receiving the professional education that would have qualified them for staff appointments in the Canadian Corps, and the alternative staff course he had established under Canadian auspices was acknowledged to be second-rate.[46]

The prime minister's representatives abroad confirmed both the volume and the validity of these complaints. In December 1915 R.B. Bennett, the Conservative member for Calgary East, noted that he had found no opposition at the front to the War Office's policy demanding that all staff officers be adequately trained.[47] Almost a year later, in September 1916, Ontario Liberal leader Newton Rowell told the prime minister that the majority of officers he had met in France regarded Sam Hughes as a definite liability to the country's war effort. In particular, Rowell's contacts, mostly junior and middle-level officers, wanted personnel matters left to their generals.[48]

Powerful criticism of the militia minister had also been voiced by Canada's high commissioner in London, Sir George Perley; but perhaps because Perley was known to be no friend of Hughes, his frequent support of Alderson (and later Byng) against the minister had carried little weight until Borden was looking for reasons to rid himself of his troublesome colleague.[49] These Perley provided in abundance during a trip to Canada in August and September 1916. Indeed, on 6 September he submitted a plan to restructure the overseas organization by setting up a small council of three or four members under a civilian but with a competent soldier on hand to exercise executive command of the army 'in a businesslike way.'[50] With Hughes absent in England, the prime minister did not want to act precipitously, but with one hook firmly in place, the high commissioner would not give up. Upon his return to Britain Perley reminded Borden of his doubts about a minister so isolated from the front making personnel decisions for the Corps. He then followed this with a strong defence of the appointments made by the British high command when it had responsibility for them.[51]

Borden's reply acknowledged that there had been many complaints about the influence of politics on CEF promotions, but the prime minister added that he was sure this had less to do with partisanship in the party political sense than with the personal favouritism shown to certain of Hughes's friends. Even so, Borden continued, this was a 'grave error' that needed correction. Perley agreed.[52] The situation was corrected, and soon. Sam Hughes was dismissed as minister of militia and defence on 9 November 1916, not long after Sir George Perley had been appointed to head a new, London-based department as minister of the overseas military forces of Canada. He, and not the militia minister in Ottawa, would exercise control over the expeditionary force. Perley at once promised Borden that the practice of favouritism would cease, to be replaced by the merit principle following the promulgation of yet another order-in-council returning authority over personnel matters in the CEF to the Canadian Corps and to Canadian military headquarters in London.[53]

When Sam Hughes left the cabinet the idea that a citizen army, led by dedicated, part-time amateur officers, was the natural and most effective form of military organization for Canada lost one of its most ardent and influential supporters. For although the former minister remained in Parliament, where he was free to excoriate his former colleagues for their disloyalty to the militia, he was a spent force who could not safeguard his dream: the creation of an army at home and abroad with a profoundly anti-professional bias. Hughes had, of course, uncovered some gems in his idiosyncratic process of selecting officers: Arthur Currie, in particular, but also David Watson, M.S. Mercer, and G.S. Tuxford. Richard Turner was less effective as a field commander than these officers, but he had qualities that made him a resolute general officer commanding the CEF in England after Hughes had gone.

However, the fact that Hughes's determination to make his own way paid some dividends is not the point at which an examination of his tenure as militia minister should stop. Many of the officers he chose at the battalion and regimental level were not fit for their appointments, although the effect of their presence in the field was fortunately muted by circumstances and conditions beyond his control. As one keen observer noted at the time, until 1918 the Canadian Corps' battles were largely set-piece affairs based on static trench lines, and as a result they rarely placed a premium on the imaginativeness or tactical good sense of platoon, company, and battalion commanders. Because of this, the tactical shortcomings of Hughes's undertrained appointees was not crucial as long as they had some talent for seeing to the needs of their men. By the time the Corps began to conduct more open warfare in 1918 some of these officers had been killed and others replaced; still others had used their time at the front to learn what they should be doing.[54]

Far more important was the way in which Hughes's disregard for the general staff's professional advice produced a thoroughly inefficient organization behind the front line. His ambition to see five, and perhaps six, divisions in France bore no relation to the country's resources and was bound to lead to a manpower crisis. The two hundred or so infantry battalions mobilized were far more than this grandiose establishment called for, yet even so they did not represent an efficient means of providing reinforcements. Many were allowed to pass the time in Britain against the day that additional divisions were formed, despite the constant need for replacements in France. Others were disbanded; but the heart-break and confusion that accompanied their disappearance and the vexing question of how to employ their now surplus officers caused unnecessary bitterness and resentment, both in France and Great Britain.

The lack of co-ordination among the three elements of the CEF in France, England, and Canada which Hughes's policies encouraged was a more serious problem still. With no uniformity in training, no mechanism to turn out the right numbers of men for each military trade, and no common promotion system, the army was in effect three independent forces. No single officer, including the chief of the general staff in Ottawa, knew the condition of the whole force, and no one could implement change throughout it. This state of affairs was exacerbated by Hughes's decision to place the training divisions in England under men eager to preserve the separate identity of their commands.

It was in fact the Canadian Corps' reaction against these and other policies that built the foundation for the development of a truly professional Canadian army. Not all Canadian officers reacted the way J.C. Creelman, a Hughes appointee, did when he learned that the minister had resigned:

There is a new contentment among us all. We walk with sprightlier step ... clear eyes ... cleaner cut ... The Mad Mullah of Canada has been deposed. The Canadian Baron Munchausen will be to less effect ... The greatest soldier since Napoleon has gone to his gassy Elbe, and the greatest block to the successful termination of the war has been removed. Joy, Oh Joy![55]

But the most successful senior officers in the Corps were determined that there must be a reordering of the system to give more authority and independence to military leaders who, because of their experience, could now be considered experts. As one former militia officer put it, 'You can have an entirely civilian army and, if it's entirely civilian its members will be dead before they are good.'[56]

7

The Canadian Expeditionary Force after Hughes, 1917–1918

The last two years of the Great War fulfilled many of Sam Hughes's expectations, although in ways that tended to satisfy his critics rather than the former minister himself. It was then that the Canadian Corps fought its greatest battles – Vimy Ridge, Amiens, Canal du Nord – after which no one could deny its reputation as one of the most formidable fighting formations in the allied armies: no mean feat for an army cobbled together from next to nothing over four years!

This was also the time when the Canadian Corps finally came under Canadian command. On 8 June 1917, two months after his victory at Vimy Ridge, Lieutenant-General Byng moved on to command the British Third Army and was succeeded by Arthur Currie, promoted from the first division. This laid to rest any suspicion that the British would never entrust a colonial, and a militia officer at that, with responsibility for a major formation. But the process leading to Currie's appointment was one Sam Hughes would have recognized. Disregarding Canada's demand that the government in Ottawa be consulted beforehand, Field-Marshal Haig made the move without reference to any Canadian political authority. His motives seem clear enough. He had never fully agreed with the claim that the Canadian government could 'interfere' (as Haig would have put it) in the internal administration of the Corps, and for Ottawa to comment on the choice of a commander would extend the Dominion's influence to the operational sphere, something the British had opposed since August 1914. Beyond that, Currie was known to have enemies in Canada, while Richard Turner, then in England, had reason to believe that George Perley had promised him a prior right to the appointment in December 1916. Haig's pre-emptive manoeuvre secured for him the Corps commander he wanted. As we shall see, Currie later suffered on this account, but for the moment it is sufficient to note that a compromise was arrived at which satisfied Currie, Turner, Haig, and the Canadian government – at least temporarily.

Byng and Currie together contributed to a recasting of the Canadian Corps' concept of operations in order to avoid the heavy casualties resulting from the line-abreast infantry assaults which dominated Allied operations in 1915 and 1916. Their innovations were not wholly original, however, so that the change in the Corps' tactical doctrine was actually an amalgam borrowed from the British, French, and (to a minor degree) German armies, along with some Canadian input.[1] Yet even if the new approaches to battle were neither wholly revolutionary nor uniquely Canadian, nor even the products of the Corps commanders' own thinking, Byng and Currie both encouraged their subordinates to use their initiative to find solutions to specific tactical problems imposed on the Western Front by the solid line of trenches stretching from Switzerland to the English Channel.

The process of innovation actually began as early as 1915, when Raymond Brutinel, a French engineer who had emigrated to Canada in 1905 and joined the Canadian service in 1914, experimented with mobile machine-guns and persuaded General Alderson that the indirect fire his motorized units could bring to bear on enemy positions would be of considerable value. The organization of this branch was advanced in Byng's time, as were counter-battery artillery procedures and the organization of the platoon to facilitate more flexibility in the employment of the infantry. Byng also introduced a new training philosophy, accepted with enthusiasm by the Corps, which recognized the essential intelligence of the non-commissioned personnel and emphasized the need to inform them of their specific battlefield objectives as well as the general flow of the fighting around them. When combined with careful rehearsal of their allotted tasks in the assault, first seen in the preparations for Vimy Ridge, this allowed attacks to proceed despite heavy casualties because the knowledge of what was being asked was not confined to the officer corps. Along with Byng's use of surprise, so that the enemy could not wait out prolonged, tell-tale artillery barrages secure in his shelters only to emerge when the infantry went over the top, the closer involvement of all ranks in preparing for battle did much to improve morale. And it was the combination of better morale and technique that saw the Corps through its most trying days in the mud and gloom of Passchendaele before the momentum changed and it went over to the attack in the summer of 1918.

Currie refined several of these innovations after he took over the Corps. The machine-gunners were organized into battalions and encouraged to develop the best tactics for their arm; the artillery's counter-battery staff came into its own, learning to fire by map reference to obviate the need for registration shots that could give warning of an impending attack; and the engineers were brought together under more centralized control to ensure that specialist construction troops could be made available wherever they were required. Beyond this, as one veteran recalled, Currie created an atmosphere which allowed for, in fact positively demanded, the movement of ideas from below. Imbued with the same spirit, his subordinate commanders 'knew, if we were going to survive ... we just had to do these things'; it was no longer good enough to defend procedures on the grounds that things had always been done this way – or because the British did them a certain way.[2]

Currie was also convinced that painstaking preparation and careful, realistic planning were necessary to save lives, and he would allow no one to tamper with his command if there was any risk of weakening his staff or destroying the fighting ability of the Canadian Corps. When, for example, the British tackled their reinforcement problem by reducing the size of their infantry divisions and urged Canada to do the same, thereby making available enough troops to field an army of two smaller corps, Currie refused outright despite the likelihood of his promotion to command the proposed Canadian Army. There were too few trained commanders and senior staff officers to provide competent leadership and support for an army, two corps, five or six divisions, and up to eighteen brigades, he explained, and it was therefore better to leave things as they were, where the Canadian Corps' performance could be guaranteed.[3]

A more serious problem arose in March 1918, when the German spring offensive tore through the British Fifth Army and threatened for a time to unhinge the Allied line completely. Casting about for any troops he could find to fill the gaps in his defences, Haig asked Currie to break up his Corps, temporarily of course, and disperse his divisions where there were holes, placing them under local British command. Persuaded that Canadians fought best when they served together under their own officers, and fearing that the dismembered Corps might never be re-established (if indeed, it was not destroyed, piecemeal, under officers he did not fully trust) Currie resisted Haig's suggestions.[4] He was not entirely successful. Two divisions were withdrawn for a short period, but Currie's unhelpful attitude soured relations with Haig. It was one thing, the British field-marshal observed, for Currie to define when Canadians fought best; it was quite another to withhold men from a decisive battle because it was likely to cause short-lived discontent. Going further, Haig added that no matter how important it was politically for a Canadian to command Canadians in their national corps, there were occasions when parochial interests must be subordinated to the needs of the Allied cause.[5]

Events proved to be on Currie's side. German capabilities were not so great as was imagined in March 1918, and their offensive stuttered to a halt without Canadian troops playing a decisive role in the defence. Indeed, the time for rest and refit and preparation for attack that the Canadians were allowed because they were not used up in the battles of early spring meant that they were more than ready to spearhead the assault when the Allies returned to the offensive on 8 August. Still, Canadian successes that day and during the last hundred days of the war did not entirely mollify Haig.

Feeling also ran high against Currie in Ottawa, where Sam Hughes still had friends, and where the seeking and granting of favours remained a way of life. Robert Borden worked diligently to secure Garnet Hughes's appointment to succeed Currie as GOC of the first division, and when Currie steadfastly refused, the prime minister made sure that the younger Hughes received command of the fifth division in England. And if this were not enough, the Corps commander was later subjected to intense pressure to move Garnet and his division to France when the British and some of Sam Hughes's friends urged the prime minister to support British proposals to create a two-corps Canadian army. Once again Currie stood firm, preferring to upset those at home than to dilute the quality of his command.[6]

These were not isolated incidents, and the constant harassment from Canada meant that Currie's tenure as Corps commander was not an easy one. In Sam Hughes's day he could have done little to withstand the pressure, but with George Perley now responsible for Canada's overseas military forces, Currie's problems were much less difficult. Given ministerial status, yet isolated from the day-to-day concern with patronage that weighed so heavily on his colleagues in Ottawa, Perley could afford to take a detached view of the army's needs and, more important, to exercise his executive authority to serve its needs. And, having witnessed the chaos and the bitterness created by Hughes's regime, he seems to have developed genuine sympathy for the plight of soldiers under heavy-handed political masters. In short, Currie had a friend at court. Bringing no preconceptions and no personal brief to his portfolio, and having no doubts about the limits of his own military expertise, Perley was prepared to offer the army professional independence so that it could fulfil its professional responsibilities.

Indications that things would be different under Perley came within weeks of his taking office. On 8 December 1916 he warned Borden that overseas headquarters was receiving far too many requests for favours bearing the prime minister's own letterhead. It was particularly disturbing that, despite Borden's promise that such partisan activity would cease, the majority of these messages sought to assist the sons of prominent Tory politicians and businessmen without the slightest regard for their military experience. That, Perley announced boldly, was a practice he wished to stop immediately.[7] When it did not – letters were still arriving almost daily – Perley raised the matter again in January, this time telling Borden that henceforth all such external interventions would prejudice an individual's chances of appointment or promotion. That was the only way, he explained, to rid the CEF of 'the present feeling of favouritism or special privilege' and to ensure that in future all personnel decisions would be based on professional merit as judged by competent military authorities.[8]

Old habits died hard, however, and in April 1917 Perley again found it necessary to caution the prime minister about the difficulties arising from Ottawa's interest in appointments. He reminded Borden that political affiliation was not a legitimate consideration in promotions, no matter what case might be made at home about the need to help friends; victory, he insisted, required the support of all Canadians whatever their partisan loyalties. If Borden needed something to satisfy his colleagues, Perley offered the argument that a successful war effort in which it could be shown that neither the Conservatives nor the Liberals had secured unfair advantages might well work to the government's favour in the next elections.[9]

The pressures on Borden were much too intense for him to follow Perley's advice completely. In June 1917, as we have already seen, he succeeded in confirming Garnet Hughes's command of the fifth division, and later that month, at the instigation of Sam Steele, he tried to block Brigadier-General A.C. Macdonell's promotion to replace Currie at first division on the grounds that the appointment belonged to Hughes.[10] This time Perley won. Garnet Hughes was not wanted at the front, he told the prime minister, while Steele's approach to Borden was sufficient cause to send the old general home.[11]

From this moment on the number of requests for favours reaching Perley's desk fell off sharply, an indication, perhaps, that his efforts were finally bearing fruit. However, another explanation is possible that cannot be credited to Perley. From late summer the manpower crisis overseas was growing and there was talk of a coalition between the governing Conservatives and those Liberals, mainly English-speaking, who accepted the necessity of imposing conscription. Under these circumstances, and particularly after a coalition Union government was formed in the fall, narrow partisanship in the area of promotions and appointments was inappropriate.[12] In the event, political interference in the Corps' personnel policies did not emerge again until April 1918, when those who had organized the heavy Union vote at the front during the general election demanded their rewards. No longer overseas minister, Perley could not prevent some of these men from receiving comfortable (but generally unimportant) positions on the staff in England. Still, his opinion had not changed:

unqualified men should not be given responsible appointments in France, he told his successor, and by and large they were not.[13]

Perley's determination to limit the number of politically motivated senior appointments in the CEF answered one of the long-standing complaints voiced by the Corps. Nevertheless, there remained the question of what to do with the hundreds of inexperienced officers still in England, who could not be left idle and yet, through no fault of their own, could not be trusted to serve in their established rank at the front. The training camps in England were also full of non-commissioned officers and men plucked from the ranks by Hughes for eventual commissioning but unwanted in their former battalions.[14]

Corps headquarters raised this issue with Perley early in 1917, asking him to reassert the policy giving battalion commanders the right to select candidates for commissioning.[15] What should be done about those already in England hoping for a posting to France the Corps commander did not say. Although the CGS in Ottawa no doubt agreed with Byng in principle, his position was becoming increasingly uncomfortable because there were also more than a thousand CEF officers in Canada appointed by Hughes still anticipating a call to France. General Gwatkin was at a loss as to how to deal with the protests sure to be made should Byng's advice be accepted.[16] The militia minister at the time, Sir Edward Kemp, was equally nonplussed, and simply asked Perley whether it was wise to choose junior officers from the ranks and whether this happened in the British army. When told that it did, he endeavoured to find an alternate route overseas for these officers, suggesting that they accompany reinforcement drafts to England and then undergo a rigorous training program before being posted to the Corps.[17]

This was similar to the plan proposed by Richard Turner a year before, but by now the majority of overseas officers wanted no part of this or any other scheme that threatened a battlefield commander's prerogative to select his subordinate officers.[18] Despite Kemp's objections, Perley sided with his staff and told the authorities in Ottawa to 'mind their own business.'[19] As a result, by the spring of 1917 almost all junior officers in the Canadian Corps were being commissioned from the ranks. At the same time Perley standardized the policy controlling all overseas promotions. A Military Secretary's branch was organized within his department to review the war records of all officers nominated for promotion in England and France and reject those without the necessary qualifications and experience; unit establishments would be firmly adhered to in order to end the 'special' appointments used by Hughes to reward his friends; and for the time being, advancement would come only to those who had seen action in France, thereby excluding everyone who had moved through the ranks in England without having experienced any fighting.[20]

From here Perley turned to the reinforcement question, directing that, in future, reinforcements would be gathered together in drafts, sent to England in the company of three or four conducting officers (where they would undergo final training), and allocated individually to frontline units as conditions warranted. To ensure that they arrived in England with the same standard of training – something which had never been guaranteed before – Perley agreed to adopt the War Office's fourteen-week syllabus and to demand that each recruit arrive in England with a certificate attesting to his progress.[21]

As a result of these changes, considered long overdue by Corps headquarters, the CEF of 1917–18 grew increasingly distinct from the 1914–16 expeditionary force, and even less like the pre-war militia and regular force. The junior officer cadre was being drawn almost exclusively from among the better battle-hardened NCOs and men, while vacancies in the senior ranks were filled by experienced junior officers. Knowledge, expertise, and merit had become the criteria for advancement, and there was simply no room at any level for those whose sole claim for consideration was their network of political ties or family friends. In short, talent and ability directly related to the task at hand had replaced political, social, and economic status or any other such ascriptive qualities in determining the worthiness of individuals nominated for the officer corps.

The influence of these changes was felt mainly in the combat arms, but in time they had an impact on the selection of officers to fill junior staff positions at battalion and brigade level. It had never been considered necessary to provide advanced staff education for those chosen to fill these appointments because, in the era of trench warfare at least, the burden they carried was not great. The static conditions at the front meant that they did not have to prepare for sudden and complex moves forward, while the lines of communication stretching to the rear remained more or less constant. Moreover, given the essential sameness of most attacks from 1915 to mid-1917, the job of ensuring adequate supplies of ammunition and other equipment was often routine. In short, with a little tutoring and on-the-job training, these lower-level appointments were no great challenge to Canadian officers who had passed through the Staff College or the best of those who had completed the militia staff course. Under Hughes there was no concerted effort to choose junior staff officers carefully, according to their experience; under Perley and the new regulations, there was. Staff course graduates tended to be selected first, but if none were available the choice was limited to the best regimental officers.

The responsibilities of senior staff appointments could not, however, be mastered on the spot by officers who lacked both advanced staffing training and considerable experience on active service. As a result, they were beyond the capabilities of militia staff course graduates and, in the beginning, of those few Canadians who had attended Camberley but had limited experience of war. Even Sam Hughes recognized this, and had asked the British for help. By 1915, however, the British army was also suffering from a shortage of trained staff officers and could not meet its own requirements, let alone Canada's. The War Office therefore established a special war staff college at Cambridge, and made its resources available to Canada. Here was a way to provide the CEF with its own trained military staff, ostensibly an important objective given the government's rhetoric about Canadianization; but the minister rejected the offer. Not only was he suspicious of all regular army training, but it seems that he also feared the creation of a group of Canadian officers well versed in British practice and attitudes. Hence his solution was to establish a wholly Canadian staff course in England to provide the Corps with the trained officers it required. Directed, however, by officers who were themselves only partially trained, and governed by the same politically motivated selection criteria imposed upon the CEF, this course could not measure up to its British counterpart, and was never recognized by imperial authorities as a legitimate staff training program.[22]

George Perley was no less sympathetic to Canadianization than Borden, but he was not prepared to sacrifice competence merely to see Canadians on the several staffs in France. Accordingly, he suspended the operations of Hughes's course shortly after taking office, and declared the certificates of qualification earned by its graduates null and void.[23] In its place he adopted the most recent British regulations. Promising regimental officers would be selected by their superiors to understudy the duties of staff captains and brigade majors; upon acceptable performance, they would move on to divisional headquarters for further training before being sent back to fill established positions at the junior level on brigade staffs. From April 1917 those who continued to prove themselves were sent to the British war staff course at Cambridge, where they prepared for divisional and corps appointments. Strict rules were enforced to reduce the likelihood of political interference. Entry to the staff course was restricted to those with staff experience at the front, while nominations for 'staff learner' appointments had to originate with an individual's commanding officer. All had to be approved by the Corps commander.[24]

There were limits to what this system could accomplish. The most senior positions realistically open to Canadian officers – GSO 1 at division and corps, and brigadier-general, general staff (BGGS) at Corps – demanded significant experience, and in the normal course of events no more than a handful of

Canadians could have been made ready to shoulder these responsibilities over the course of the war. Fully aware of this, Perley cautioned Ottawa not to set its hopes too high. With Borden's concurrence, he approached the War Office asking that a number of Canadians be given GSO I training; BGGS appointments could, for the moment, be forgotten.[25] The War Office could hardly refuse so reasonable a request, and as a result by the summer of 1917 several Canadian officers were understudying GSO I positions with British divisions.[26] Moreover, when Colonel R.M. Sims, the Canadian government's representative at Field-Marshal Haig's headquarters, suggested that the minister should control the selection of candidates for higher staff training, Perley's response was unequivocal: the political heads of the militia and the expeditionary force, he wrote, had no business involving themselves in matters of purely professional concern.[27]

Perley's confidence in his staff, and his consistent view that they knew best on military matters, may well have influenced the organizational structure he chose for his overseas ministry. As will be remembered, one of Sam Hughes's last acts as militia minister had been to create an Acting Overseas Sub-Militia Council to improve the administration of the CEF in England and France. Borden had rejected Hughes's solution as a remedy for the CEF's troubles, no doubt because of the individuals appointed to the council. That did not mean that the prime minister objected to the actual structure Hughes had recommended; it was, after all, patterned after its parent organization in Ottawa. Indeed, when he proposed either General Gwatkin or Major-General Fiset, the deputy minister, as chief of the general staff overseas, it was obvious that he expected the overseas ministry to be organized along familiar lines.[28]

Perley fooled everyone. First he rejected Gwatkin, Fiset, and any other officer from Canada because they had no experience abroad during the war. Next, he chose to employ as many permanent force officers as possible because of their greater familiarity with staff work. Brigadier-General P.E. Thacker and Colonel A. Kemmis-Betty, Staff College graduates both, were named to head the adjutant general's branch, while Brigadier-General A.D. McRae, quartermaster general in London, was retained because he had done good work despite interference from Canada. Finally, Perley appointed no CGS, no 'first among equals.' Instead, after Arthur Currie had refused, he brought Major-General Turner to London and named him general officer commanding the Canadians and chief military adviser to the minister. All other officers at headquarters (including the AG and QMG) were subordinate to him.[29]

This was precisely the same military hierarchy that had existed in Canada before Frederick Borden's reform of 1904, and it was precisely the organization that many had blamed for the sorry state of civil-military affairs in the

Dominion from 1872 to 1904. Why Perley should have chosen this structure in spite of the trouble his predecessors had with Herbert, Hutton, Dundonald, and other GOCs has never been explained. It may be that after the confusion of the Hughes era he desired a straightforward, uncomplicated, and unambiguous military hierarchy that, because of the GOC's predominance, would protect Turner from rivalries, jealousies, and any disinclination to co-operate on the part of his subordinates. Or Perley may have simply followed British practice where there was only one chief of the imperial general staff under whom served the BEF's commander-in-chief, and the general officers commanding-in-chief of the various army commands and geographic areas with which the Canadian Expeditionary Force in England could be compared. Whatever the reason for his decision, however, Perley made it clear to Borden that with Turner as GOC and Walter Gow as deputy minister he had no need or desire for an overseas council acting as a collegial decision-making body.

Perley's overseas department and Turner's military headquarters did not win universal approval. Some charged the two with interfering in the Corps' internal affairs, either to assert the principle of civilian control or because Turner believed he held the senior Canadian appointment overseas. To others the new overseas ministry seemed to be a vast wasteland, a hot bed of political favouritism in which room was found for more surplus and unfit officers than even Sam Hughes and John Carson had collected as hangers-on. Finally, there was considerable criticism of the precedent involved in naming Perley to the cabinet when he would not be available routinely and regularly to answer questions about his department in Parliament.[30]

The latter complaint was well founded on constitutional grounds, but hostility to the new organization overseas was not motivated primarily by deep concern about the damage being done to the Canadian political system through the appointment of an absentee minister. Rather, the criticism levelled at Perley and his department reflected, in the main, a desire for revenge on the part of Hughes's followers.[31] There is no evidence to support their claim that Perley and Turner maintained, let alone intensified, the kind of partisanship in CEF appointments that prevailed under Hughes's regime, while the assertion that overseas headquarters grew to meet the minister's desire to manage a large personal empire was a complete fabrication. In fact, the streamlining measures put forward by Brigadier-General McRae and approved by Perley cut so deep and affected so many Tory office-holders that Edward Kemp was wont to complain that they could only have been inspired by an anti-government, pro-Liberal bias. This, of course, was absurd: Perley was loyal to his party even if he was no blind partisan.[32]

Nevertheless, there was some truth to the stories about bad feeling between

Turner and Corps headquarters, although not while Byng was in command. Turner was not about to challenge his former chief while Perley worked amicably with Byng's headquarters to improve administration behind the frontline and in those areas outside its jurisdiction. The relationship between London and the Corps deteriorated following Currie's promotion, yet even so there is little to link this to any kind of consciously conceived and orchestrated plan on the part of Perley and Turner to restructure the overseas organization in order to bring the Corps more firmly under Turner's direct control. Rather, the difficulties that arose seem best explained by the understandable but unhappy fact that by June 1917 Turner and Currie, whose careers had progressed in much the same way at much the same pace, were personal rivals.

Each had commanded a brigade in the first contingent; each had suffered a bad battle in which his leadership was called into question; and each had nevertheless survived to take over a division, Turner in August 1915, Currie in September. Both were considered for the GOC appointment in London. Currie, in fact, had been Perley's first choice for the position because he was more capable and because he was 'generally preferred by officers at the front,' an important consideration given the overseas minister's desire to bring harmony to the CEF. Turner, on the other hand, was 'more popular' with the Conservative party, in part because of Currie's presumed Liberal sympathies.[33]

Reluctant to surrender command in the field, and suspecting that political intrigue lay behind the proposed transfer, Currie refused Perley's offer,[34] whereupon the minister turned immediately to Turner. The GOC of the second division was no more eager than Currie to leave the front, but once Turner was assured by Perley that his seniority would count for something if the Corps became available, he relented.[35] When the vacancy arose, however, Byng and Haig selected Currie without notifying Perley. By then Currie had had an additional six months' experience denied to Turner; he had commanded the first division well during this period; and he remained the choice of his colleagues.[36]

Perley accepted the fait accompli giving Currie the Corps, but at the same time he strove to safeguard Turner's personal prestige. The latter was appointed lieutenant-general just ahead of Currie, thereby maintaining his nominal seniority in the *Militia List*, and Currie was persuaded to acknowledge Turner's status as Perley's chief military adviser. In addition, Turner was given some authority to oversee all overseas promotions, although it was never intended that he should exercise a general veto over Currie's selections.[37] Still, command of the Corps was the real plum, and it is unlikely that any compromise could have compensated completely for its loss.

Currie's feelings of insecurity are also easily understood. Though few knew it, he was under a cloud in 1917 because of dubious financial dealings before the war, and would ultimately depend upon fellow officers and departmental officials to bail him out. The Corps commander was at the same time under fire from a coterie that had coalesced around the interests of Sam Hughes, Garnet Hughes, H.D.B. Ketchen, and other Tory war-horses. Considerable pressure was exerted on him to find places for these latter two in particular, and the animosity produced by his failure to do so lasted throughout the war.[38]

All this made Currie prone to over-react when there were even slight differences with Ottawa and London, a propensity easily seen in the one fully documented quarrel between Turner and Currie to take place while Perley was overseas minster. Discovering that Turner had approved the promotions of several supply officers without reference to Corps headquarters, Currie exploded. 'Why do *you* suggest?' he asked Perley, speaking of overseas headquarters in general, when the Corps commander was 'the most cognizant of all the factors'. 'Surely, it is for me to say who should be recommended,' not the minister's subordinates who were 'too enthusiastic for their friends'.[39] In fact, according to British practice, these appointments were quite properly within the purview of McRae (as QMG), Turner, and Perley. But such arguments did not appease Currie; the crime had been committed and that was that. In the end, Currie was persuaded to drop the matter only because he trusted Perley's assurance that good men had, after all, been appointed, even if by the wrong authority.

This did not augur well for the future. Although Perley had worked assiduously to establish an administrative and management system that could institutionalize harmony between the Canadian Corps and overseas headquarters, he had failed. Increasingly, Turner and Currie co-operated only because of the minister's personality and the atmosphere of trust he had cultivated with each of them individually; this, too, would soon disappear.

Worn out after a year combining the roles of high commissioner and minister responsible for the CEF in Europe, George Perley left the overseas department in October 1917. He was replaced by Edward Kemp, Hughes's successor as militia minister in Ottawa, who was followed there by Major-General S.C. Mewburn, one of the pro-conscription Liberals who had joined Borden's Union government. Kemp's arrival in London produced a noticeable change in attitude on the part of the civil side of the overseas ministry. Like most ministers of militia before him, Kemp suspected that the soldiers would always try to shake free of civilian control and usurp power that rightfully belonged to the politicians. Convinced that this process was well under way in Perley's administration, he lost little time in trying to restore what he considered to be the proper civil-military balance.

Turner had the new order explained to him on 17 November 1917. Clear limits would be set on the GOC's executive authority, Kemp declared, and henceforth the minister was to be consulted on all matters involving new policies, expenditure of funds not already approved, communications with either the War Office or Ottawa, and 'points of such magnitude' that they called for political involvement.[40] Kemp's position was constitutionally sound, but it worried Canada's adjutant general in England nevertheless because it re-opened the prospect of political interference. Major-General Thacker moved quickly, therefore, to protect the professional independence the army overseas had already won under Perley. Among other things, he advised Turner, Currie must be brought back into the fold, under tighter control from Canadian headquarters in London, for as long as no single officer was supreme over both the Corps and the Dominion forces in England, Kemp could divide and conquer. Thacker's solution was simple. Turner's position should be elevated to GOC-in-chief; Thacker himself should be made GOC administration; and Currie should be directed to report to Turner, who would henceforth be responsible for co-ordinating military policy, organization, and administration in both France and England.[41]

Turner would not go that far. Instead, he asked only that Kemp confirm his right to communicate directly with authorities in France on purely military matters.[42] Perhaps Turner knew that Kemp would never accept Thacker's far-reaching design for reorganization. Perhaps he did not want to antagonize Currie. Whatever the case, Thacker's forecast that relations between Canadian headquarters in London and the Corps would not be the best – and that Kemp would take advantage of this to step in – proved accurate.

In February 1918 Currie complained that Turner's headquarters continued to meddle in affairs which Perley had defined as concerning the Corps commander and Field-Marshall Haig alone.[43] Turner responded that, as Kemp's chief military adviser, he must have access to Haig to obtain information, to present the views of the Canadian government to the British high command, and, if necessary, to comment on operations particularly as they affected the expeditionary force. Furthermore, he charged, Currie's reports to Kemp could not be accepted 'at face value,' coloured as they were by the Corps commander's fierce loyalty to his officers and men.[44]

Kemp was already aware that Turner and Currie no longer worked effectively together. He had told Mewburn as much in January and, influenced by developments in February and March, he submitted a more gloomy report still in April. The problem, he explained, was that Turner was unsure of his authority to deal with the Corps, while Currie was uncertain of whom he should look to for direction. Turner had tried to smooth things over by refraining from issuing instructions directly to the Corps commander, choosing instead to relay messages through the government's representative at Haig's headquarters, Colonel R.M. Sims.[45] But Currie did not co-operate with this officer either, and in fact resented his presence at the front even more than he objected to Turner's activities.[46] Kemp was equally annoyed with the soldiers' attitude to civilian authority. In February 1918 he charged that the senior officers in France and England had been away from Canada for so long that they had lost sight of their constitutional responsibilities. For them there was only the 'military idea,' the belief that only they knew how to manage the war effort.[47] Kemp did nothing for the time being, but when the situation had not improved by early spring he decided to act, to settle the Currie-Turner rivalry once and for all.

On 1 April 1918 Kemp created an overseas military council modelled after the Militia Council in Ottawa. He would in the future be involved directly in the day-to-day affairs of the CEF, and all decisions would flow from the council instead of having some emanate from the minister's office and others from Turner's. There was, however, one difference between the overseas organization and that in Canada. Kemp specified that he wished Turner to be named his chief of staff, and not chief of the general staff.[48] Precisely what significance this had for Kemp we do not know. In the continental armies a 'chief of staff' had greater prestige and power than a chief of the general staff in the British system: he was more than a first among equals because he co-ordinated the work of the AG and QMG and was considered their superior. In Britain and Canada the CGS, AG, and QMG sat as equals on the army and militia councils, each responsible for his own branch, and all with the right of direct access to the minister. If Kemp was aware of this subtlety, he may have been sending a signal affirming that Turner had not been demoted and remained in authority over Thacker and McRae. On the other hand, it is possible that Kemp was attempting to emphasize the military's subordination to the civil power by defining Turner's position as personal staff officer to the minister rather than as the head of a quasi-independent general staff that might yet stand in opposition to its political master. Whatever the reasoning, Turner's executive authority as chief of staff was no longer what it had been as GOC.

Fixing the relationship between the Overseas Military Forces of Canada and the Canadian Corps was Kemp's second priority, and it was itself a two-stage process. Although it had always been understood that Field-Marshal Haig would control operations and that he should be consulted about any changes in policy that might affect the Canadian Corps' fighting efficiency, by 1918 Sir Robert Borden was anxious that British civil and military authorities alike recognize the Dominion government's ultimate responsibility for all of Canada's overseas forces. This happened in April, when the War Office and Haig formally acknowledged that the Overseas Military Forces of Canada were a single entity comprising the Corps, non-Corps troops in France, and the CEF in England – and that all reported to Kemp as minister.[49]

With this settled and with Turner's status defined, Kemp was free to attempt to bridge the gap between Turner and Currie. The problems of the past remained. Currie still resented all efforts by Canadian headquarters in London to give direction to his command, either directly or through Colonel Sims, while Turner and his staff did not fully trust Currie and certainly objected to his dictatorial style. In Kemp's view the only solution was to create a Canadian Section representing the government, his ministry, and all branches of the staff at Haig's general headquarters in France. This would be the halfway house for Anglo-Canadian and Corps–OMFC communications, in this way allowing the Canadian government direct contact with Haig and the OMFC similar contact with the armies in France without suborning the military hierarchical relationship between Currie and the commander-in-chief in the field and without giving rise to a direct Currie-Turner confrontation.[50]

Still, this solution had not been easy. It took three months of discussion with Turner and his colleagues before Kemp felt able to go ahead with his reorganization scheme, and even then, he informed the prime minister, it had been necessary to exercise 'great patience' and to stave off more than one threatened resignation before he implemented the plan.[51] Similarly, Kemp had had to reassure Currie that the Corps would not be saddled with a 'budding bureaucrat' in the Canadian Section at GHQ. In fact, the officer selected to replace Sims, Brigadier-General J.F.L. Embury, had been chosen in the main because he was acceptable to Currie.[52] Yet tension remained until the end of the war.

The formation of Embury's Canadian Section at Haig's general headquarters was the last in a series of developments confirming and strengthening Canada's administrative control over its expeditionary force and declaring the Dominion's right to have direct access to those who controlled the Canadian Corps' operations. In turn, the impressive performance of Canadian troops in battle accelerated the process by which Canada became a truly independent member of the British Commonwealth. Having entered the war because Britain was at war, the Dominion took part in the peace negotiations and signed the Treaty of Versailles in its own right because Robert Borden's demand for at least this much autonomy could not be denied.

It has been argued that only the creation of an overseas ministry as an institution could have successfully reformed the organization and administration of the CEF and thereby laid the foundation for the Canadian victories of 1917–18 which were so important when the prime minister staked his claim.[53]

That puts the case too strongly. To be sure, Borden's decision to set up a separate overseas department was instrumental in negating Sam Hughes's influence over the expeditionary force, which was in itself essential for improving the Corps' fighting efficiency. Similarly, commanders and their staff officers in England and France were helped considerably by having a minister resident in London, close to the centre of the Allied war effort. However, the creation of an efficient military organization from the front line to the most rearward unit, and the nature of the reforms eventually adopted, depended less on the mere existence of an overseas ministry than on what the minister supervising the department was willing to do. Had Sam Hughes or someone sharing his point of view been posted to London in December 1916 instead of Perley, there is reason to question whether the rules and regulations governing the overseas military forces would have changed at all. Contrary to custom, however, Perley chose to give the soldiers their heads; because of their experience at the front, they in turn promulgated personnel policies based almost exclusively on merit. To his credit, Perley supported the soldiers as strongly as possible whenever the politicians at home showed signs of resurrecting the traditional practice of rewarding individuals because of their party affiliation or social standing.

Sir Edward Kemp's opinion of his military advisers was more akin to Hughes's than George Perley's. He believed that his predecessor in London had allowed the general staff too much power and influence, and when he left England after the war he convinced Robert Borden that Richard Turner should not be offered employment in the peacetime army because the general's 'peculiar temperament' made it 'very difficult to make him realize the limits between civil and military authority.[54] Sam Hughes could not have put it better. Yet despite his consistent effort to restore what he considered to be the proper civil-military balance in the overseas ministry, Kemp scrupulously avoided interfering in matters primarily of professional military concern. He did not force Currie or Turner to make promotions they believed to be wrong, for example, and he offered welcome support in the fight against pressure from London and Ottawa to create a two-corps army. In this way he, too, nurtured the professional independence the soldiers had struggled to achieve under Hughes, and which had first flowered under Perley.

The overseas army's growing freedom to govern itself, directly attributable to the performance of the Canadian Corps on the Western Front, suggested that a profound change had occurred in the management of Canada's military affairs. By 1918 the soldiers had won the respect of the politicians because of their competence in battle, and their advice on military matters was seen to be responsible and objective. In effect, Perley, Kemp, and (at home) Mewburn had acknowledged that they did not know as much as – or more than – their senior military staff, and in so doing affirmed the army's status as a professional organization well able to fulfil its responsibilities. For its part, the overseas army, and particularly the militia element within it, had broken with tradition and imposed upon itself professional standards of conduct, behaviour, and, most important of all, expertise. Competence, not connection, was the criterion for advancement. And when Currie gave up the chance to command an army because he was convinced that Canadian fighting efficiency would suffer, there was no finer demonstration of the professional ethos that requires loyalty to service before self.

Canada and its army had learned the lessons that had prompted the professional reform of the main European armies a half-century before. Surrounded by potential adversaries, the countries of Europe dared not forget what experience had taught them. But when the Canadian Corps came home in 1919, it was returning to a country that had no obvious enemies, and for which, as a result, there was no natural, pre-ordained standard of military preparedness. Secure in North America, Canadians could forget the lessons of the Great War at very little risk to themselves.

The implications of this for the peacetime army were considerable. Having learned how to soldier in the trenches of France, and accustomed to leading well-equipped formations and units at close to full strength, would regular officers be content if the country chose to return to a traditional, militia-oriented, underfunded, underequipped, and undermanned military organization? Having demanded and secured a promotion system based on merit, how would they react if political, family, social, or business connections again became criteria for advancement? Could they accommodate themselves to an environment in which, for political reasons, their advice on defence policy was ignored. When the guns stopped firing on 11 November 1918 and those who would return to the peacetime permanent force contemplated the future, they chose to expect, and work for, the best.

PART IV

THE PROFESSIONAL ARMY'S STRUGGLE FOR LEGITIMACY, 1919–1939

8

Post-war reconstruction and the higher organization of national defence

Planning for the peacetime reconstruction of the Canadian army began at least a year before the war in Europe was over. Freed by conscription from beating the bushes for volunteers for home defence or the expeditionary force, and benefiting from the new spirit of co-operation with the overseas ministry, Willoughby Gwatkin turned his hand to what he knew best: laying the foundation for efficient mobilization in the next crisis. The CGS knew that he faced a number of special problems because of what had happened since August 1914. For one thing, Canada now had two distinct armies – the militia at home and the CEF – which were organized along different lines and had few traditions in common. There was no room in the smaller peacetime establishment for all units from both forces; but such were the loyalties involved, there was no easy and obvious solution as to which should survive. Perhaps, Gwatkin suggested, the two organizations could be integrated, to combine the historic roots of the militia's named regiments with the unit identities, battle honours, and esprit de corps of the CEF's numbered battalions.

Gwatkin was concerned about such things because, in his view, they affected the nature of a country's military spirit. It was important that a young country like Canada lose neither the militia myth embodied in such institutions as the Queen's Own Rifles and Royal Grenadiers nor the enviable fighting record of the 2nd and 8th battalions, CEF. There was, however, one aspect of the old militia myth, embodied in Sam Hughes's dramatic call to arms in August 1914, which Gwatkin was determined to erase. Despite the initial popularity of the minister's action and the applause he garnered because of the first division's rapid deployment to England, the CGS regarded Hughes's mobilization plan as a failure and a dangerous precedent: it had made no allowance for proper training of the expeditionary force before it went overseas; there were no provisions for replacements and reinforcements; and the unthinking rush to send as many Canadians as possible to the front had sown the seeds of the recent conscription crisis.

Hoping to take advantage of the generally sympathetic view of the army then prevailing, and persuaded that Sam Hughes's dismissal and the adoption of compulsory service together indicated a willingness on the government's part to think about defence in a new way, Gwatkin submitted his draft proposals in November 1917. These called for a scheme of national defence so firmly entrenched in legislation and so complete that, once adopted, it would prove difficult for future ministers to toy with. Strong garrisons would be established on both the Atlantic and Pacific coasts and comprehensive defence schemes developed for each militia district so that, in the matter of home defence, politicians would never again feel the need to resort to the improvised, and exaggerated, measures that had plagued the CGS for the past three years. Similarly, Gwatkin asked that the basic form and organization of future expeditionary forces be settled now, to allow the general staff to work out the best structure for the post-war army and to begin planning for peacetime training. To this end he recommended the construction of several permanent military areas large enough to accommodate full-scale divisional manoeuvres.

The military establishment required to undertake these responsibilities was going to be much larger than before. The permanent force, in Gwatkin's view, should be expanded to a minimum of twenty thousand officers and men, with infantry battalions and representative units of the other arms and services located in each of the military districts to act as instructors and as the nucleus of the field army. But using the First World War as his model, and noting in particular that the pre-war professional armies had long since disappeared, having been overwhelmed by masses of conscript soldiers, the CGS concluded that the heart and soul of the country's defences should be provided by a completely revitalized militia. Manned at war strength at all times, adequately equipped and trained in the use of modern weapons, and led at first by experienced veterans, the militia was expected to be able to put battle-ready formations of all arms into the field at extremely short notice either for the direct defence of Canada or as part of an expeditionary force for service overseas. In order to hasten the process of revitalization – in fact to build a firm base that could attract soldiers from the Canadian Corps to the militia after the war – Gwatkin recommended that the district commands be offered immediately to senior permanent force officers then in France. Still, the crucial feature in Gwatkin's plan, upon which all else depended, was his contention that the military force he was describing could only be maintained if the government was willing to retain conscription after the war. The period of full-time active service, he hastened to add, could be limited to as little as four months, the time needed to conduct basic training, but it was essential that all adult males spend a further two years compulsory service in the part-time militia before their military obligations could be considered fulfilled. Anything less than this, he warned, and the army would not be ready for battle on the outbreak of war in the future.[1]

The government did not act on Gwatkin's advice before the war was over. Management of the country's war effort was a large enough task, and arriving at decisions on fundamental questions of military policy so far in advance was something with which Canadian politicians were neither familiar nor comfortable. General Currie had also had his say. Having learned of Gwatkin's memorandum through the overseas ministry, he issued a strong warning against transferring permanent force officers to the military districts in Canada no matter how helpful they might be to the CGS. For the regulars to leave the front for secure appointments at home before victory had been won, he explained, would tarnish their image forever; if they stayed in France until the end, however, there was a chance that the rivalry and bitterness that marked relations between regulars and militiamen prior to 1914 could be avoided in the future.[2]

Gwatkin wisely refrained from engaging Currie, or the cabinet, in further discussion on the matter until the war was over. But as soon as he saw an opportunity, he asked the deputy minister whether it would be possible to bring forward legislation introducing peacetime conscription during the next session of Parliament, when the country and its political leaders were still used to the idea of compulsory military service. Gwatkin offered to draft the bill himself if it would speed things up. Much to his delight, and surprise, the idea was received warmly and with enthusiasm by the militia minister, but with one proviso. It was essential, Gwatkin was told, to solicit opinions from the overseas ministry and the Canadian Corps, as they were also part of the country's military hierarchy.[3]

Senior officers overseas had also been thinking about Canada's post-war military organization and, as Gwatkin surmised, these veterans of the Canadian Corps were particularly concerned with maintaining the identities, battle honours, and traditions of their wartime regiments. 'Better that a dozen peace regiments [that is, the unmobilized militia in Canada] should go to the wall,' declared Major-General A.C. Macdonell, commanding the first division, 'than the CEF units be lost.'[4] Brigadier-General James H. MacBrien, commander of the 12th Brigade, agreed. Although Macdonell was senior, in fact it was MacBrien's opinion that carried the greater weight. Named chief of staff to Kemp in December 1918, he was asked to draft the overseas ministry's proposals on military organization for the post-war era.

Like Gwatkin, MacBrien believed that the Great War had proved once again the importance of peacetime preparedness, either to deter aggression or to enable an army to do well in its first encounters with the enemy. As a result he, too, favoured the idea of creating a national army supported by conscription. His plan was therefore similar to Gwatkin's in its basic recommendations, but went much further in trying to militarize Canadian society. Army training was to begin at adolescence, for example, when boys would enter the cadets, and reach its peak at eighteen, when all young men entered the regular force for a minimum of four months. Three years compulsory part-time service with the militia would follow, after which they could leave the army but would remain subject to recall to active duty in the event of a crisis. Within a decade, MacBrien calculated, there would be sufficient numbers of trained soldiers in the country to allow for the mobilization of up to fifteen divisions for the direct defence of Canada. Permanent force strength under MacBrien's plan would rise to thirty thousand, all ranks, with all officers being drawn from either the Royal Military College or training programs run in conjunction with civilian universities. Regimental training would be conducted in Canada, augmented by exchanges with the British army, while staff education would be the responsibility of the British army's staff colleges at Camberley and Quetta, India. With this kind of education and training available, given guarantees of modern equipment, and after allowing permanent force pay and pension benefits to rise to appropriate levels, MacBrien was sure that Canada would have a well-motivated and respected regular professional army able not only to teach well but also to hold its own on any battlefield.[5]

What was this army for? To MacBrien, as well as Gwatkin, there was reason to maintain sufficient military force in Canada to at least cause the Americans to stop and think about taking action against Canada if, as some feared, British and American interests some day clashed. Secondly, both were convinced that Canada might be called upon to participate in another major war overseas, and both wanted the army to be better prepared than it had been in August 1914. The two generals also agreed that communism was a potential threat to Canada, and they saw a large army as an effective internal security force. Most important of all, however, Gwatkin and MacBrien were convinced that compulsory military training would, in the long run, persuade Canadians that defence was the responsibility of everyone; and as long as it was applied equitably and universally, as a matter of routine, peacetime conscription might even break down the barriers that had emerged during the war between Canada's English- and French-speaking communities.[6]

Perhaps more than Gwatkin, MacBrien realized that this was a revolutionary program unlikely to be adopted before certain structural changes in military and political organization had taken place. Within the militia department itself, for example, it was important that the army spoke with one voice, so that the minister did not receive conflicting advice from his general staff officers. Accordingly, he urged that the status of the senior officer at headquarters be elevated to that of a commander-in-chief, who alone would submit policy proposals to the minister.[7]

But this was only a partial solution. MacBrien also understood that no matter how much goodwill might exist between the militia minister and his generals, or how sympathetic the minister was to the army, the overall support the armed forces could count on from the government depended ultimately on cabinet's interest in defence questions and its general attitude toward the military. A co-operative and helpful minister could easily be ignored and overruled by colleagues ignorant of or hostile to the armed forces' aims and objectives. Nothing would be gained by hiding the general staff away. That was sure to arouse suspicion, while cloaking the army's plans in a veil of secrecy and keeping them from other departments would do nothing to convince the latter of the genuine needs of the army.

To solve this problem, MacBrien recommended the creation of an interdepartmental organization patterned after the British Committee of Imperial Defence to analyse the strategic situation affecting Canada. A second body would study the country's war potential. Civil servants would be represented on both committees, of course, and would therefore be in a position to comment on military policy, but MacBrien was not worried by this prospect. Instead, he was confident that encouraging other departments of government to share responsibility for the state of the country's defences and its survival in war would lead them to err on the side of generosity rather than restraint.[8]

MacBrien's recommendations were submitted to Kemp, who passed them to Ottawa for future consideration. In the meantime, the general was selected by Prime Minister Robert Borden to represent the Dominion at a War Office-sponsored conference aimed at drafting a 'considered scheme for imperial defence' which would, in due course, be presented to the Imperial War Cabinet.[9] MacBrien was warned, of course, to make no commitments of any kind, George Perley noting that even though the conference's final report would not be binding, it was important that the government did not run the risk of 'embarrassment' from a document that asked for more in the way of military expenditure than the Canadian treasury could bear.[10] More suspicious still, Edward Kemp declared that it was 'impossible for [a soldier] ... to voice the opinion of the Government on the general question of post war organization.'[11]

As it was, the empire's Post-Bellum Committee failed to submit a final report, embarrassing or otherwise, because the three British services could not agree among themselves how best to share the responsibility for imperial defence.[12] Still, MacBrien was able to make some progress when he talked with the British army representatives about what Canada should be doing for local defence, and how it might contribute to the defence of the empire as a whole. While careful to qualify his remarks with the warning that it was for Ottawa to decide in each case, MacBrien went so far as to discuss specific numbers. For home defence, he suggested, an army of about fifteen divisions was being considered, while the expeditionary force establishment might be as large as seven divisions.[13] As speculative as these discussions were, this was precisely the kind of detail Perley and Kemp had wanted to avoid – and with good reason. As we shall see, MacBrien's statement, which was never agreed to by the Canadian government, soon came to represent a commitment among soldiers on both sides of the Atlantic and was the touchstone for general staff planning in London as well as Ottawa.

Arthur Currie certainly knew about Gwatkin's plan for military reorganization before he returned to Ottawa to take up the appointment of inspector general of militia and chief military adviser to the minister. He may also have been in touch with MacBrien while the latter was preparing his paper in London. Whatever the case, Currie had no argument with the basic changes the two had recommended. Moreover, he believed that he was in a good position to carry out their reforms, and to usher in the new era of civil-military relations MacBrien in particular was looking forward to. Although his formal welcome home was not all that it could have been, and the Hughes faction was still out for revenge, Currie had the loyalty of most of his subordinates, particularly those who had been overseas throughout the war, and the goodwill of Canadians at large. He was, after all, a victorious battlefield commander, with a status enjoyed by no other Canadian officer; he had time and again proved that he would not sacrifice the Dominion's interests to accommodate British policies; and as a former militia officer who had demonstrated professional competence he was one individual who might be able to build a bridge between the citizen army and the permanent force. As such his voice would be exceedingly difficult for any political party to ignore.[14]

Currie's commitment to reform and his willingness to act were evident immediately upon his arrival in Ottawa. Although the government had made no decision on what its post-war defence policy would be, a committee headed by Major-General Otter had been struck to reorganize the militia, to find room in the peacetime army for at least some CEF battalions, and to ensure that the battle honours and traditions of those units that could not be saved were transferred to appropriate militia regiments. Currie was dissatisfied with the prolonged deliberations on these questions, but more than that, he believed that the Otter Committee's terms of reference had been defined too narrowly. Traditions, identities, and symbols were important, he agreed, but it was time to address the more fundamental issues of war and peace establishments and preparing the army for the next conflict. Accordingly, Currie asked MacBrien to breathe new life into the Otter committee and to extend its mandate beyond the integration of Canadian Corps units into the militia. Because of this, the so-called Otter Report, which was accepted by the government, contained much of the substance of MacBrien's earlier studies. Most significant of these was the size of the post-war active reserve, set at three hundred thousand to accommodate conscription, and organized into the fifteen divisions considered the minimum required to provide for the direct defence of Canada.[15]

With this foundation laid, Currie directed the general staff to begin drafting the several defence plans sketched out in Gwatkin's and MacBrien's memoranda. In the meantime, his task was to build the army for which these plans were designed. Recalling the sorry state of the permanent force in August 1914, it was easy to see that its greatest deficiency had been lack of experience in the artillery, cavalry, and infantry regiments, either because the South African veterans had left the army or because they had been appointed to the staff, where they were no longer able to offer professional guidance to their junior colleagues. Currie hoped that the Great War had changed all that; the Canadian Corps' development into a thoroughly efficient fighting organization had spawned a trained and experienced officer corps numbering in the thousands, whose tactical ideas and organizational capabilities were already being held out as exemplary models in British staff colleges.[16] The problem was to entice them to join the regular army. Few had committed themselves to a military career (indeed it was likely that many had shared in the general contempt for the permanent force before the war), and all they knew of soldiering was their wartime experience. Not for them, Currie reasoned, the demoralizing pre-war routine of teaching the militia and administering half-strength companies. Instead, the most dedicated and professional officers among them – those he wanted most – would probably consent to join the peacetime army only if there were reasonable prospects of 'real soldiering' with modern kit at something close to full war establishment. And, having participated in the more open and mechanized battles of the last few months of 1918, they would be satisfied with nothing less than the opportunity to hone their skills through intense training in the kind of fighting presaged by these battles.[17]

Currie's hopes and plans clearly hinged on the government's fulfilment of the promises it seemed to have made when it adopted the Otter Report. Less obviously, but no less important, Currie also knew that he had to rid the army of those pre-war regulars, now in senior positions across the country, who had not gone to France (or had not done well there), but who nevertheless believed that they should be allowed to complete their military careers. Of course they were not all to blame for their predicament, many having been kept in Canada against their will; as a result there were grounds for the argument that they had a right to continue in the service until they qualified for a full pension. But Currie was adamant. Retaining such officers would block the appointment and promotion of better qualified men from France; indeed, their very presence would perpetuate a spirit of mediocrity within the regular officer corps that he was not prepared to accept.

Currie's course of action was direct, if not ruthless, and he fully expected to be unpopular by the time he had finished.[18] Working closely with MacBrien and a selection board chaired by Otter, he supervised a review of all applications for permanent force commissions and recommended retirement for most of the pre-war regulars who had missed active service. In their place he nominated Canadian Corps veterans.[19] Unhappily, his firings and hirings were not accepted by the government, still trying to define its policy, and this delay eventually took its toll. 'I am afraid that we are not going to get into the Permanent Force ... as many [veterans] as I had hoped,' he told a friend. 'Reorganization has taken so long that many chaps got tired of waiting ... and it seems harder than one thought possible to get rid of some officers of the Permanent Staff and Permanent Corps.'[20] The situation was little better six months later. 'Political pull,' he complained to the director of military operations at the War Office, had prevented 'clearing out' the deadwood, and he doubted whether he could produce a permanent force officer corps able to 'win the respect of the militia.' The part-time soldiers with overseas experience knew 'what a thoroughly trained officer was,' and were unlikely to be fooled by indolent regulars with pretensions of expertise.[21]

This was only one of Currie's disappointments. In 1919 the government decided, the Otter Report notwithstanding, that it would not adopt compulsory military service in peacetime. Then, in June 1920, the militia minister declared that despite the recent increase in the regular army's establishment to ten thousand from forty-five hundred – still a far cry from the twenty to thirty thousand recommended by MacBrien and Gwatkin – no more than five thousand men would be on strength at any one time. Furthermore, although pressed hard by the general staff to procure weapons and equipment for all fifteen divisions enumerated in the Otter Report, the government undertook only grudgingly to accept a British offer to return the equipment of the four Canadian infantry divisions and the calvary brigade that saw active service on the Western Front during the war – less all mechanical transport.[22]

The politicians, it seemed, had been affected by the lessons of the Great War hardly at all. Their response to demands for increased military preparedness was a question: Defence against whom?[23] When they provided their own answer – no one – the position of the army was clear. The defeat of the Central Powers, it was believed, had ushered in an era of peace abroad, while few could take the threat of the United States seriously. The level of military spending and preparation called for by the general staff, therefore, was regarded as an unwanted, unjustified, and unaffordable luxury.[24]

Currie and his colleagues were disheartened by this turn of events; but the real shock came when the returned soldiers of the CEF, who had been expected to support the general staff's campaign for a larger military establishment, failed to do so. Most, it appeared, had no inclination to continue their military service in any form, and perhaps because of the ghastliness of their war experience, they had little interest in compelling others to serve. Reluctantly, Currie had to admit that the veterans' lobby in favour of the army would be weak.[25] The inspector general was also guilty of seriously under-estimating the opposition of long-serving militia officers to any scheme likely to lead to profound changes in the basic nature and role of the old part-time force. Sam Hughes was still speaking out strongly against the regulars, describing them as 'an excrescence on the country,'[26] and many agreed with him. Among these was Lieutenant-Colonel O.M. Biggar, assistant judge advocate general and one of the prime minister's closest confidants. Although he sympathized with the general staff's desire for compulsory military service, he knew that no government would adopt conscription voluntarily and in peacetime. That headquarters nevertheless continued to ask for the largest possible regular army when universal service had been rejected, when there was no obvious external threat, and when the danger of revolution had passed, strained his faith in the general staff's credibility. He was also afraid that the staff's insistence that only a large regular army could provide real security would become widely known and ultimately cause the zeal for part-time soldiering to diminish to the point where the militia would surely die. Then only a small standing army would remain, useless for defence, and in violation of the country's traditions.[27]

Biggar's argument was well reasoned, and it won the day. Despite its earlier acceptance of the Otter Report, with its blueprint for a huge army of thirty thousand regulars and three hundred thousand militia reserves, by mid-1920 the government was offering the general staff very little to work with: a regular force of no more than five thousand men; a militia of fifteen divisions on paper, but fewer than fifty thousand active members; and war equipment for four divisions. Currie drew the appropriate lessons. For all intents and purposes it was 1888, 1905, and 1913 all over again, and time to educate the politicians and Canadians at large on the deterrent value of military preparedness. Impatient, reluctant to 'grope in the dark' until things had improved, and unwilling to treat his office as he was obviously meant to – as a sinecure, an easy and harmless reward for his wartime service – Currie resigned in August 1920.[28]

MacBrien, who had supported Currie behind the scenes and was one of the chief architects of post-war military reorganization, was appointed chief of the general staff that same month. If he was serious about reform, his job was going to be difficult, and there are some who would argue that he was possibly the worst choice for the delicate task that lay ahead of him. James Eayrs, for example, notes that his undoubted soldierly qualities and his reputation as a soldier's soldier were 'not those needed for success in the frustrating environment of peacetime administration', where 'aplomb and coolness under fire, ... crisp competence and ... courage' were irrelevant. Instead, it was important to understand the workings of bureaucracy, and exercise great tact and patience, both of which were foreign to MacBrien's character. As a result 'the imperturbable field commander became the impulsive desk officer increasingly impatient and choleric.'[29] Indeed, he so lacked 'the cunning of restraint,' a recent study suggests, that he alienated all who stood in his way and consequently failed at everything he tried.[30]

There is some truth in this interpretation. MacBrien was single-minded, almost to the point of pig-headedness, and his intransigence made compromise next to impossible. But the stereotype of the unyielding soldier is not altogether accurate, and in fact obscures some of the more complex, and rational, motives underlying his behaviour. For MacBrien knew perfectly well what he was doing and what was required before the military profession in Canada was treated with the respect he believed it was due. He also recognized that the key to change was to somehow alter the workings of bureaucracy, whose processes he understood quite well.

MacBrien's education in these matters had come in England, at the same Post-Bellum conference where he had outlined his long-term goal to build a seven-division expeditionary force in the Canadian army. For besides looking at tactics and organization, the participants had also examined the problems of command, civil-military relations, and the higher direction of war that had come to light over the previous four years. And based on what he heard, MacBrien came away convinced that institutional reform was the secret to preventing the general staff from being isolated and ignored in the future. What was required, in particular, was an institutionalized, routine, and (he hoped) powerful forum that would involve several departments in maintaining the efficiency of the army.

The British Committee of Imperial Defence (CID) was the obvious model to draw from. Chaired by the prime minister and including senior members of cabinet as well as the heads of the army, navy, and air force, the CID's task was to identify, analyse, and solve defence problems at such a high level of political responsibility that its decisions carried great weight with the full cabinet. Moreover, the army's concerns could not stay hidden in departmental files, the preserve of an eccentric like Sam Hughes. There were risks in involving in these deliberations officials from other departments who might be hostile to the military, and some soldiers might complain about excessive civilian control; but to MacBrien it was essential that the government as a whole understand the objectives and premises of military planning, that it be made aware of the competence underlying the general staff's advice, and that it recognize the potential for harm if the staff's recommendations were ignored. This was the essential first step that had to be taken before specific plans or requests for equipment were likely to be approved.[31]

It was equally important for the army to influence public opinion. Accordingly, representatives from headquarters appeared before service clubs, professional societies, and militia associations emphasizing the need for military preparedness, while the *Canadian Defence Quarterly*, a journal technically independent of the department but actually managed by general staff officers, featured articles and editorials supporting MacBrien's point of view. The immediate return on these investments was poor, however, because the staff found itself either preaching to the converted or confirming pre-existing prejudices against the army.[32] The decisive battle was clearly the one aimed at re-educating the government.

The frock-coat/brass-hat quarrel in Britain during the Great War and the Byzantine machinations within the War Office itself between the supporters and detractors of Sir Douglas Haig was proof enough that the mere existence of an organ like the CID would not guarantee harmony between soldiers and politicians.[33] The problem, MacBrien and his colleagues at the Post-Bellum conference agreed, lay in the structure imposed on the British army by Lord Esher fifteen years before and adopted, with some modifications, in Canada. The collegial principle of his Army Council and general staff system ran against the clean and definitive lines of authority in the traditional military chain of command, and at headquarters at least the right of all the heads of the various staff branches to deal with the secretary of state for war directly meant that he could receive conflicting advice. If this became known in the CID, the government might be persuaded to do nothing until there was consensus among its chief military advisers or, worse still, pick and choose potentially irreconcilable bits of advice from this or that branch of the staff. For the CID to work properly, and in the best interests of the service, the Post-Bellum conference concluded, the army must speak with one, united voice.[34]

A number of participants argued that a return to the pre-Esher appointment of commander-in-chief was the best solution, and MacBrien himself hoped that Currie would be treated as such upon his return to Canada. Others at the conference, perhaps more aware of the pitfalls involved in re-establishing an appointment that had caused so much friction only twenty years before, called for subtler, yet still meaningful, change. Rather than revive the office of commander-in-chief, they said, the status of the chief of the imperial general staff in Britain (and consequently the Canadian CGS) should be elevated so that he enjoyed unequivocal authority and precedence over all other senior staff officers. For want of better terminology this was called the 'chief of staff principle,' but in fact the officer holding the proposed 'chief of staff' appointment would be a commander-in-chief in all but name. The notions of collective responsibility and collegiality on the army and militia councils would be laid to rest; and the AG, QMG, and MGO, having lost their right of direct access to the politicians (except with prior approval of the chief of staff) would become subordinate officers, accountable to the chief even in the day-to-day management of their own branch of the staff. With a united front thus provided to the minister and to the CID (or its counterpart in Ottawa), it was assumed that the army should fare better, in Britain and in Canada.[35]

Currie's appointment as inspector general when he returned to Canada went some way to meeting these demands. He was senior to his colleagues at headquarters and, more important, was designated the government's chief military adviser. Still, MacBrien saw it only as a weak compromise.[36] The AG and QMG had not surrendered their right to speak directly to the minister and were therefore in a position to disagree with Currie at the highest level within the department. Furthermore, MacBrien was convinced that Currie's appointment had been tailor-made for him because of his wartime record and did not, in fact, reflect any genuine systemic change. He was right. When MacBrien succeeded Currie he did so not as inspector general, but as CGS; and all the old limitations inherent in that office were retained. The AG and QMG, to be re-garded as co-equals again, had complete jurisdiction over their own branches of the staff, and MacBrien had no power to direct or co-ordinate their activities. And, since none of these officers formally took precedence over the other, even as a token chief military adviser, the army once more had three official voices, not one.

There is no mystery as to why this happened. Currie's departure left no wartime heroes to reward with extraordinary appointments; consequently, the government had no reason to make concessions and concentrate military authority in the hands of a single officer who, like the pre-war GOCs, might choose one day to contest the limits of ministerial authority. It was not for MacBrien to contest the government's decision, and he prepared himself to do as much as he could for the army as CGS. In less than two years, however, he was presented with an opportunity to increase his authority and, indeed, to take precedence over every other officer in all three Canadian services. This promised more than any Canadian soldier had ever dreamed possible.

Inter-service co-operation had never been the hallmark of the Canadian armed forces since the birth of the navy in 1910. Responsible to its own minister, the Royal Canadian Navy had consistently refused to take part in a joint analysis of requirements for coast defences before 1914,[37] and although the situation improved for a time during the war, the post-war Joint Service Committee soon became mired in disputes over minor details of little strategic importance.[38] Inter-service co-operation was also a problem in both the United States and Great Britain after the war, and in each country there were well-publicized debates over the benefits of combining the fighting services in one department where they would be forced to work together.[39] Aware of these deliberations, and thinking that integration might be especially beneficial to Canada's small defence establishment, Currie urged that the services be brought together.[40] Gwatkin, now inspector-general of the air force, and Walter Hose, director of the naval service, agreed, but the proposal did not go forward under Robert Borden's Union government.[41] It was revived shortly after Mackenzie King's Liberals took office when, with support from the militia and naval ministers, their deputies, and the three service chiefs, the prime minister easily persuaded his cabinet colleagues that the idea was sound. As a result, just as the British and Americans rejected integration for fear that it would actually intensify inter-service rivalries, the bill reorganizing Canada's defence structure passed through Parliament: the Department of National Defence would come into existence on 1 January 1923.[42]

MacBrien hoped that the revised organization would free money for the army by reducing administrative costs, but he was also worried about conflicting loyalties within the new department. Under the old structure the army at least had its own spokesman in cabinet; but now, if the minister favoured the navy, there would be none. That was the worst case. The more likely prospect was that any major dispute between the army and navy would lead to a re-evaluation of all departmental activities, even those pertaining to the army alone, while the minister sought to effect a compromise or to choose between competing programs. Anxious to avoid this at all costs, and seeing advantages for the army if the navy and air force could somehow be controlled, MacBrien hit upon the straightforward solution of having himself appointed departmental chief of staff with authority over all three services, all planning, and all submissions to the minister.[43]

Commodore Hose objected strenuously. Although the director of the naval service was to be a member of the new Defence Council (which would replace the single-service Militia Council) and would retain operational control over the RCN, it was obvious that MacBrien intended to subordinate the navy's interests to those of the army. Had the CGS not argued that the post of chief of staff must be reserved for the head of the militia – the senior officer from the Dominion's pre-eminent service – and that the Defence Council should not exercise collective responsibility over policy? Threatening his resignation, Hose countered with an alternative that substantially denied the fact of integration. He and MacBrien would have equal status; the navy would determine its own conditions of service and provide its own administrative and supply services; and the two would share the department's budget as circumstances dictated.[44]

Taken aback by this unexpected discord and unwilling to commit himself yet, the minister asked Lieutenant-Colonel R. Orde, judge advocate general, to resolve the impasse. The JAG's remarks were not helpful. Finding merit on both sides, Orde would not choose between the two, but simply restated each argument. Hose was justified in worrying about the professional direction of the navy should a militia officer exercise control, Orde noted, while MacBrien was right to believe that co-ordination would suffer if the two service chiefs had equal status. One or the other case would have to be accepted, imperfect as they were; but if Hose's proposal were accepted, the deputy minister could always be asked to co-ordinate the two services' policies, programs, and estimates.[45]

Hose lost this battle when MacBrien's scheme was adopted on 24 November 1922. Adding insult to injury, Hose was not informed of the decision until 17 January 1923, and then only after he demanded confirmation of a rumour he had heard two weeks before. This was not a propitious beginning to an era of supposedly improved army-navy relations. But instead of resigning, as he had originally intended, the director of the naval service chose to remain in uniform and combat MacBrien from within.[46]

Hose made the correct choice. G.J. Desbarats, recently appointed deputy minister of national defence, was an enthusiastic supporter of Hose and the navy, having already served as the latter's deputy minister. He was also a strong advocate of the supremacy of the civil authority and so was more than willing to fight what he perceived to be MacBrien's illegitimate seizure of power. Desbarats's tactics were masterful. Exploiting defence minister George Graham's complete indifference in his portfolio, he simply refused to implement the cabinet directive confirming MacBrien's responsibilities as chief of staff and then interposed himself between MacBrien and the minister, appropriating the task of co-ordinating service policy to his own office in the process. It was now MacBrien's turn to protest, but Graham did nothing to enforce the appropriate clauses of the National Defence Act. Desbarats picked up on this and, in a carefully worded memorandum, noted coolly that since the minister was raising no objections to his deputy's actions, there was clearly no obstruction and no usurpation of MacBrien's supposed prerogatives.[47]

MacBrien was disgusted by the unholy alliance between Hose and Desbarats, and his personal relations with the two deteriorated beyond recall. Indeed, he was goaded into stupid behaviour – as was Hose when, for example, he refused naval participation in the country's Armistice Day ceremonies because the administrative order for the parade had been written by the army.[48] But emphasis on this aspect of the quarrel misses the significance to MacBrien of Desbarats's intervention. A civilian without even a minister's claim to constitutional responsibility was making policy, and the army's professional advice was being ignored as a result. The general staff was therefore in precisely the position it had striven so hard to escape: nothing was systematic, and decisions rested entirely on the whim of the minister or his deputy. Because of this, there seemed little point in seeking a wider audience with other government departments. Worse yet, MacBrien became so deeply distracted by the departmental in-fighting that he failed his responsibility to the militia. At one point, for example, he refused to settle a dispute between his subordinate staff over which of two defence schemes should take priority – war with the United States, or planning for an expeditionary force in the event of another world war.[49]

The Hose-MacBrien quarrel lasted until 1927, during which time nothing of importance was accomplished by the Department of National Defence. Then MacBrien provided his own solution to the problem. Distraught at his inability to make integration work as he thought it must, angered by what he saw as moral weakness on the part of politicians who would not enforce the National Defence Act, disillusioned by Desbarats's behaviour, unforgiving of Hose, and beset by financial problems, he resigned. He had failed to change the workings of bureaucracy and was convinced that the general staff would suffer for years to come.[50]

MacBrien's successor was Major-General H.C. Thacker. Bothered by ill-health and having no stomach for politics, Thacker had not wanted to accept the appointment as militia chief and did so only when he realized that he would serve on a purely caretaker basis until Brigadier A.G.L. McNaughton had completed an apprenticeship in command of a military district. Thacker did not expect to accomplish much during his tenure, and he did not. When he left Ottawa in 1928 he recalled that his experience there had been every bit as distasteful as he had anticipated: too much politics for an old professional soldier.[51] Still, Thacker took one step for which McNaughton never forgave him. Although MacBrien had insisted that his successor should continue to hold the appointment of chief of staff, Thacker readily accepted Defence Minister J.L. Ralston's suggestion that he become militia chief of the general staff and give up all claim to authority over the navy and responsibility for co-ordinating defence policy.[52] That opened the way for Hose's eventual nomination as chief of the naval staff (CNS) and equal status with the CGS. With little fanfare, then, and even less protest, the Department of National Defence was reorganized along the lines put forward by Hose five years before. Compounding the error, in McNaughton's view, Thacker had resurrected the Militia Council as a forum in which matters of particular interest to the army could be discussed. Not only did this accentuate the separation of the army and navy within the department, but it also restored the adjutant general's and quartermaster general's right of access to the minister.[53]

McNaughton's opinions on the proper organization of national defence headquarters had been formed during years of close association with MacBrien, first on the Otter committee, and then during the period when he served as the latter's deputy chief of the general staff. Like his mentor, and despite the contrary teachings of the Imperial Defence College, McNaughton held firm to the belief that unity and co-ordination would have to be imposed on the Canadian forces, preferably through a 'super chief of staff.'[54] He also agreed that the future of the army depended upon the nomination of an army officer as this chief of staff. Voluntary co-operation, as MacBrien's experience had shown, would probably favour the navy despite the fact that, as McNaughton saw things, the navy added little to Canada's security. It would always be too small to provide effective seaward defence against a major power, and judging from the Great War it was likely to be folded into the Royal Navy anyway. More to the point, McNaughton foresaw few contingencies below the level of a major war that justified naval expansion. Ralston did not agree, prompting McNaughton to consider his own resignation within a year of his appointment.[55]

Like Hose six years before, McNaughton chose finally to remain in the service; and just as Hose had been rescued by Desbarats's arrival as deputy minister, McNaughton's career was rehabilitated when R.B. Bennett's Conservatives won the election of 1930. With the help of W.D. Herridge, a good friend from the Canadian Corps who happened also to be the prime minister's brother-in-law, the CGS found himself numbered among the government's closest advisers. Bennett in particular was impressed by the general's intellect and his broad general knowledge.[56]

Quick to capitalize on an opportunity when he saw one, McNaughton set out to put all these connections to the best possible use. He began by setting in motion a series of transfers that brought his men into the other senior appointments at headquarters. These moves were widely criticized within the army, and when asked to comment even Arthur Currie – an acknowledged admirer of the new CGS – admitted that 'all was not well' in Ottawa. But he advised against carrying the issue further because the CGS was filling the vacuum left by yet another weak minister, D.M. Sutherland, and because the prime minister was known to prefer dealing with strong men. Besides, Currie added, McNaughton stood 'head and shoulders' above his colleagues; that he was in control was undoubtedly for the best.[57]

Having acquired thoroughly loyal subordinates at headquarters, the CGS next turned his sights on the navy. In 1930 he persuaded Bennett that the CGS alone should speak for all three services at the forthcoming imperial conference, and then used that platform to secure general agreement that Canada's army and air force should be re-equipped before the navy. The performance was repeated in 1932, when McNaughton convinced the government that the Dominion could best meet its obligations to the Geneva disarmament conference by making massive cuts in the naval estimates and only token reductions in the army and air force budgets.[58] Finally, when recommending a return to MacBrien's chief of staff system in 1935, he stipulated that the senior appointment should go only to the army and air force: no sailors need apply.[59] Although departmental reorganization was not implemented, his view that the Royal Canadian Navy 'should not be developed' was listened to. By 1935 the naval estimates were such that the service was on the verge of disappearing.

The deputy ministers in the department between 1930 and 1935 fared little better at McNaughton's hands. Insisting that the doctrine of civilian control did not extend to these officials, the CGS argued that Desbarats and Colonel L.R. LaFlèche (appointed in 1933 upon the advice of General Percy Lake) should be content to administer the civilian side of the department. It was not for them to have 'some undefined position of control' in policy-making.[60] McNaughton therefore ignored them on such matters, making his case to the minister direct. On other occasions he even bypassed the minister and went straight to Bennett. Because of this, he recalled later, he was satisfied that the deputy minister 'could do no harm.'[61]

All these manoeuvres could not be concealed, especially as Desbarats and LaFlèche had their own circle of influential friends. Eventually, the story of McNaughton's activities reached the press, with the Liberal Vancouver *Sun* in particular complaining that the CGS had wrested 'effective domination away from the deputy minister [who] was technically and legally the head of the department.' Such 'brass-hat domination,' the *Sun* continued, was 'disturbing, if not entirely unconstitutional.'[62] But well connected as he was, the CGS had little to fear from such outbursts.

As things turned out, McNaughton was probably too well protected and too closely identified with Bennett and the Tories. As the election of 1935 drew nearer, the prime minister realized that the CGS had actually become a political liability. Not only was McNaughton under attack for his extraordinary influence and his unprecedented seven-year term as CGS, but there was also savage condemnation of his heavy-handed and overly enthusiastic administration of the government's unemployment relief camps along military lines. The image of the country's poor being bawled out by thuggish regular force sergeants was not pretty, and it seemed inevitable that the Liberals would replace the CGS if they won.[63] Accordingly, whether it was to serve Conservative political interests by getting rid of an unpopular figure, or whether it was to protect a valued colleague by placing him in the public service before the opposition took over, Bennett asked McNaughton to transfer to the National Research Council and to hand over the appointment of CGS to Major-General E.C. Ashton in May 1935.[64]

Mackenzie King's Liberals won the election, and within a short time McNaughton was convinced that they had undone most of what he stood for. The navy began to expand, slowly it was true, but this was taken as a vote of confidence in its future. LaFlèche was also lending a hand in making policy. In McNaughton's view General Ashton was wholly responsible for this debacle because he lacked the courage to stand up to the politicians. '[He has] broken the organization which I laboured for years to build up,' McNaughton told Thacker, 'against the time when it would be necessary to rehabilitate our defence forces.'[65]

McNaughton's criticism was unfair. The former CGS had conveniently forgotten that he had had his troubles with Mackenzie King's government eight years before. He was also blind to the fact that, despite having argued that systematic change was essential to reduce the army's reliance on the happy accident of a CGS and his minister (or prime minister) getting along, his own success between 1930 and 1935 depended heavily on the cultivation and manipulation of Bennett's friendship. And even then McNaughton had failed to persuade the prime minister to restore the appointment of chief of staff. Ashton could hardly be blamed for his lack of political friends.

Still, McNaughton was right when he identified his successor as coming from a different mould. It was not Ashton's style to pick fights unnecessarily. He did not want to cast the navy into oblivion, having accurately assessed the prime minister's interest in carving out a niche for that service in home defence. Similarly, while doubting the wisdom of divorcing the Royal Canadian Air Force from militia control, he chose not to prolong his opposition to the elevation of its senior officer to the post of chief of the air staff. Finally, Ashton realized that the Liberals had an instinctive bias against the army because of the casualties it was likely to suffer in a major war. Casualties raised the manpower question; manpower problems were inexorably linked with conscription; and conscription recalled the memory of a nation divided and a Liberal party in disarray only twenty years before. For all these reasons, the CGS chose compromise instead of confrontation in his dealings with the government and the other services.[66]

Ashton's approach paid handsome dividends. The defence debate of 1937 proved the accuracy of his predictions as the government decided to finance only the strengthening of the country's coastal defences, in which the navy was to play an important role. The goodwill produced by the CGS's co-operative spirit meant, however, that it was possible to work with the navy and, as we shall see, to ensure that army staff work was not limited to making plans to garrison the country's frontiers. More important, when it became obvious during the Czechoslovak crisis of 1938 that the formal requirement to pass all submissions to defence minister Ian Mackenzie through his deputy impeded operational planning, Ashton was able to enlist the enthusiastic support of the CNS and the air force to correct the situation. Mackenzie was told of the problem and directed the three chiefs to report to him. LaFlèche would be kept abreast of developments, of course, but only as a courtesy.[67] The role and status of the deputy minister had thereby been redefined so that military advice would come from service personnel without passing through a civilian intermediary. There was also no doubt that responsibility for co-ordinating the efforts of the army, navy, and air force lay with the chiefs of staff, not with the deputy minister.

The requirement for speedy and unimpeded communication during a crisis had convinced Ian MacKenzie that he must have direct access to his military advisers. Correct as it was in this light, the defence minister's decision to bypass the deputy was made that much easier because the services were finally working together, in harmony, toward a common goal. Mackenzie did not have to take sides among them, or risk opening any wounds whenever it was time to choose a course of action. No doubt it would have been better for MacBrien to have recognized as much when he and Hose began to brawl in 1923. As it was, the intense rivalry between the two did nothing to enhance the professional reputation of the armed forces within or outside their own department.

The extremes to which Hose and MacBrien carried their feud were particularly unhelpful in establishing a good working relationship with the Department of External Affairs, the army's potential rival in assessing the impact of international developments on Canada's national security. Finding common ground with the government's leading foreign policy advisers after the war would have been a difficult enough task as it was, since they perceived no clear threat to Canada requiring extensive military preparations in the Dominion. Canada's membership in the League of Nations complicated matters further, since the League held out the prospect of a future in which disputes could be resolved without resort to war. The League's creators were not naive, however, and had carefully allowed for the concept of collective security, by which League members would band together to impose their will on any country bent on aggression. Armed forces thus had to be available to enforce the League's mandate, a consideration the soldiers were quick to point out when they justified a larger defence budget. But the view in External Affairs was less certain. Did it follow that obligations to the League required a relatively minor power like Canada to prepare for the commitment of its military resources? Was that not the responsibility of the great powers, whose support of collective security carried more weight and punch?

Beyond that, the two senior officials in External Affairs between the wars, O.D. Skelton and Loring Christie, had already developed a deep and abiding distrust of men in uniform, and the goings-on in the Department of National Defence did little to alter their perceptions. Skelton's opinions reflected a long-standing anti-imperial and nationalistic bias which saw the Canadian militia's intimate association with the British army as one of the more important ties binding the Dominion unnecessarily to the mother country. Furthermore, Skelton was convinced that the Canadian general staff's dedication to helping Great Britain in time of peril would ultimately strengthen the imperialist cause in Canada and thereby make it impossible for Ottawa to formulate a foreign policy of its own. As long as Canadian policy served British goals, there could be no unity at home. The Great War had proved that, and in Skelton's view no 'responsible Canadian statesman [could again] risk civil war in Canada by taking part in a struggle in the English Channel.' Wondering 'how many hypotheses [put forward by the general staff] make a commitment,' he insisted that the military be warned to assume very little about the nature and extent of Canadian participation in future wars and to withhold these assumptions from London.[68]

Loring Christie was no less hostile to the general staff and to its campaign to convince Canadians 'to think on the martial side,' to ignore the restraining hand of diplomacy, and eventually to see the world through 'general staff eyes.'

If the army succeeded, he observed, international agreements would become 'agreements to fight'; collective security would be no more than 'collective coercion'; and a 'war psychology' would grip the nation, rationalizing all wars as 'preventive.'[69]

Christie was particularly upset when he discovered in the 1930s that the general staff was drafting mobilization plans for an expeditionary force, and he tore at its memoranda with vigour, exposing every possible flaw in logic and every hint of commitment to help the empire. It was pure folly, he declared, for the Canadian army to use the pretext of a major war 'as the ordinary and permanent design and strength for [its peacetime] organization' when major wars were rare and 'extraordinary' events in international relations to be dealt with if and when they occurred. Far better, he added, for the staff to accept 'as the law of our life' that Canada's response to such an eventuality would be determined by the government when it happened. Minor crises, on the other hand, were the norm of international politics, and so deserved to be the basis for planning. Besides, he continued, it was possible to predict these 'with some confidence.' But if the general staff continued to wander in the realm of the 'extraordinary' and unpredictable, there was good reason to question 'whether a Canadian soldier need bother thinking at all.'[70]

Christie was no pacifist, and no advocate of unilateral disarmament. He also knew that it was impossible to prevent the general staff from 'concocting paper schemes' even if the army lacked the men, money, and equipment to implement them. Still, he thought it wise and productive for the government to 'pin [the soldiers] down to something that can be intelligently described in public ... might be of some value in promoting national unity,' and might incidentally 'stimulate the military mind, force it to the initiative, and perhaps even extemporize better.' At the very least the government would be filling a potential vacuum by announcing a policy of this sort, and so guarding against a situation in which army preferences became official policy by default for no other reason than the politicians had failed to provide leadership in another direction. In Christie's view, that direction had to be home defence; anything else would be 'extremely wasteful as well as unintelligible to the public.'[71]

The general staff was no less eager for a firm statement on defence policy. As Major-General Thacker explained, the general statement holding self-governing dominions responsible for their own defence agreed to routinely at most imperial conferences was not sufficient, yet it was all the army had to go by. Without something more specific, he continued, it was

impossible for the responsible military officers to deal fully or intelligently with such important questions as the organization and establishment of the Militia, both peace and war; the preparation of regulations for mobilization and the arrangement of any Expeditionary Force that might be required [to help the empire or the League].[72]

Here, however, was the problem. Although the army desperately wanted guidance, by the end of the 1920s its senior officers all agreed that it was woefully wrongheaded to assign priority to home defence. The country was in no danger of attack, while fiddling with defence policy to promote national unity was perverse. The greatest threat to peace was in Europe and Asia, where both the League and the empire's community of interests were being challenged. It was there that the army should be prepared to act, the general staff maintained, all the more so because public opinion would demand action in the event of a crisis. If the government could not keep Canada out of war, and if the dispatch of an expeditionary force was therefore inevitable some time in the future, did it not make sense to plan before the event, for strategic, political, and practical reasons?[73]

Born of mutual distrust as well as a fundamental disagreement over what was best for the country, the wide gulf between the army and the foreign policy advisers in External Affairs was not easily bridged. Frequent association between the two sides on an interdepartmental committee might have broken down some barriers and so improved the level of mutual understanding, but from 1919 to 1935 no such opportunity arose. External Affairs rejected every initiative the general staff took in the 1920s to create the Canadian equivalent of the CID, while in the early 1930s R.B. Bennett preferred to deal with McNaughton on an informal, personal, non-institutional basis. Instead of having to work together because they were thrown together, therefore, the two departments were free to continue their long-range sniping. The diplomats accused the soldiers of war-mongering, and the general staff countered that Skelton, Christie, and their kind were isolationists and obstructionists.[74]

The situation changed, somewhat unexpectedly, with the election of Mackenzie King's Liberals in 1935. Often made out to be dogmatically anti-military, King in fact had a consistent view of what Canada's defence responsibilities should be: the Dominion must, he believed, be capable of making a significant contribution to its own defence while avoiding all commitments in advance to participate in foreign wars. The prime minister was therefore prepared to listen when Ian Mackenzie passed on the warnings issued by McNaughton and Ashton that the armed forces had deteriorated to such an extent that their ability to defend Canada was now highly doubtful.[75] Shocked by the army's sorry state, King was convinced that he must do something, but he was not sure how far to go or how best to proceed with rearmament. Accordingly, he waited for eight months before announcing that he would chair a cabinet-level interdepartmental Canadian Defence Committee which would undertake a thorough review of the country's military policies.[76]

The army had won, but its immediate victory was only partial. The creation of a high-level committee such as the prime minister proposed, with all the moral and executive authority generated by his interest in and leadership of its activities, had long been the general staff's goal. But it was only a single step – and not necessarily the most crucial one – in increasing the army's influence in the policy-making process. For one thing, the CDC would probably have to limit itself to the broadest kind of strategic analysis, leaving it to others to draft regulations dealing with censorship, control of shipping, and economic and military mobilization in time of crisis. If this was left to the individual departments concerned, the army's requirements or preferences could be ignored, either inadvertently or purposely. More important, there was always the risk that the committee would become a kind of clearing house for memoranda submitted independently by the various branches of government. Although the army's program would at least be guaranteed a hearing under these circumstances, the process of discussion and deliberation could very easily remain more adversarial than co-operative, with the general staff presenting its case and External Affairs, given its biases, presumably offering an alternative more to the government's liking. What influence would be won then?

The way out, MacBrien had always argued, was to force interdepartmental collaboration at a level lower than the CDC, in a set of sub-committees asked to examine specific planning problems and to arrive at a joint solution which would then be passed on to the CDC. This had the advantage of involving less senior (and perhaps therefore more malleable) staff in the discussion of military policy, and it would also expose all the participating departments to the many specific details upon which the army built its case. Convinced of the logic of its arguments at all levels, the general staff was sure that as the representatives from the civilian departments became familiar with the soundness of military planning, as fact was added to fact and as fitting conclusions were drawn, the prevailing Colonel Blimp image of the army officer would disappear. In short, to the general staff, the gradual process of educating and winning over the government as a whole depended very much on the creation of this sub-committee structure.

Despite his obvious willingness to lead the Defence Committee, and having authorized the creation of the sub-committees asked for by the general staff, the prime minister issued clear instructions to his foreign policy advisers not to participate in the work of these bodies.[77] He gave no reason for this decision, but Ashton chose not to press for an explanation despite his disappointment. Too much was at stake to risk alienating the prime minister or causing him to dissolve the CDC in a fit of pique at the army. Yet it was also essential to avoid giving the impression that the sub-committees could work effectively without representatives from External Affairs. Accordingly, the CGS delayed the first of the scheduled sub-committee meetings in the hope that the prime minister would come around of his own accord. For if Mackenzie King, at his own initiative, directed his officials to co-operate, Ashton was confident that they would take their task seriously.[78]

When nothing was heard from the prime minister's office, Ashton realized that there was a danger in this tactic. If King failed to act, the work of the sub-committees would be surrendered by default. Unwilling to accept a self-inflicted defeat, but still suspicious of King's purpose, Ashton and his staff tried six times between April and November 1935 to convince External Affairs of the importance of its participation in the sub-committees. When an answer finally arrived in December, it was uncompromisingly negative. Holding fast to the rather purist notion that diplomats could not strive for peace if they also were involved in preparation for war, External Affairs declared emphatically that the co-operation the army called for was 'not practicable.'[79] Undeterred, Ashton contacted External Affairs again, and within a few weeks was rewarded with a positive response – of sorts. Representatives from the department would sit on the proposed sub-committees after all, but only if two preconditions were met: the sub-committees would have to be divorced completely from the CDC; and any recommendations arising out of their work were to be passed to cabinet above the signature of the defence minister alone.[80]

The architect of this reply, O.D. Skelton, had fashioned a crafty compromise, but his manoeuvre did not fool Ashton. The CGS saw that as long as it was Ian Mackenzie who was bringing advice to cabinet, External Affairs would no longer share technical responsibility for military planning and so could argue that the existence of a collective, interdepartmental agreement on national security was fiction. Who would deny that the sub-committees, under Mackenzie's 'control,' were not mere ciphers mouthing the general staff's point of view? Just as important, the act of removing the sub-committees from the protective umbrella organization of the CDC would rob them of the moral authority the Defence Committee enjoyed by virtue of the prime minister's involvement. Skelton's formula, then, was only marginally better than having no sub-committees at all.[81]

Ashton was desperate to make a start, but before accepting any offer he played a small game himself. The separation of the CDC and the sub-committees was reasonable, he told Skelton, so long as External Affairs was represented on all the sub-committees, chaired those in which it had a natural, primary interest, and provided the staff for the permanent secretariat. This time Skelton was no fool: the secretariat's duties included the drafting of all submissions to cabinet, and if that were done by his staff it would seem that External Affairs had already agreed with everything brought before the prime minister and his colleagues on the CDC. Together, Skelton and Christie advised King to reject Ashton's terms, which he did. Convinced, finally, that he had achieved the best possible terms, and fearful of losing what had already been gained, the CGS capitulated. The Department of National Defence, and more particularly Colonel Maurice Pope (following in his father's path), would supervise the interdepartmental discussions on military preparations, and Ian Mackenzie would submit Pope's memoranda to the cabinet.[82]

The sub-committees did useful work before Canada declared war on 10 September 1939. The government's War Book outlining the emergency steps to be taken by each department was ready on the ninth, as were enabling laws and provisions to deal with enemy aliens, control shipping, introduce censorship, and protect vital industries, utilities, and transportation networks. Nevertheless, these were not the studies of specific military problems the general staff had been hoping for in addition to the necessary, but essentially administrative, organization of the civil government for war. They were therefore of only marginal value to the soldiers.

The work of the Canadian Defence Committee was an even greater disappointment. After a good beginning on 26 August 1936, when the way was opened for the limited rearmament program announced in the House of Commons the following February, the next five meetings before Canada's declaration of war became mired in budgetary detail and cost accounting at the expense of a thorough review of military policy and the army's mobilization schemes.[83] The CDC's failure to discuss the general staff's contingency plans was probably its greatest shortcoming. It meant that although Ian Mackenzie knew that the army was making arrangements to mobilize an expeditionary force for overseas service in another major war, this fact was not made clear to the other government departments. As a result, both Skelton and Loring Christie claimed genuine surprise when they learned, on 29 August 1939, that the army favoured committing at least two divisions to the war expected in Europe. As Christie recalled, this was 'something of a hairpin curve from the ... line of propaganda [issued by the army and the government] about attacks on Canada.'[84] Unrepentant still, Skelton fumed at the prospect of Canadians dying in a conflict that was 'not our war.'[85]

Mackenzie King was no happier. Having long argued that the Dominion's military liabilities must be strictly limited in the next war, he was taken aback by the revelation that the army had all along been thinking about extensive commitments abroad. Ian Mackenzie was blamed for having connived with the soldiers and failing to resist them 'as he should.'[86] Lack of communication which the interdepartmental structures were supposed to prevent had thus laid the groundwork for another round of improvisation and for further undermining of the general staff's mobilization plans.

As we shall see, it did not happen that way. Though King, Skelton, and Christie all favoured restricting Canada's military role, preferring her to be a centre of war production rather than a source of manpower, their view of the Dominion's proper contribution ultimately did not prevail. Instead, beginning in September 1939, the three service chiefs worked together to ensure that the army's defence scheme calling for an expeditionary force was not put aside, and by August 1945 there were five divisions and two armoured brigades overseas, not much short of the general staff's pre-war estimate of the country's maximum military effort. In addition, tens of thousands of Canadian sailors and airmen were battling the enemy on the Atlantic and in the skies over Europe. This was hardly war at the cheap.

All this suggests that Currie, MacBrien, and McNaughton had been right about the importance of the services speaking to the politicians with one voice, but perhaps it also indicates that three separate service chiefs working in harmony carried more weight than one imposing his will on the other two. The general staff was also correct in thinking that the creation of an interdepartmental national security 'bureaucracy' would one day be helpful in overcoming traditional civilian antipathy to the military. But unable to curb their expectations, the generals wanted too much too soon. It would be wrong, therefore, to attribute Canada's extensive contribution to the Second World War simply to inter-service co-operation or the co-opting of officials like Skelton and Christie. Popular support for Great Britain so strong that it could not be ignored was the key, and on this point the general staff had been right. Ultimately, then, and as always, public opinions and perceptions rather than the existence of a useful organization chart defined the status of the military profession and determined the limits of its influence.

9

Military planning, 1919–1939

Military planning in Canada immediately after the Great War was chiefly in the hands of Colonel James Sutherland Brown, director of military operations and intelligence (DMO&I) at militia headquarters. Of all the responsibilities assigned to the general staff, his was easily the most misunderstood and the most open to suspicion and criticism. For one thing, the very idea of planning for war aroused antipathy in a society still trying to recover from the wounds of 1914-18 and desperately wanting to believe that the League of Nations had ushered in a new era of peace and prosperity. For another, Brown worked in secret, and uninformed speculation about what he and his colleagues were up to made for natural exaggeration. Strategic planning was viewed in the worst possible light.

The bad reputation of military planners was further damaged as details about the origins of the Great War were released throughout the 1920s. The way in which almost all the governments of Europe had become prisoners of their general staffs after the assassination of the Archduke Ferdinand was indictment enough. Evidence that at least some of these general staffs leapt at the opportunity to give meaning to the hours they had spent drafting mobilization schedules and railroad timetables added an element of incredulity, if not disgust, to this impression. General staffs and strategic planning, it seemed, went hand-in-hand with militarism gone wild.

Although it had played no part in the coming of the Great War, the Canadian staff was lumped in with all the rest, and militia headquarters' rejoinder – that to do nothing might actually invite attack – won few converts among a population that perceived no clear external threats to its security. Moreover, the army's emphasis on what it could do to protect imperial interests or support the League of Nations overseas was equally uncompelling to a group of politicians and senior public servants who believed that such adventures would threaten national unity.[1] Indeed, there were some who thought it was dangerous for the army to develop even notional, suppositional, or theoretical defence plans aimed only at improving its talents in this area. As we have seen, O.D. Skelton was afraid that these hypothetical considerations would become political commitments by default, while Loring Christie would have been happier if the army were enjoined against thinking altogether.[2]

Because of the secrecy surrounding his work, Sutherland Brown's plans were not widely discussed during his lifetime, and it has been left to present-day historians to examine them in detail, and in particular his draft covering the contingency of war with the United States. First off the mark was James Eayrs, to whom Sutherland Brown was the archetypical cigar-butt strategist in uniform, whose broad, sweeping arrows on large-scale maps bore no relation to reality, and whose emotional anti-Americanism made it impossible for him to sort out the crucial difference between the capabilities and the intentions of Canada's continental neighbour. As a result, he consistently committed what James Eayrs characterizes as 'the more unusual of the strategic intelligencer's sins': to mistake a friend, the United States, for an enemy, and then plan for war against this friend. Compounding this initial error was 'strategist's cramp ... a kind of creeping paralysis of the imagination,' which prevented Brown's colleagues at headquarters from recognizing his biases even though these 'challenged most of the assumptions held by others within the military establishment.'[3]

The one general study of military staffs between the wars repeats this view. 'The Canadian problem only came up briefly in the United Kingdom,' writes D.C. Watt:

Otherwise the defence of Canada against its over-mighty neighbour to the south was left to the fertile imagination of ... Colonel J. Sutherland ('Buster') Brown, whose conviction of the inevitability of war with the United States, unshared by any other member of the Canadian Defence Establishment, led him to draft Defence Scheme No. 1. This envisaged a grandiose invasion of the United States ... Not bad for a militia of 38,000 whose budget in 1921–1922 had permitted a full nine days' training a year.[4]

The sense of ridicule underlying these accounts scarcely needs pointing out. In Canada, they suggest, the most delicate task of strategic planning from 1920 to 1927 (when Sutherland Brown was posted to London) was left in the hands of an unstable officer bent on committing a woefully inadequate Canadian army to an invasion of the United States, and fully expecting to win. Unhappily, although there are grounds to question the premises and provisions of Defence Scheme No. 1, the urge to jest at Sutherland Brown's expense has seriously distorted the picture of military planning in Canada from 1919 to 1939. It ignores the fact, for example, that similar plans were being drafted in the United States, both because they were deemed necessary, and because such exercises were useful in maintaining the general staff's expertise.[5] Secondly, the authorized version suggests that only Brown believed in the possibility of war between Canada and the United States.

This was not the case. Gwatkin and MacBrien had both emphasized the importance of drafting a comprehensive set of peacetime defence plans for all possible contingencies when they drew up their plans for the army's post-war organization, and when Currie returned to Ottawa in 1919 he set his staff to work on them. Priority, for the moment, went to internal security because of the fear of communism and extended labour unrest,[6] but once conditions at home had improved, Currie turned his attention to the United States. Here he received unhelpful advice. The Royal Navy, Lord Jellicoe explained during his tour of the Dominion, now believed that the American threat to British and imperial interests was 'so remote' that planning for war with the United States no longer entered the Admiralty's calculations. As a result, it was hardly worth while for Canada to worry about the problem either, particularly if the Dominion could not count upon receiving British naval support.[7]

The Admiralty's view reflected, of course, the wartime partnership between Britain and the United States and the expectation that relations between them would remain good. Currie did not disagree entirely, but his view of the United States was different. To the Admiralty, the American border was thousands of miles away; from Ottawa, it was just over an hour's journey by train. To Currie and his staff this represented a crucial difference: for Canada the United States was a contiguous foreign power against which at least some preparations had to be made. This was a fact of life for all continental nations, whose former allies could become enemies, and it was a condition with which all the countries of Europe were familiar. Indeed, even the United Kingdom was influenced by similar considerations. With Germany defeated and Russia in disarray in 1919, the War Office had identified France as a potential adversary because it was the major power closest to England, and because the two countries had fought before. The parallels were obvious. Planning for war with the United States was a legitimate responsibility of the Canadian staff, Currie maintained, even if it was no concern of the Admiralty.

The question of whether, if war broke out, Canada could expect British help, without which the battle would surely be lost, was still very much in the air. The Canadians did not want to believe Jellicoe, but it seemed that he spoke for Britain. The relief was understandable, therefore, when shortly after Jellicoe's pronouncement Field-Marshal Sir Henry Wilson, chief of the imperial general staff, reaffirmed the British army's interest in protecting the Dominion. Agreeing that a resort to armed force might some day be necessary to resolve an Anglo-American or Canada–U.S. dispute, it was to him 'unthinkable' that Britain would stand idly by if Canada came under attack.[8] With this reassurance, and at Currie's behest, Sutherland Brown began the first sketches of what would become Defence Scheme No. 1.

Clearly the DMO&I was not acting on his own. Nor was he blindly anti-American, or spoiling for a fight. Brown readily acknowledged that the United States was 'presently friendly' and that there was no immediate reason for relations to deteriorate. However, he explained, he could not accept the argument that, because most disputes with the Americans had been settled peacefully in the past, they would necessarily be resolved amicably in the future. The danger, as he saw it, was that American industry was becoming increasingly dependent upon easy access to Canadian natural resources which, if denied, might create popular support for armed intervention. This was all the more likely if there was no Canadian army worthy of the name standing in the Americans' way. 'Unpreparedness for rightful defence,' he cautioned, was an 'incentive to unjust aggression.'[9]

Yet Brown did not take the problem of defending Canada lightly. The long border with the United States could not be manned everywhere, while the vulnerability of the Dominion's population centres and transportation corridors was obvious. It was also clear that British help was essential to offset the hugh manpower advantage enjoyed by the Americans. The strategic problem, therefore, was how to gain time to allow the British to react before it was too late. Brown had already examined this question at the Staff College in 1914,[10] and the solution he devised then was written into Defence Scheme No.1. Persuaded that a purely defensive strategy was doomed to failure, he preferred to throw the enemy off balance using surprise and shock action. 'Flying columns' of militia battalions would be thrown across the border in a controlled penetration to a depth of a few hundred miles so that if all went well, and the U.S. army was caught unprepared, the Canadian force would have the chance to prepare ground of its own choosing for a fighting withdrawal. By the time it had been pushed back to the border British operations should be under way against the American east coast and Indian and Australian contingents on their way to attack California. Although Canadian territory in the west would probably have been lost in the mean time, Brown was convinced that if the militia stood firm from the Great Lakes to the St Lawrence and the British and imperial forces did good work on the coasts, a reasonable peace settlement was likely to follow.[11]

Brown circulated the first draft of his plan to the district commanders in

April 1921. Although almost all agreed that preparations of this sort were required, most were appalled at the tasks they had been allocated. Given the sorry state of the militia, they doubted whether offensive operations were, in fact, possible, and, ignoring Brown's warning that 'extreme caution' would lose the war, they called instead for a defensive strategy.[12] The DMO&I's colleagues at militia headquarters were more supportive. Currie and MacBrien both understood that Brown's plan depended, ultimately, on the government's providing complete mobilization equipment for all fifteen divisions on the militia order of battle; in addition, it presupposed that the militia battalions themselves would be up to strength. In other words, Brown was not advocating that Defence Scheme No.1 should rely upon the existing undermanned and ill-equipped citizen army for all time; the immediate concern of the district commanders about the wisdom of committing this force to battle, while valid enough, could therefore be put aside. Currie and MacBrien also realized, with Brown, that when all fifteen divisions had been re-equipped the army would be ready to meet any lesser emergency.[13]

In his later years, McNaughton claimed that he was convinced of the lunacy of Defence Scheme No. 1 almost from the time it was first circulated. The agreements arrived at in Washington that same year which imposed parity in capital ships on the Royal Navy and its American counterpart had, in his view, so undermined Britain's ability to help Canada that Brown's assumptions were no longer valid.[14] This was wisdom after the event. In April 1923, two years following the appearance of Brown's first draft, and when McNaughton, as deputy chief of the general staff, was Brown's immediate superior, he was still describing the Americans as 'consistently imperialistic' and having a policy 'aimed at the hegemony of the Americas.' More to the point, he had not yet discounted the possibility that Canada would receive British help in the event of war with its neighbour, and because of this asserted that the Dominion's position remained 'far from hopeless.' Canadian prospects would be even better, he added, if the Americans became permanently entangled in Far Eastern affairs which forced them to disperse their military resources over a wide geographic area. Still, the risks involved in using the armed forces to settle a dispute with the United States would be significant, and the government would be well advised to attempt all solutions short of war.[15] These sentiments were echoed in 1925 by Lieutenant-Colonel H.D.G. Crerar, then on exchange duty at the War Office. A protégé of McNaughton, Crerar told his colleagues in London that while war with the United States would place Canada in a 'more than desperate situation,' her position would not be altogether hopeless. Indeed, the outlook might actually be encouraging, given adequate 'preparation, energy, and boldness' and the traditional 'spirit' and 'hardiness' of the

Canadian people.[16] This, of course, was Sutherland Brown's point precisely.

Brown revised and refined Defence Scheme No. 1 throughout 1922 and 1923, adding continuously to the intelligence he had gathered about military installations and vital points in the border states during his reconnaissance trips there two years before.[17] The plan was more detailed as a result, but it was still fundamentally flawed. Although there had been legitimate reasons for keeping the first, imperfect draft secret, even from the minister, in fact Defence Scheme No. 1 seems never to have been shown to the political head of the Department of National Defence in any form. The general staff correctly assessed the political climate as being intuitively hostile to this contingency plan in particular, and MacBrien, obsessed by his sustained quarrel with the navy, had little time, energy, or inclination to persuade the government otherwise – if, indeed, that was remotely possible. Consequently the case for improving the militia so that it could undertake the tasks set down in Defence Scheme No. 1 could only be made in vague, imprecise, and abstract statements about self-defence, and these generalizations were unconvincing to those who believed that Canada had no enemies. Defence expenditures fell, and by mid-decade the militia was in a sorrier state than it had been in April 1921.

The district commanders were, as a result, unhappier than ever that they were still being asked to plan operations south of the border. Brown's offensive strategy, in their view, was now impossible.[18] At militia headquarters, meanwhile, McNaughton was convinced that the time had come to switch tactics. With the campaign to re-equip all fifteen militia divisions an obvious failure, and perhaps even the cause of increased antipathy to the army, it would be better, he argued, to exercise self-restraint and request mobilization stores and modern weapons for only one division and build from there. Moreover, he added, there was some justification for defining a field force of this division, a cavalry brigade, and an artillery brigade as satisfying all of Canada's strategic requirements.[19]

Brown was stunned by McNaughton's recommendations. The question of whether the army should be prepared to defend the Dominion against the United States – which it could not do with only one division – was not, he told MacBrien, for the general staff to answer. Responsibility for the defence of Canada lay with the government, and if the army was to be so small and weak that it could do little more than roll over at the first sign of American aggression it was up to the politicians to say so. McNaughton, on the other hand, was advocating that the army emasculate itself, and voluntarily relieve the politicians of a fundamental obligation to the Canadian people. That was not only unwise, Brown was saying, it also represented an abrogation of professional responsibility on the army's part.[20]

MacBrien had every reason to address this dispute immediately. On the one hand, McNaughton's suggestion that one division was sufficient for all of Canada's strategic requirements called into question the seven-division expeditionary force the chief of staff had put forward as Canada's likely contribution to another war in Europe during the 1919 Post-Bellum conference at the War Office. For another, there were reasons to re-evaluate Defence Scheme No. 1. Reductions in British as well as Canadian defence expenditures were steadily weakening the imperial forces available to meet the United States, while the goodwill apparent in all relations with the Americans undermined the rationale of Brown's scheme. Moreover, McNaughton was undoubtedly correct when he argued that Canadians in the 1920s would simply not stand for massive increases in defence spending for so unlikely a contingency as war with their closest (and a good) neighbour. MacBrien, however, did nothing; but as his instructions to give priority to direct defence were not countermanded, Brown refused to act on McNaughton's recommendations, asserting instead that his own views best reflected MacBrien's intentions. Formally, therefore, the army remained committed to Defence Scheme No. 1 and the acquisition of equipment for the full fifteen-division militia.[21]

Three years passed before the issue was raised again. During the initial stages of budget preparation in September 1926 the director of equipment asked the quartermaster general whether his estimates should be predicated on fifteen divisions or some smaller force.[22] Asked for his opinion, McNaughton replied that one division was enough because there would be 'sufficient time [in the future] to deal with the question of expanding ... to cover the ... eleven [infantry] divisions' that remained on the books.[23] In 1924 MacBrien had hinted that McNaughton might be right but said nothing to Brown.[24] This time he told the DMO&I to begin work on a plan to mobilize a small, one-division expeditionary force.[25]

Brown protested this directive for the same reasons he had stood against McNaughton in 1923. It was entirely wrong, he told MacBrien, for the army to decide, unilaterally, that it should not prepare to defend Canada against a contiguous foreign power. Policy at that level was a political responsibility. Next he reminded the chief of staff that if the government could be persuaded to underwrite the cost of the military organization contained in Defence Scheme No. 1 all other contingencies would be covered, including the one-division expeditionary force McNaughton was so concerned about. Then Brown played what he considered to be his trump card. Remember, he told MacBrien, that 'last time we had Sam Hughes to blame' for all the army's troubles; next time, however, 'we shall be the culprits' if mobilization for home defence went awry because, having chosen to ignore the problem, the general staff had no recourse but to improvise. Against the Americans that would ensure the country's defeat.[26]

MacBrien was stung by this remark, and immediately informed Defence Minister J.L. Ralston that the lack of a direct threat to Canada was no justification for retrenchment. Although some in the government might think that a fully equipped fifteen-division militia was too heavy a burden, the chief of staff declared that it was neither excessive to the country's requirements nor beyond its capacity to maintain. Indeed, MacBrien concluded, Ralston should do his utmost to obtain formal cabinet approval of the general staff's contingency plans and to complete the rebuilding of the militia 'or there would be chaos' in the event of war.[27]

Some months later, at Ralston's behest, a tri-service Joint Staff Committee was established to co-ordinate defence planning, and at its first meeting in October 1926 the members agreed that the defence of Canada was more important than planning for an expeditionary force, even though the latter was the 'more likely' contingency. The requirements of a home defence army included everything needed for an overseas contingent, it was argued, and concentration on the former would protect the staff from being held responsible for 'the many mistakes made in the last war' that 'were not the fault of the Military Authorities.'[28] Sutherland Brown had won. The army would not give up Defence Scheme No. 1, nor retreat voluntarily, as McNaughton wanted, from its position that all fifteen militia divisions should be equipped for war. However, the resolution of this long-standing dispute in Brown's favour soon meant nothing, as Ralston was unable to obtain additional money for the army. Sutherland Brown himself left headquarters to attend the Imperial Defence College, and MacBrien resigned. His successor, Major-General H.C. Thacker, had no interest in keeping Defence Scheme No. 1 up to date, regarding it as 'chimerical to say the least.' Instead, he preferred to begin work on the expeditionary force unless the government gave firm instructions to the contrary.[29]

Thacker's sojourn at militia headquarters lasted little more than a year, when he was replaced by McNaughton. Brown's nemesis reiterated Thacker's order not to complete Defence Scheme No. 1, at least until the government had spoken. But despite his later denials McNaughton continued to worry about the United States and its desire for paramountcy in the Americas.[30] Indeed, it was only in October 1929 that he finally decided that to continue thinking about preparing for war with the United States was irrational – for reasons that had nothing to do with changed perceptions on his part of what the Americans wanted and what they would do to get it. Rather, his decision was a direct reaction to an announcement by British Prime Minister Ramsay MacDonald that the Royal Navy's bases and facilities in Halifax and the Caribbean would be shut down as a demonstration of Britain's goodwill towards the United States.

McNaughton was troubled, and annoyed, for two reasons. On the one hand he was furious that the British, without prior consultation with the Dominion, had surrendered Canada to the American 'sphere of influence'; for their withdrawal from Halifax had removed an important imperial prop on which Canadian military success against the United States had always depended. As a result, the British had actually dictated to Canada 'on the possibility of taking such measures for our own defence as we may think proper' – strange words from a man who, in later years, claimed that he had discounted the validity of Defence Scheme No. 1 and denied the possibility of British assistance nine years before.

No less extraordinary was the way in which McNaughton brooded about the response of the British public to MacDonald's statement, and his concern that it would make the scenario written into Defence Scheme No. 1 all the more likely. The CGS was convinced that most Englishmen would resent what appeared to be a complete sell-out to the United States and would force their government to forge alliances with other European powers to counter American strength. If that led to war, as McNaughton believed it could, the CGS thought that Canadians might prefer to remain neutral – another extraordinary statement – but he was sure the Americans would attack anyway. Having failed to build up the army described in Defence Scheme No. 1, and unable to count on 'an added effort from our associations with the British Empire' because of the closure of the Royal Navy's bases, Canada would be overrun, and quickly. A recent staff study proved, moreover, that even Japanese assistance would be of little value.[31]

In other words, the Dominion was bankrupt, militarily, because the government had, on its own, looked at the country's defence problems in precisely the same way as McNaughton: the worst case, now seemingly at hand, had been discounted and ridiculed because it was all so implausible. Yet even though the successful defence of Canada against the United States was obviously a forlorn hope, McNaughton would not renounce the American bogey altogether. Sufficient preparations had to be made, he told Ralston, that the Americans would at least have to 'pause and count the cost' if they ever chose to ignore Canadian neutrality and attempted to occupy or control Canadian territory. This advice was not recanted at any time during the seven years McNaughton held the appointment of chief of the general staff.[32]

Still, even this defence of Sutherland Brown as a staff officer who initially was only doing his duty, and who later worried that the army was emasculating itself, is incomplete. It fails to place Defence Scheme No. 1 in context with the other plans under consideration in the 1920s and, for that reason, obscures the fact that Canadian military planning between the wars served two distinct, albeit similar, purposes. One was the simple operational requirement to have something ready in the event of a crisis. The other, adumbrated by Brown in his remark to MacBrien about having Sam Hughes to blame, was the major lesson learned from the army's experience in August 1914, when a 'civilian throng ... little better than a mob' had milled about in confusion and disarray because the minister had dumped the mobilization plans produced by Gwatkin and Gordon-Hall. Subsequently Hughes used the power and influence he had seized at Valcartier to extend his control to the expeditionary force in England and France, where his policies had proved so damaging to the Canadian Corps. Although conditions improved under Perley, and Kemp was not always hostile to the army, 1918 had seen the re-emergence of a certain amount of civil-military distrust. Accordingly, much as they wanted to, the senior officers who returned to Ottawa after the war could not bring themselves to believe that Sam Hughes was a special case, a unique political ego running amok in military affairs. His ghost continued to haunt them, and the spectre of ministerial meddling in the future was cause for concern.[33]

Restructuring the organization of the Department of National Defence and seeking closer ties with External Affairs was, as we have seen, one of the strategies adopted by these senior officers to institutionalize what was, for them, a better civil-military relationship. A second was to make it difficult for future ministers to do what Sam Hughes had done, but without involving the army in a formal, messy, and probably futile fight with the politicians over the nature of ministerial prerogative. That kind of battle had never been won before, and was unlikely to succeed in the years to come. An appealing solution, therefore, was to draft a series of defence schemes so comprehensive, so clear-headed, and so tied to the army's organizational structure that they could not be abandoned with ease, on a whim, in the event of a crisis. Hence Sutherland Brown's insistence that the question of direct defence should not be divorced from the question of equipping the fifteen-division militia in Defence Scheme No. 1. For the same reason MacBrien should, perhaps, have realized that McNaughton's advice to concentrate on a one-division expeditionary force threatened the seven-division pledge of 1919.

As it was, under Thacker's direction militia headquarters had already turned its attention to the question of overseas expeditionary forces by the time McNaughton became chief of the general staff. Sutherland Brown had sketched out a scheme to raise a brigade group to support the British in Turkey in 1922,[34] and in 1927 followed this up with a plan to organize a division for service in China to protect British interests there in the event of a Sino-

Japanese war.[35] Conflict was avoided for the moment, but Brown's efforts were not wasted. Two years before, the government had informed the general staff that it was not to draw up plans in concert with the War Office or other the Dominions 'for different hypothetical situations,'[36] an instruction clearly breached by Brown's China draft. But after seeing the DMO&I's work, Ralston approved 'in principle' the completion of the administrative outline for mobilizing a large expeditionary force, knowing full well that some co-ordination with the British army would be required. The task fell to Brown's successor, Colonel H.H. Matthews.[37]

McNaughton was understandably pleased with this turn of events. For the first time the army had formal political approval to make contingency plans; but even more important, the soldiers were free to consider what McNaughton always believed was the most likely contingency: a major war somewhere outside North America in which Canada would participate in concert with the rest of the empire. At the same time Ralston had indicated his willingness to allow the army to think in terms of a seven-division expeditionary force, not just the one division McNaughton put forward some years before as a bargaining tactic. Still, there was the question of what to do with Defence Scheme No. 1, which Ralston had probably not seen, and the large militia establishment it entailed. Whether Brown's draft could simply be abandoned without a political decision to forget direct defence and to assign priority to overseas commitments, unlikely from a Liberal government, was one problem. Reducing the militia from fifteen to seven divisions involved difficulties of another kind. Loud, long, and bitter protests were sure to come from the regiments scheduled to disappear from the order of battle and from all those friends of the army who did not understand that the sacrifice of eight paper divisions was meant to produce seven divisions totally prepared for war. Ralston, for one, was acutely aware of the probable backlash against the government in the face of such a drastic cut, and he therefore advised the CGS not to be carried away by his youthful exuberance.[38] A tentative reorganization of the infantry into seven divisions was sketched out by Colonel Matthews, but nothing further was accomplished before the defeat of the Liberal government in 1930.[39]

The election of R.B. Bennett's Conservatives promised much for the army. The Tories were traditionally the party of empire; it seemed likely, therefore, that the new administration would approve the general staff's plan to reorganize the militia to fit its scheme for an expeditionary force of seven divisions. Because of the onset of the Great Depression, however, as well as the difficulties sure to be encountered in disbanding the infantry regiments excessive to the proposed establishment, McNaughton chose to be patient. The main thing was to select the right moment.

The opportunity arose in 1931, when an interdepartmental committee was struck to prepare the government's submission to the disarmament conference sponsored by the League of Nations and scheduled for Geneva the next year. Chosen along with the minister to represent the Department of National Defence, the CGS saw at once that this was the forum to which he should make his case. He handled the situation magnificently. Through Lieutenant-Colonel H.D.G. Crerar he first cautioned the committee not to anticipate too much from the conference. Self-defence, he explained, was 'an inalienable right' which no nation would surrender readily. Accordingly, if agreements to disarm were reached at Geneva they were sure to be limited, and would probably permit the participating countries to maintain larger and better-equipped armies than that called for in current Canadian planning.[40]

McNaughton then appeared before the committee himself, and provided a detailed outline of the deficiencies in personnel and equipment that were effectively hobbling the fifteen-division militia. This litany of shortages certainly set the scene for a stern lecture savaging the idea of disarmament for an army in such poor shape as Canada's, but suddenly, and unexpectedly, the tone of McNaughton's message changed. Many of the problems just described, he declared, could be disregarded because a fifteen-division militia was no longer needed. The United States had been removed from the list of potential enemies, and as a result the force could be reduced to seven fully equipped divisions 'for overseas employment in support of ... the British Empire, or possibly to implement a decision of the Council of the League.' This had been clear within the regular army for some time, he explained, but expectations of a hostile reaction on the part of militia officers concerned that their regiments might disappear as part of any cut-back had delayed the whole process of reorganization. Now that reductions could be linked to the League of Nations' quest for disarmament, he suggested, strong arguments could be made for proceeding with them. Canada would subsequently have a smaller, less expensive military establishment that none the less met her requirements fully; she would also shine at Geneva.[41]

The committee saw nothing wrong with McNaughton's forthright statement regarding the expeditionary force, but the Conservative government was no more eager than the Liberals had been to deal with irate militia officers about to lose their regiments. The CGS was therefore told to move slowly and cautiously in implementing any plan to reduce the militia from fifteen to seven divisions. McNaughton agreed, but at the same time warned that the seven-division establishment would have to be equipped as soon as possible if the militia and its friends were to accept the new organization. Furthermore, the government must realize that the seven divisions were to be regarded as both the maximum and the *minimum* force necessary to satisfy Canadian interests.[42]

No one challenged this statement. Confident that he had won the army's most decisive encounter since the war, and fixing his eyes resolutely on the map of Europe, the CGS directed the district staffs to determine which units deserved to remain on the smaller order of battle. At headquarters meanwhile, the general staff was to ensure that whatever arrangements existed for the direct defence of Canada could not interfere with plans to mobilize an overseas expeditionary force. The army's priorities were clear. 'The most serious or important issue for which we ... require to be organized,' McNaughton informed the CIGS in December 1932, 'concerns itself with the mobilization and dispatch of a Canadian Expeditionary Force to take part in an Empire war of first magnitude.'[43]

Drafts of Defence Scheme No. 3 (to raise a seven-division expeditionary force for service overseas) were sent to the district commanders in April 1931, who were enjoined to take no action because the plan had not yet won government approval. In the event, there was little for the district staffs to do. Unlike Defence Scheme No. 1, this latest plan had no operational focus because it was not designed for a particular theatre or campaign; instead, it was a simple statement of the expeditionary force's order of battle and a guide for the orderly selection of the units that would fight wherever they were required by the British or Allied high command. Despite this, the district staffs complained that the plan asked too much of them. Only six days had been allowed between the receipt of the first notice to mobilize and the assembly of battalions at local headquarters, and in that time the district staffs would undoubtedly face a barrage of protests from regiments left out of the force.[44]

Headquarters took note of these objections, revised the plan, and sent copies of the new version to the militia districts in June 1934 with the reassurance that militia reorganization to suit the scheme would follow shortly. The district staffs were therefore to begin taking the executive action proscribed three years before. The most efficient militia units had to be identified so that they would join the permanent force in the first two divisions. (The general staff was determined to place the regular army in the thick of the fighting from the outset, to strengthen its image.) At the same time, the names of likely commanding officers were to be forwarded to Ottawa. For although the CGS acknowledged the government's right to make the final selection of officers for the overseas contingent, he wished to influence its choice by having a complete roster of preferred candidates on hand.[45]

Drafts of two other contingency plans were prepared at the same time. The general staff had long feared the implications of Japanese expansion, and throughout the 1920s had warned that Japan's drive for hegemony in the Pacific could lead to war with Britain and the Commonwealth. It was necessary, therefore, to strengthen the defences on Canada's west coast. By the 1930s the situation had changed somewhat. Japan was still expanding, but it seemed more likely that her interests would bump into those of the United States without necessarily involving Great Britain. With the practical demise of Defence Scheme No. 1 in 1931, the staff recognized that it was more useful to shift the focus of the embryonic Defence Scheme No. 2 from direct defence against Japan to the protection of Canadian neutrality in a u.s.–Japanese war. Failure to enforce this neutrality, McNaughton warned later, was sure to lead to the occupation of British Columbia by the Unites States.[46]

The redrafting of Defence Scheme No. 2 was completed in 1933, but the plan did not win government approval until 1936. In the intervening years the Department of External Affairs failed to define the extent of the territorial waters that had to be defended when Canada declared neutrality. This was a crucial matter in British Columbia, where the 1871 Anglo-American Treaty of Washington bisecting the Strait of Juan de Fuca assigned Canada sovereignty over areas the Japanese could argue were international waters. Failure on Canada's part to keep the Japanese out of this region – her obligation as a neutral according to the 1871 treaty – would justify an American response in force; while obstructing the Japanese was an act of war according to the rule of international law establishing the three-mile limit. In the end, External Affairs declared its intention to adhere to the terms of the Treaty of Washington. Defence Scheme No. 2 was revised accordingly, and once the navy and air force had agreed upon their roles in coastal defence the plan was approved by the minister in May 1938. The final version was nevertheless worded with care so that reinforcement of British Columbia would not interfere in any way with implementation of Defence Scheme No. 3.[47]

Defence Scheme No. 4 was the direct successor to Sutherland Brown's proposals to mobilize small expeditionary forces in 1922 and 1927. By the 1930s the contingency was narrowed somewhat to include only an attack by a minor power on imperial interests or internal unrest within the empire, particularly if fomented by 'a subordinate coloured people.' Canadian interests would not be threatened in either case, and in fact the general staff considered that Dominion participation in such conflicts should be avoided. But harking back to the South African War, when public opinion forced Prime Minister Laurier's hand, the CGS was determined that the army should have a plan ready that would not conflict with Defence Scheme No. 3.[48]

The drafting of Defence Scheme Nos. 2, 3 and 4 provided Canada with a panoply of plans, but of the three only Defence Scheme No. 3 was to receive continuing and serious consideration. Its complete implementation and the reorganization of the militia to conform to its requirements would be needed to provide what the general staff regarded as the minimum military force for Canada. McNaughton tried valiantly to persuade Bennett's Conservative government to act on the matter but, consumed by its efforts to fight the depression and respecting the power of the part-time militia, cabinet set the matter aside. Accordingly, McNaughton had little reason to be satisfied when he left the service in 1935. Still organized on the basis of fifteen divisions technically committed to home defence, and lacking all modern equipment, the army was actually in worse shape than when he had been appointed.[49]

McNaughton's successor, Major-General Ashton, did not delay in raising the matter as part of his review of military affairs for the incoming Liberal government, and in November 1935 urged Ian Mackenzie to forge ahead with militia reorganization as soon as possible. Seven divisions, declared Ashton, 'were adequate to meet our heaviest probable commitment, namely the dispatch of a Canadian Field Force overseas.'[50] Although the government knew that it would face some difficulty with the militia, reorganization was approved with little delay. Nothing, however, was said about where the army might be used.[51] Indeed, officials within the Department of External Affairs were beginning to realize that they had been neatly outmanoeuvred by McNaughton during the disarmament discussions a few years before. His contention that the cabinet committee meeting of 14 June 1933 had authorized an overseas force of seven divisions was specifically disavowed, Loring Christie observing that 'further explicit words' were required before it had the government's official stamp of approval. King's cabinet also made it clear that there had been no commitment to re-equip the militia with modern weapons. Whether the government recognized seven divisions as Canada's minimum requirement was also in doubt.[52]

Fearing the collapse of the staff's planning, Ashton unleashed a steady stream of memoranda to Mackenzie highlighting the deplorable state of the army's equipment and making a strong case for Canadian self-sufficiency in weapons' production. At least once he also asked the government directly to approve headquarters' plans for a three-to-seven division expeditionary force, soon called a 'field force' to obscure its relationship to commitments overseas.[53] The barrage was effective. Ian Mackenzie passed everything to King, who finally reviewed defence policy in August 1936. McNaughton's parting message of the year before was particularly influential, convincing the prime minister that he 'would deserve to the shot [if] I did not press for immediate action and should war come on with nothing accomplished meanwhile and this were revealed.'[54] Consequently, King asked the army what it wanted over the next ten years and how much it would cost.[55]

The Joint Staff Committee replied that the compilation of accurate estimates depended on whether preparations for an overseas expeditionary force were to be included, and added that a three to five-year forecast was safer than ten, given the current international situation. Assuming that seven divisions were mobilized and sent abroad, expenditures (including increased militia training) were set at $163 million, not including tanks or modern mechanized transport. The absolute minimum, which entailed upgrading coastal defences and equipping two divisions for mobile warfare, was $98 million.[56]

Ian Mackenzie presented these figures to cabinet in November 1936 and made a strong case for including equipment for the expeditionary force in the next budget. That the country's coastal defences needed improvement went without saying, he explained, but the government must also remember that public opinion would demand active Canadian participation in any major war overseas. The defence minister therefore plumped for the $98 million program, declaring that 'everything ... asked for, was "required,"' including what he described as the 'insignificant' allocations for a two-division expeditionary force.[57] Cabinet deferred its decision, but on 2 December Ian Mackenzie acceded to Ashton's request to base all future mobilization planning on the defence schemes as they stood, including the seven-division expeditionary force, as long as this was not made public. Mackenzie also told Ashton to raise the question again in February, when departmental estimates would be considered in more detail.[58]

Ashton looked to the future with confidence. His disappointment with the government's formal statement on defence policy during the February 1937 budget debate was therefore understandable. Both the prime minister and the minister of defence took great pains to explain that the marked increases in defence spending presented to Parliament had nothing to do with an expeditionary force – none was under consideration, they declared – but were limited to improvements to direct defence at home.[59] Bound by this pronouncement, the general staff quickly re-evaluated Defence Scheme No. 3 to see what could be salvaged. Strict adherence to the government statement of policy suggested that Defence Scheme No. 2 should be revised to include both defence of neutrality and direct defence in the event of war – a simple and uncomplicated solution. But since it made no provision for an expeditionary force, everything the staff had been working for since 1919 would be sacrificed by following this course. Accordingly, the decision was made to rewrite Defence Scheme No. 3 in such a way that the expeditionary force elements, already cloaked by their designation as a field force, were hidden further. The two divisions would still be equipped for a major war abroad, but the rewritten plan would stress their deployment at home, for the defence of Canada.[60]

This was a master stroke. Ian Mackenzie accepted the new version of Defence Scheme No. 3 in March 1937, noting with pleasure its emphasis on home defence. However, he continued, 'I realize that whereas Government policy is at the moment concerned with the defence of Canada and the protection of Canadian neutrality, it is the duty of the staff to prepare for every possible contingency. I therefore approve the plan in principle and detail.'[61] In short, he had given the staff great freedom of action, and as a result it could legitimately prepare for what was commonly believed to be the most likely conflict in the future.[62] All that had been lost was the altogether unlikely prospect that all seven divisions of the original Defence Scheme No. 3 would be equipped in peacetime.

Even so, the army's position remained incongruous, and somewhat uncomfortable. Publicly, and particularly as far as the prime minister was concerned, strategic planning did not go beyond direct defence at home. Privately, and with Ian Mackenzie's blessing, the staff was to continue planning for an overseas war, but this had to be concealed, even from the rest of the cabinet. While such equivocation may have been good diplomacy, it played havoc with the army's justifications for new equipment. Indeed, as Maurice Pope commented, many of the procurement requests put forward 'strain[ed] the capacity of an archangel to make a convincing case' that they were intended solely for home defence.[63]

The 1937 defence budget had, of course, addressed the question of improving Canada's coastal defences, but it said nothing about providing the field force with mobilization equipment, even for home defence. Ashton at once warned Mackenzie that 'a very serious gap' was developing 'between official policy and the actual implementation of that policy.'[64] But rather than modify the army's plans, he added, it would be better if the government found it 'expedient to extend the scope of their present policy' beyond a concern for static coast artillery to support for the embryonic field army.[65] In an effort to make this alternative more palatable still, the CGS instructed his director of operations to revise Defence Scheme No. 3 yet again. The field force now became the even more innocuous 'mobile force,' and its two divisions were allotted 'the primary role of dealing with enemy landings on Canadian soil,' something for which the government should have little trouble finding money. Still, an 'incidental' commitment to service overseas remained in the scheme, as did a schedule for expanding the mobile force to seven divisions.[66]

This was manoeuvring of the most delicate sort, and in time the conflicting objectives adduced for the mobile force involved militia headquarters in an almost impossible conundrum. By 1938 the general staff was convinced that the army would soon be called upon to fight abroad; yet general rearmament was a realistic expectation only if the government was persuaded of the likelihood of a direct attack on Canada, a contingency that ran the risk of turning the politicians against dispatching troops overseas altogether. Because of what was at stake, however, the general staff took the gamble and began to exaggerate the forms and scales of attack projected on Canada's coasts in the event of war in order to support its case for additional equipment. At the same time the soldiers seized every opportunity to remind the government to procure matériel from the United Kingdom before the British rearmament program closed that source of supply.[67] But no matter what headquarters did or said, the defence minister was unable even to guarantee the acquisition of modern coast artillery, let alone to persuade his cabinet colleagues to buy tanks, trucks, and field guns for the mobile force.

Government policy changed abruptly with the war scare over Czechoslovakia in September 1938. Senior army officers were sent to Washington with instructions to buy whatever coast defence artillery was available, while the air force looked for bombers and maritime patrol aircraft. There was even talk of ordering equipment for the mobile force. But when the crisis had subsided and the talk of war receded, things returned to normal. The officers in Washington were recalled, their emergency spending warrants revoked, and nothing more was heard of upgrading the mobile force. Moreover, in no time at all the prime minister was objecting to the most routine correspondence between Ashton and the chief of the imperial general staff. King's preoccupation with national unity and autonomy apparently defined such exchanges of information as a greater threat to Canada than anything the European dictators might do.[68]

The army was also shaken by the Munich crisis, but for entirely different reasons. Kept in the dark about the machinations required to safeguard the existence of the expeditionary force, the district commanders on the coasts accepted the exaggerated forms and scales of attack promulgated by the general staff early in 1938 as an accurate forecast of what they were likely to face, and once war seemed imminent they arrived at the logical conclusion that the forces at their disposal were too weak to keep an enemy off Canadian soil.[69] Accordingly, they asked for reinforcements, the GOC at Halifax demanding so many extra battalions to 'line his beaches with infantry,' sneered an officer at headquarters, that he actually threatened the mobilization of the mobile force.[70] Fortunately for headquarters, the dissatisfaction of the men on the spot with the number of troops allocated to them was not discovered by cabinet, and so was not turned against the underlying rationale of Defence Scheme No.

3, an important consideration when the possibility of facing raids was regarded, by the general staff at least, as so much 'moonshine.'[71]

At the same time headquarters received a flood of offers from veterans'
organizations and the militia to recruit volunteer contingents should war break
out. Prompted by the best of intentions, but in complete ignorance of the
general staff's plan, these overtures were ignored during the actual period of
the Munich crisis. But they were cause for considerable concern. Given the
precedents of 1899 and 1914, when 'special service' forces were mobilized, it
was always possible that the government would seize upon such informal offers
of service and ignore Defence Scheme No. 3 when war broke out and an
expeditionary force was called for. Accordingly, Major Ken Stuart, assistant
director of military operations, implored the CGS to make Ian Mackenzie
understand that only the mobile force should form the basis of an overseas
contingent. Otherwise, he cautioned, 'even if one of these [offers] is accepted,
chaos will ensue, and we shall end up in the condition we found ourselves in
1914.'[72]

Ashton acted quickly. On 28 September he sent the minister a history of
Defence Scheme No. 3, reminded him of his promise that the army could work
on plans for an expeditionary force, and then repeated the warning that mobilization had to follow the general staff's guidelines if complete disorder was to
be avoided. It was time, Ashton said, for Mackenzie to take Defence Scheme
No. 3 to cabinet complete with its nuances about an overseas commitment so
that the government would not make the mistake of relying upon volunteer
'special service' contingents when war was declared.[73] It was equally important
for militia battalions to know that they had a definite and useful role in the
general staff's plans to prevent hasty (and misguided) offers of service from
that quarter. The CGS therefore asked Mackenzie's permission to disclose the
general intent of Defence Scheme No. 3 to the most senior citizen soldiers.[74]

Beyond this, the army was determined to exploit the government's obvious
nervousness during the recent crisis. Ashton asked for a doubling of the permanent force's effective strength to ninety-seven hundred, and for the immediate purchase of complete mobilization equipment for the mobile force, including tanks. He also recommended substantial increases in the training
budget.[75] Major Stuart was even bolder. In a private letter to Mackenzie he
declared frankly that a seven-division militia and the two-division mobile force
were 'hard to justify' if their primary role was home defence: both were excess
to requirements. This was not the fault of the military authorities, he pointed
out, because they had been compelled to devise a military structure over the
previous decade without any firm guidance from above, and had simply
guessed as best they could. Now that the army's organization and the govern-

ment's apparent intentions were so out of harmony, however, something had to be done; but rather than tinker with the former, Stuart argued, the government should change its policy 'to take notice of the increasing likelihood of major war.' Suspecting that Ian Mackenzie was actually a friend, but that the rest of cabinet would need convincing, Stuart played an 'American card' to clinch his case. If President Roosevelt was manoeuvring the United States into a position 'to intervene against the dictators,' he asked, could Canada do less? The cabinet should follow the American lead and buy equipment for four divisions: two for home defence, and two for service overseas.[76]

Ian Mackenzie made no reply, but three months later the general staff dropped all pretence that it was planning for the Canadian army to remain at home in the next war. 'Under existing strategic conditions there is no risk of an armed invasion of Canada in strength,' the new CGS, Major-General T.V. Anderson, told his colleagues in February 1939. As a result, there was no need to worry about mobilizing the mobile force 'for the defence of Canada in Canada,' despite what had been introduced into Defence Scheme No. 3 only a few months before. The general staff was now to concentrate on training and equipping the mobile force according to standards set for a war in Europe. Troops for coastal defence and internal security were to be found outside the mobile force (and the follow-on four divisions of Defence Scheme No. 3) as circumstances warranted.[77]

Recalled to headquarters for the specific purpose of revising Defence Scheme No. 3 to fit this reorientation, Colonel Crerar took a long look at current British doctrine before submitting his final draft. Based on developments in the United Kingdom, he eventually dispensed entirely with the horsed cavalry division (allowing, however, for its possible conversion to armour) and rewrote the war establishment for the remaining six infantry divisions to adhere to British requirements for increased mechanization. Concurrently the director of military training was instructed to draw up a syllabus that would prepare both the militia and the permanent force for war 'in a temperate climate' against a 'civilized enemy.' Germany was the target.[78]

Whether these changes responded to the growing evidence that Britain would commit an expeditionary force to Europe, or whether they simply reflected Major-General Anderson's distaste for the dissembling demanded of his predecessor to justify Defence Scheme No. 3 is not entirely clear. What is certain is that the new version of the plan was not cleared with Ian Mackenzie before or during the process of revision, and it could in no way be construed as the army's response to a shift in government policy. So far as the general staff knew, the cabinet continued to give priority to coastal defence, influenced no doubt by the prime minister's desire to find alternatives to the commitment of an expeditionary force overseas.

By 21 August 1939 General Anderson was convinced that the government would not have its way. As he told his colleagues, the allocation of even one division of the mobile force for home defence could 'not be justified on purely military grounds,' while the political rationale for doing so was equally weak. Once a major war had broken out, Canadians were 'not likely ... to be satisfied' if the Canadian army remained 'idly at home and Great Britain is seen to be fighting for her existence.' Furthermore, he was confident that the preparatory work completed by Crerar was so exhaustive that ministerial improvisation was unlikely. In his view, the spectre of Sam Hughes's blunders being repeated had been dashed.[79]

Everything seemed to be lost five days after Anderson's rosy forecast. On 24 August O.D. Skelton advised Mackenzie King to send only air force units overseas in the event of war and to keep the army at home to counter the major German raids he anticipated would be launched against the Dominion.[80] The next day the British gave notice that they were implementing the precautionary stage of their defence scheme, and as a result measures were taken in Canada to warn the units already selected for the mobile force that mobilization was at hand. General Anderson affirmed that these preparations were, in the first instance, for home defence, but his intention was to recommend that the government send the two divisions overseas.[81] On 26 August, however, a story in the Ottawa *Evening Citizen* suggested that early the next morning cabinet would decide the nature and extent of Canada's commitment to the war looming on the horizon. The service chiefs had heard nothing about this meeting, and knowing well the prime minister's predisposition against committing the army to Europe, Colonel Stuart realized with horror that the government might be intending to act without consulting its military advisers. At worst, the army would surely be confined to Canada; at best, the general staff could be faced with yet another improvised call to arms. Stuart therefore advised Anderson to submit his recommendations at once 'before a decision based on faulty evidence was reached.'[82]

The CGS's memorandum was on Ian Mackenzie's desk that morning. While acknowledging that government policy made no provision for an expeditionary force, Anderson predicted that the outbreak of war would produce 'an immediate and overwhelming demand for active intervention in harmony with the United Kingdom.' If the British committed their army to Europe, English Canada would expect no less a contribution from Ottawa. Admittedly, there had once been reason to doubt whether the British army would return to

France because an influential school of thought in Whitehall 'had consistently deprecated British intervention [on the continent] with land forces on a large scale.' But this 'facile and attractive' argument had been largely undermined by recent events in Czechoslovakia, and the 'somewhat complacent theory of a limited war' had been replaced by British determination to stand firm against the dictators on the German border.

The CGS was nevertheless worried that a mistake was about to be made because the inherent unsoundness of the theory of limited war was not understood in Canada. After all, the prime minister was still preaching the view that 'the great days of expeditionary forces are over,' and that air forces held the key to victory. Anderson, of course, did not agree with this forecast. But even if it were true, he continued, neither the RCAF nor the RCN were in any shape to offer effective assistance overseas in the early – and crucial – months of fighting. Accordingly, the government would not be helping the allied cause if it chose to dispatch only naval and air contingents abroad. Moreover, Mackenzie King seemed still to believe that Canada had a 'problem of home defence' in the event of a European war – utter nonsense, in the CGS's opinion – and so was inclined to keep the army in Canada, where it would never meet the enemy, and where it would contribute nothing to winning the war. Anderson therefore impressed upon the minister the importance of sending the army to Europe early enough to make a difference – in other words, as soon after mobilization as possible – and of adhering to Defence Scheme No. 3 *in toto* so that there would be no repetition of Sam Hughes's disastrous decision to ignore professional advice.[83]

For political reasons, Ian Mackenzie rejected Anderson's submission. He was not prepared to present cabinet with a document that disclosed the army's consistent preoccupation with the expeditionary force (despite the government's instructions to the contrary) and criticized the prime minister for his misreading of British policy as well as for his failure to understand the futility of limited war. Moreover, something positive had to be said about the contributions air and naval forces could make. Still, Mackenzie agreed with the CGS's main line of reasoning, and indicated his willingness to support the army if a toned-down memorandum was substituted for the one he had just read.[84]

Anderson wisely followed his minister's advice. On 29 August all three service chiefs submitted a joint paper incorporating most of Mackenzie's recommendations. The expeditionary force was duly described as a 'secondary and incidental' consideration in the army's planning, with priority going to home defence, while the part to be played by the RCN and RCAF overseas was played up. But, the chiefs continued, public opinion '[would] overwhelmingly demand ... active intervention in the direct aid of Great Britain' now that the

British had recognized the 'inherent unsoundness of the theory of limited war' and were committed to sending their own expeditionary force to France. As far as the army was concerned, Anderson acknowledged that the government might wish to avoid sending a two-division corps to Europe at the outset, but he implored the cabinet not to upset existing plans to mobilize such a force, and reminded it of the great advantage to be gained from sending two divisions overseas immediately. That was his recommendation.[85]

The complete mobile force was placed on active service, as planned, the following day. But Prime Minister King was still determined to limit Canada's liabilities (and therewith the casualties that could provoke another manpower crisis) in the war, so that on 16 September it was decided that the expeditionary force would be kept small. Only the first division would proceed to England, while recruiting for the second would soon be halted. It was not until January 1940 that the government announced its intention to send the latter overseas, but the creation of an even larger Canadian army as envisaged in Defence Scheme No. 3 was not approved.[86]

The staff work which lay behind the various Canadian defence schemes was not nearly so complex as that undertaken by the main protagonists in the Second World War. This was as it had to be. Since the Canadian army would be a small force operating in association with larger armies according to the scenarios set forth in Defence Scheme Nos. 3 and 4, militia headquarters could do little else but draft administrative instructions for the efficient mobilization of the contingent: the real plans of war had to be left to the Allies. Canadian control of events was more or less assumed in Nos. 1 and 2, but even these lacked clarity and a certain amount of objectivity. Such was almost to be expected. The planning section at headquarters was so small (often only two officers) that its director rarely enjoyed the time to escape routine administrative responsibilities. There is no excuse, however, for the army's failure to undertake demographic studies to determine whether the manpower required for its planning commitments, and particularly for the seven divisions of the original Defence Scheme No. 3, was actually available. Moreover, the plans drafted between 1919 and 1939 never gained the formal approval of the governments of the day. It is doubtful whether Defence Scheme No. 1 was ever seen by a responsible minister, while of Mackenzie King's cabinet only Ian Mackenzie seems to have understood the real implications of Defence Scheme No. 3. The prime minister's expressions of shock, surprise, and dismay when he discovered the general staff's preoccupation with an expeditionary force on 29 August 1939 were genuine enough, and could easily have prejudiced him completely against the army.

As it was, the absence of political support affected the process of military planning significantly. While the German army was dedicated to 'institutionalizing military excellence' in its staff work,[89] Canadian planners believed they must first establish order, organization, regularity, and routine to legitimize their position as *the* advisers to government on matters of national defence. A good plan overturned by amateurish improvisation would not be worth much. As a result, the plans produced at headquarters between 1919 and 1939 were written with this aim in mind as much as they were with an objective consideration of strategic realities. In fact, at times it seemed that a bad plan was considered better than no plan at all if only because it furthered the cause of planning itself.

Sutherland Brown always argued that the adoption of the Otter Committee recommendations on militia organization meant that he could assume the existence of a fifteen-division army for operations against the United States. McNaughton did not necessarily disagree with the requirement for so many divisions, but when he saw that a fully equipped army of this size was a pipe dream, he decided that it would be wise to reduce the establishment to the seven making up the expeditionary force. When Ashton saw that this was equally unrealistic, the two-division field/mobile force was born. For a time even this had to be referred to very cautiously, and great care was taken to emphasize its role in home defence. General Anderson changed this orientation; even so, on 10 September 1939 he did not know what portion of the Canadian army would be sent overseas.

The reluctance of Canadian governments to spend money on defence from 1919 to 1939 meant that all these plans were more shadow than substance. Equipment was not available to back up either the army's or the government's intentions. Inevitably, then, the process of preparing the troops mobilized in the fall of 1939 went less than smoothly. At times it could even be described as chaotic, although for different reasons than in August 1914. Equipment was scarce; uniforms were not available; and training was often unrealistic. Moreover, the future of the second division was left in limbo for several painful months. Defence Scheme No. 3 had not, in fact, been implemented *in toto*.

Yet that does not mean that the officers on the general staff in Ottawa had worked in vain. Their contention that the English-speaking population in Canada would not allow the government to keep Canadian soldiers from active participation in a major war proved correct, and the preparations they made ensured that there was some order when the call to arms finally came. Furthermore, the influence of Defence Scheme No. 3 was strong when the fall of France in June 1940 demanded an increased commitment on the part of Canada. The third, fourth, fifth, and sixth divisions originally pledged by

MacBrien in 1919, and which remained in the plan despite its many revisions, were all mobilized (along with parts of a seventh and eight), and by the end of the war the equivalent of six divisions were in battle. In essence, then, the general staff had ultimately succeeded. The Canadian army of 1939–45 was organized along the lines the army itself preferred, according to the program the army had set out for almost twenty years. What was not readily apparent, however, was that the general staff's keen interest in protecting its mobilization plans had actually weakened the army's potential as a fighting force. Having concentrated on departmental organization and contingency planning as the means of achieving professional independence, the staff had little time or inclination to worry about how the army should be prepared for war. It forgot that professional soldiers were not just civilians in uniforms.

10

Training and education, 1919–1939

The general staff's preoccupation with military planning and the higher organization of defence from 1919 to 1939 was understandable, and perhaps logical. Creating a comprehensive set of defence schemes and solving the country's long-standing problem of civil-military distrust seemed the best guarantees against improvisation during a crisis, and the only way to reverse the traditional practice of under-funding the army. Success in these endeavours, it was believed, would allow the army to undertake realistic and extensive training with modern equipment for the next war. That, after all, was its primary raison d'etre.

As we have seen, however, defence budgets remained pitifully small for most of the twenty years between the two world wars, and the government gave little guidance to the general staff as to what its military policy actually was. That the army would be called upon to defend Canada under certain circumstances was certain, but whether this held for all situations, including war with the United States, was not clear. Similarly, although no government was willing to commit itself in advance to come to the aid of Great Britain in a major conflict, the possibility was never ruled out. The proper organization for the army was in doubt because of this. Modern, mechanized divisions would obviously be required for any European war, but were they as useful for clearing up small, scattered enemy intrusions on Canadian soil? Similarly, coastal defence installations were crucial for the defence of Canadian neutrality, but less so for the indirect defence of Canada overseas or for operations in support of the League of Nations. Such lack of direction over where, against whom, under whose command, and in what strength the army was likely to fight complicated the job of drafting its training syllabus, while the lack of modern equipment, particularly in the 1930's, made it difficult to achieve realism in field exercises.

Yet this was no excuse for failing to produce an officer corps well versed in the art and science of war and able to lead effectively. Planners are not omniscient, and because of this all armies must be ready for contingencies not provided for in their formal defence schemes. The fact that Canadian soldiers were not tied to a specific plan – as, for example, the French army of the 1930s was to the Maginot Line – was, in a sense, liberating; there was room for creativity. Similarly, the study of battlefield tactics does not require an army to possess every weapons system expected to be used in the next war, although that would obviously help. Critical reading of foreign military journals provides some knowledge of new technologies that can be incorporated into training schemes, and simulations are always possible. It was far better, in other words, to drop flour bags from airplanes and to designate trucks and automobiles as tanks and armoured cars in the 1930s than to ignore air power and armoured warfare altogether. The Canadian army was never so poorly equipped, so starved for funds, that such measures were altogether impossible. As a result, Canadian officers were in a position to learn and practise at least that body of fundamental professional knowledge applicable or adaptable to most battlefields even during the hostile environment of the interwar years.

When he returned to Canada as inspector-general in 1919, Arthur Currie was confident that he had the nucleus of a competent officer corps in those Canadian Corps veterans who had indicated their willingness to serve in a reconstituted peacetime permanent force. Unhappily, the post-war army was so small that there were few new positions available for these individuals, while the fact that the regulars who had not seen action at the front were not retired left few vacancies in the old establishment to be filled. When he resigned in 1920, Currie was convinced that the regular army had been sentenced to years of mediocrity.[1]

In fact, the future proved less bleak than Currie forecast. The financial constraints imposed by the government from 1922 on which sealed the fate of the fifteen-division army and precluded the purchase of new equipment actually revitalized the officer corps over the next few years. Forced to release more than one hundred officers, Major-General MacBrien adhered to Currie's plan and weeded out mostly those whom the former Corps commander had identified as the worst of the old, pre-war regulars. Although replacements could not be made immediately, this weeding out created an officer cadre more uniformly experienced and competent by 1924 than Currie had dared hope only four years before. Some CEF veterans had been squeezed into the army and, with fewer long-in-the-tooth pre-war regulars above them, were in a position to advance through the ranks to positions of influence, where their experience actually counted for something.[2] But this, by itself, could not guarantee the maintenance of high professional standards in the army. If these veterans were to remain in touch with contemporary developments; if the succeeding generation of junior officers was to learn its profession; and if merit was to be justified as the only grounds for promotion, the army had to have a well-conceived and critical system of professional education and training.

The seeds of such a system had been planted before 1914 and were re-established shortly after the war. Subalterns for the regular force would come from the Royal Military College of Canada or the officer training programs established in civilian universities. The army of the future would therefore have an officer corps with at least three years of post-secondary schooling, a high standard for the time but one considered essential for success in the complex technical battlefield of the future. Promotion to captain and major would depend on passing British army examinations (marked in Canada), although active service in the Great War in these ranks could count as an equivalent qualification.[3]

As far as staff education was concerned, Canadian officers would continue to attend the British or Indian staff colleges. When, by the mid-1920s, Canadians began to experience some difficulty in passing their staff college entrance exams, a preparatory course was introduced at RMC, often in conjunction with the 'theoretical' portion of the militia staff course. The latter was always open to regular officers on a refresher basis, and although it was a much diluted copy of the Camberley syllabus, it gave more than the few selected for staff college an opportunity to study staff duties.[4] From 1926 one or two Canadian officers a year were chosen to attend the Imperial Defence College, a kind of post-graduate school where senior officers from the British, Indian, and Dominion armies studied problems of imperial defence and national strategy.[5]

One exception was made to the wholesale replication of the pre-war officer training system. At the turn of the century candidates for battalion or regimental command had been required to pass the British tactical fitness for command course at the Senior Officers School, Shoeburyness. Just before the war, however, a parallel course was created in Canada to qualify officers at home. It could not compare with its British counterpart because there were no brigades to manoeuvre in the field and because the directing staff lacked experience, but the existence of separate Canadian military institutions pleased Sam Hughes, who defended them vigorously. The Great War produced an experienced Canadian officer corps, and given the pride the Canadian army had in its performance, particularly at the tactical level, the reopening of the Canadian course seemed to be justified. But once it was clear that there would be no brigade on the ground in the post-war army, the general staff concluded that a completely critical evaluation of an officer's potential would be impossible in the Dominion. Accordingly, except for those who had already commanded a major unit at the front, officers in the combat arms would have to qualify in England before taking up a lieutenant-colonel's command.[6]

The structure of this educational system was essentially the same as before the war, yet it promised much more. For the first time the RMC staff included Canadian officers with significant battle experience, a factor of no little importance in the early training of impressionable officer cadets.[7] Designed to update the practical knowledge of middle-level British officers returning from imperial outposts, the tactical fitness course at the Senior Officers School was more comprehensive and challenging than before the war, and so suited Canadian requirements admirably.[8] Finally, there were major changes at the Staff College, in the main because of the belated recognition that the pre-war syllabus had been too pat, and too much geared to set-piece school solutions.[9]

There were nevertheless clear limitations to what even the most ambitious and rigorous program of courses and examinations could accomplish. Beyond that, the rules implementing promotion by merit had been broken before in Canada, leading the assistant adjutant general in 1922 to wonder whether individuals 'with sufficient political backing' would again rise to the top without reference to their experience and competence.[10] As it turned out, he need not have worried. Undoubtedly because of the bad example set by Sam Hughes, politically motivated promotions and appointments proved to be a thing of the past. Indeed, the one occasion when partisan favoritism was alleged in some quarters – that McNaughton was named chief of the general staff because he was a Liberal – was ridiculed even by the Tories.[11]

There is always a danger, however, that a comprehensive system of courses and examinations will produce an ethos which defines successful completion of these hurdles as the sum total of professional development. Such purely theoretical training, cautioned the editor of the *Canadian Defence Quarterly*, 'will not enable us to appreciate many ... practical difficulties ... and will prevent us from arriving at definite conclusions.'[12] General Archibald Montgomery, soon to be Britain's chief of the imperial general staff, had the same kind of fear about Camberley. 'I have always looked on the Staff College' he remarked in 1926, 'as a place where an officer can learn to be a junior staff officer and where he also learnt, not how to be a higher commander, but how to gradually fit himself for it in later years.' Whether an officer who took full advantage of his two years ever rose to the top 'must depend entirely on his own efforts ... He has to put in a great deal of study of military history and get all the experience he can,' Montgomery continued, 'but no officer can be made into a higher commander by compulsory education, especially at the age of 45.'[13]

Annual manoeuvres at the brigade and divisional level had been anticipated as one of the by-products of peacetime conscription, and these would have added to the theoretical education it was relatively easy to offer Canadian officers. But the rejection of compulsory service in 1919 forced the regular force into its pre-war routines. The under-strength regiments and battalions were again broken up into penny-packet companies and squadrons and scattered around the country. In this way they were intended to provide schools of instruction easily accessible to the militia, and dispersed, secure bases for operations in aid of the civil power. War considerations, it was clear, had little weight in the army's organization.[14]

The general staff made a concerted effort to win increases in the army's budget to permit at least one permanent force concentration a year, but appropriations from 1920 to 1926 were never large enough to permit this. As a result, the companies, squadrons, and batteries of infantry, cavalry, and artillery never came together as battalions or regiments, while in some years even the smaller sub-units were unable to spend the hoped-for two months at summer camp.[15]

The dullness of the administrative routine that remained invited the regulars 'to moulder away quietly in disuse.'[16] As long as a few Great War veterans were left in the regimental messes there could be some useful shop talk, but as the years drew on retirements and promotions began to remove these men, leaving behind platoon and company commanders who had never seen a battalion under arms. The effects of this were already apparent in 1926. Junior officers who had entered the army after 1919 had so little experience, and so few chances to learn, that they were failing their promotion exams at an alarming rate. Most were incapable of employing the most minor platoon and company tactics effectively.[17] By 1927 the rot was so deep that headquarters began to give up in despair. With current limitations on training, the *Militia Report* for the year explained, it was 'impossible to attain efficiency.' Warning that the army's remaining expertise was in danger of total erosion, the report questioned whether it was at all worth while to conduct field exercises at any level. Those for 1927 were cancelled.[18]

The army was not entirely responsible for this sorry state, as even the most inspired leadership would have had extreme difficulty in overcoming the soul-destroying conditions of service imposed by the government's constraints on spending. Still, effective leadership of any kind was lacking from 1924 to 1927. Embroiled in fights with the navy or each other, the chief of staff, his deputy, and the director of military operations paid little attention to the state of their army. The director of military training, for example, was given no guidance whatsoever from colleagues who, as late as 1930, were still asserting that Canada could put a 'formidable force into the field ... which would prove a match for the best of professional troops.'[19]

That simply was not so. The cancellation of the 1927 training exercises because of the army's dreadful performance the year before was proof enough, but more was in the offing. Defence Minister J.L. Ralston persuaded his cabinet colleagues to set aside funds for permanent force camps in 1928 and 1929, and these were held in each of the two summers. The results were far from encouraging. Following the first exercise Major-General Thacker reported that the regulars had done poorly in all aspects of field operations: orders were neither concise nor direct; communications between units had been haphazard at best; and there was little recognition of the need to co-ordinate artillery and cavalry support for the infantry.[20] McNaughton agreed, and before the 1929 exercise he admonished the regulars to demonstrate that they had learnt something about all-arms operations from the Great War and from their reading of the most recent British army pamphlets. If they failed, he explained, they would have to return to fundamentals, leaving more advanced (and more interesting) manoeuvres until the state of the army's training and organization warranted them.[21]

Neither Thacker nor McNaughton had exaggerated. Major H.G. Eady, a British officer then touring Canada, attended the 1928 camp, and his report was at least as devastating as those submitted by the two Canadian generals. Although the officers he saw were very keen, he pointed out that all the permanent force units were 'quite unfitted' for the tactical schemes they had attempted, and even less ready for actual military operations. The cause was not hard to find. The manoeuvres had been 'too ambitious,' Eady explained, because the regulars' 'reduced establishment ... and the way in which they are scattered' precluded 'preliminary training to fit them to undertake more involved combined schemes.' Eady was not sure, however, that McNaughton's solution of returning to fundamentals would work. He doubted, for example, whether the permanent force could ever be used 'as complete units for war' or whether its officers would have adequate opportunity to learn their profession. At the moment, peacetime service in the Canadian army furnished them with little more than 'the means of obtaining some regimental life and also a little combined training.'[22]

In the event, defence budgets plummeted with the onset of economic depression in October 1929, bringing a halt to all permanent force regimental and combined arms training.[23] Emphasis was on honing individual skills without benefit of any collective practice. The non-permanent militia was similarly affected, so that the regulars were unable to derive even the marginal benefits that came from supervising its summer camps. Left once more to concentrate on administration and interior economy, the permanent force became 'hopelessly bureaucratic,' one officer recalled; 'it seemed ... impossible to perform even the simplest operation without issuing a four-page written order.'[24]

The permanent force did not return to the field until the summer of 1938, when the gradual return to prosperity and the increasingly tense international situation led to larger defence budgets. Assembling at Camp Borden, Ontario, for a month, the regulars were to train as a 'skeleton infantry brigade' for three weeks and then, with the help of two Toronto militia units, as a 'mixed force of more normal proportions' for the last four days. Things did not go well. Doctrine taught but never practised over the preceding eight years had not been learnt, causing sloppy and ill-advised tactical deployments. At one stage, it was reported, 'field guns at a road piquet were sited so as to face each other, threatening each other.'[25]

The exercise was nevertheless enlightening, no doubt because so much was new. For the first time tanks, armoured cars, anti-tank guns, and quick-firing artillery were involved, albeit in dummy form, giving the regulars some taste of modern war. But it was not enough. This was the last dry run before mobilization in September 1939, and thus the only chance for the majority of Canadian officers to prepare for the battles they expected to be fighting shortly after war broke out.

The commandant of the 1938 concentration was not happy that his troops had to resort to the use of simulation. 'Full value for the funds expended,' he reported, 'cannot be obtained so long as the present limited establishments are imposed and modern equipment is lacking.' Colonel Elkins added that these deficiencies were too well known in militia headquarters to require further elaboration. Indeed they were.[26] They were also well known at the political level, having been the subject of countless memoranda and reports to the defence ministers of the day over the past fifteen years.

It would be easy to blame the permanent force's lack of modern equipment and its resulting unfitness for modern war entirely on government reluctance to spend for defence, and with some justification. The material well-being of the army was clearly the government's responsibility, all the more so because the system of parliamentary votes for inclusive items such as 'equipment and stores' offered the general staff little room to establish its own spending priorities. But that explanation paints too neat a picture; it ignores the uncertainties produced by a rapidly developing technology, and hides some problems the regulars created for themselves.

The situation had not been so serious immediately after the Great War. Despite vigorous opposition from the Liberal benches, the Union government had accepted enough war surplus from the British armies in France to outfit four infantry divisions and a cavalry brigade in Canada. No tanks or mechanized transport were included, but there was sufficient equipment for both the regulars and the militia to practise operations not unlike those in which the expeditionary force had recently been engaged. Moreover, headquarters itself was not upset by the fact that armoured fighting vehicles had not been shipped to Canada. Doubting the reliability of the current generation of tanks and motor vehicles, MacBrien argued that it was unwise to alter organization and tactical doctrines in anticipation of technological change that might very well fall short of expectations. Given the cost of mechanization, this was not an unreasonable concern for the head of a small, underfunded army. At the same time, however, MacBrien was not altogether comfortable with the trends of modern warfare. In a statement that could have been made by the stereotyped British Colonel Blimp Canadians loved to ridicule, he noted that there was 'a definite limit to the degree to which the mechanical can replace the human element' in fighting, especially when reliance upon mechanical things would inevitably produce a soldier 'less inclined to make use of his own weapon.'[27]

Problems first arose when it became evident that the fifteen-division army envisioned in Defence Scheme No. 1 might not be fully equipped to Great War standards. On the one hand McNaughton, then deputy chief of the general staff, maintained that the military should make only what he considered to be realistic and limited demands on the government for money so as to avoid annoying a less than sympathetic Parliament. By doing so, the army might obtain complete mobilization stores for one infantry division, one artillery brigade, and a cavalry brigade, after which it could work gradually toward a multi-division army.[28] Sutherland Brown consistently advised the opposite on the grounds that the army should not voluntarily surrender what was required for what was in his opinion its primary strategic role – defence against the United States.[29]

This dispute was not resolved for five years. MacBrien agreed first with McNaughton, then with Brown, and then, as we have seen, let the matter hang. With such inconsistency at the top, a unified and coherent policy could not be evolved. While all agreed with MacBrien that the army was 'in danger of being left hopelessly behind unless this important matter ... [was] taken up in the near future,' they could not come together to make common cause.[30] The question of what equipment to buy had been subsumed by arguments over how much.

Even so, deciding what should be purchased was not easy in the early 1920s. Despite doubts expressed about mechanical reliability, advances in technology were making mechanized vehicles far more dependable then they had been during the war. But innovations came so quickly that few designs were ever stabilized. The decade was thus one of experimentation, with many armies, including the British, relying on old stocks while awaiting the results of these tests before establishing new doctrine. Even when it became obvious that tanks, armoured cars, and mechanized transport would have firm places in the new order of battle, few new models were freely available. The Canadian staff therefore decided to wait until these reached mass production rather than saddle the army with more obsolete equipment.[31]

There was also a problem over whose equipment to buy. Some officers like Sutherland Brown and Thacker held firmly to the principle of imperial uniformity and argued that, apart from modifications to suit climatic differences, Canada should accept British designs whenever they were perfected.[32] Others, no less convinced of the value of uniformity, were nevertheless impatient with Canada's debtor role. The Canadian militia was 'old enough,' MacBrien noted, '... not to have some other land do it all,' and should be developing some of its own designs.[33] In the event, with no money on hand for complex work of this kind, the staff contented itself with conducting a survey of the country's industrial potential for future reference, experimenting with a Canadian-designed, all-purpose, six-wheeled truck, and carrying out trials of other vehicles' performance in snow.[34]

The lack of a clear role for the army produced its own set of complications and disagreements. Cavalry enthusiasts argued that mounted troops were likely to be of more use to Canada than tanks in an American war because the hilly, forested terrain of the east had too few good roads for armoured fighting vehicles.[35] Officers with a greater appreciation of the value of mechanization made a case for concentrating on the development and training of 'guerrilla swarms' using motor cycles, automobiles, and armoured cars for a war with the United States; this was cheaper, and probably more effective, than extensive expenditures for the more sophisticated kinds of armoured fighting vehicles.[36] But if the most likely contingency was an overseas war waged in conjunction with an imperial expeditionary force, the army would have to adopt British establishments, organization, and equipment. But from 1922 the British army had been prohibited by the ten-year rule from thinking in terms of a continental war, and these establishments did not exist.[37] As a result, the general staff branch in Ottawa was unable to pass precise plans or organization tables to the quartermaster general, who in turn was unable to make specific recommendations as to what kit was needed – even after the North American contingency had been relegated to the lowest priority.[38]

The 1920s were, therefore, lost years from the standpoint of equipment. Only basic items were procured: helmets, web equipment, rifles, gun and small-arms ammunition, and four Canadian-made six-wheeled trucks. These, of course, were insufficient to maintain, let alone expand, the 1921 inventory, and so the situation had actually deteriorated.[39] The QMG's report for 1926 held good for the entire ten years.

War stocks are being rapidly depleted ... While the armament and military stores returned from overseas have been well-preserved ... little progress has been made in recent years ... The expenditure on stores since the war has been limited to immediate and necessary annual supply.[40]

Because of its tensions, because 1920s experimentation had begun to bear fruit, and because of the influence of McNaughton, the 1930s was a somewhat different decade. A scientist-engineer as well as a soldier, the CGS was acutely aware of the implications of modern weapons on the battlefield. He was also thoroughly convinced that if Canada went to war again she would do so in Europe against an industrial state with a highly mechanized army. He therefore laid Defence Scheme No. 1 to rest, and directed his staff to work cohesively to persuade the government to purchase the modern arms necessary for an expeditionary force. At the same time, he pressed the government to support a domestic weapons industry so that the Canadian army would not be wholly dependent on overseas sources of supply.[41]

The depression precluded major capital expenditures of this kind, however, and through the early 1930s the army was limited to maintaining what it had and to procuring only a few trucks and light tracked vehicles.[42] McNaughton's frustration and displeasure were apparent in his final report as chief of the general staff. 'The situation ... with respect to equipment and ammunition,' he told the minister, 'is one that can be viewed only with the greatest concern':

And with the rapidly deteriorating international situation the position is becoming more and more disquieting. In the past years, the Defence estimates ... have been barely sufficient to keep the mechanism of defence alive. Apart from the essential overhead, it has been possible only to provide for the training of a minimum cadre ... it has not been possible to add to our meagre stock of equipment. Generally speaking, the opposite has been the case and reserves have been used up.[43]

The assessment of McNaughton's successor was equally blunt. In two lengthy memoranda submitted soon after he took over, Major-General Ashton outlined the army's many deficiencies, repeating the now familiar litany of 'no tanks, no armoured cars, no mortars, and no aircraft.' Some equipment, he pointed out, was so old as to be useless for modern war: Canada's field artillery, for example, had horse-drawn guns that were outranged by more modern, mechanized pieces by as much as four thousand yards.[44]

Nevertheless, the emphasis on mechanization had not died during the lean years of the early 1930s, and the commonly held assumption that Canada's next war would be in Europe gave the staff's thinking a clearer focus than had been evident in the 1920s. Work progressed on the scheme to reorganize the militia to conform to the requirements of Defence Scheme No. 3, and this would bring six tank regiments along with other armoured formations into Canada's order of battle.[45] A thorough investigation of the various types of armoured cars followed and, in August 1936, the Canadian Armoured Fighting Vehicle School was created at Camp Borden.[46] The next month the general staff's first draft estimates of the equipment needed to mobilize an expeditionary force of two divisions were ready: eighty-five million dollars for basic equipment, twenty-one million for light machine-guns, field artillery, and anti-tank weapons, and a further seven million for fourteen tanks to be used only for training.[47]

These submissions carried some weight, but total procurement fell far short of what had been requested. Moreover, approval to purchase some of the smaller items, for which Ashton commended the government, did not reflect the administration's whole-hearted support for building up the field army for overseas service.[48] Indeed, quite the opposite was the case. When the government announced its defence policy to the House of Commons in February 1937 it gave clear notice that priority would go only to matériel connected with the direct defence of Canada. Since this included a two-division mobile force, the general staff had reason to hope that the army would enjoy at least some mechanization. But even the limited rearmament program presented to Parliament was cut back to the point where coastal defences in British Columbia could be improved only by cannibalizing existing facilities elsewhere. Nothing whatsoever was obtained for the field force.[49]

The situation had improved only mariginally by August 1939. Suspicious of what the Americans called 'merchants of death,' anxious to avoid any commitment to supply the British army, and inclined to view weapons manufacture as unproductive (and perhaps even damaging to the growth of a normal, balanced mixed economy), the government resisted the general staff's pleading that Canada become self-sufficient in weapons production.[50] When the one venture into the field – the manufacture of the Bren light machine-gun – ended in a scandal reminiscent of Sam Hughes's worst days, the government's prejudices were confirmed.[51] In peacetime, at least, the Canadian army would have to look elsewhere for its weapons. But by 1939 no foreign supplier could confirm delivery. Neutrality laws passed by the U.S. Congress were a major deterrent against placing orders with American firms, while the rapid expansion and rearmament of the British army took up most of the United Kingdom's output. As a result, although some orders were placed with English factories following the Munich crisis, they could not be filled before 1942. Other designs suitable to Canadian requirements were still in the developmental stage, so these too remained unavailable. Consequently, Canadian officers could do no more than read about modern war even as the army was being mobilized in September 1939.[52]

It was not enough. Although Major-General D.W. Spry and Brigadier Willis Moogk recalled that as junior officers they had studied 'General J.F.C. Fuller and other up-to-the-minute experts, fire and movement, and other modern ... tactics,' so that they were 'well in advance of the schedules ... followed in England in 1940,'[53] their experience could not be applied to the army as a whole. If the regular army's training exercise at Camp Borden in the summer of 1938 illustrated anything, it was that the officer corps could not apply what it had read.

Of course, there were a few officers who could make the most out of abstract concepts. Of these, the most impressive were Lieutenant-Colonel E.L.M. Burns and Captain G.G. Simonds, both of whom were to become corps commanders during the Second World War. In a series of articles published in the *Canadian Defence Quarterly*, they conducted a debate over the organization and tactics of armoured formations which addressed questions that would be raised in precisely the same terms by General Bernard L. Montgomery following the desert campaign of 1942. Sheer intellectual effort had convinced both Burns and Simonds that British doctrine was in danger of producing divisions that could attack or defend, but not do both. The two could not agree on how to solve this dilemma, yet both were able to make the mental leap from an organization chart to what conditions would be like on the third or fourth day of a battle. Their analysis called upon their own limited experience as well as a broad understanding of the pamphlets and articles available in the headquarters and RMC libraries. More important, neither was afraid to criticize or offer alternatives to current British doctrine.[54] Such incisiveness could not be expected of all officers, however, and in general the Canadian army of the 1930s was as Maurice Pope described it: 'British through and through with only minor differences imposed upon us by purely local conditions.'[55] All manuals were British, as was tactical training; and learning about 'what was' at second hand from Britain left little time to think about what might be.

Yet the most compelling reason for easy compliance with British doctrine was one which the general staff in Ottawa fashioned for itself, and which has been well defined by Burns. 'The discussion is in terms of what should be done with the British division,' he wrote in the introduction to one of his *Canadian Defence Quarterly* articles. 'It may strike the reader as rather presumptuous for an officer of a Dominion that has no military formation higher than a Brigade to propose reorganization the British divisional system,' he admitted; however,

the British regular division is the prototype of all the divisions of all the forces of the Empire, it having been agreed long ago at Imperial Conference that organization and training should be uniform. Hence, a Dominion officer who feels it his duty to suggest improvements in military organization must argue the case for a change in all the Empire's forces, taking cognizance of the whole range of that army's duties, from first-class warfare to the suppression of religious maniacs in abominable deserts.[56]

While Burns, Simonds, and (to some extent) Ken Stuart were not afraid to tackle problems confronting British planners, most Canadian officers drew back from commenting on imperial practices, fearing that Canadian independence in military affairs would obstruct the close association expected between Dominion and British formations – a closeness demonstrated in the Great War and essential for the next. Canada, they argued, would be a source of weakness to the empire 'whenever Imperial practice [was] contravened.'[57] Their concern was so powerful that the Canadian general staff checked regularly with the War Office to ensure that its military organization and doctrine followed the British model as closely as possible. This was why the Canadian army abandoned the machine-gun brigade organization developed and discovered to be so useful during the Great War. The War Office had discarded it for purely financial reasons, lamenting the fact that such a step was necessary, but Ottawa followed suit automatically, even though conditions in Canada did not warrant such a move.[58]

Wholesale reliance on the British for organizational and doctrinal guidance was detrimental enough to the growth of a thoughtful and critical military profession in Canada. That British thinking was in a state of flux during the 1930s simply muddled things in Canada further. The rules of the game changed frequently, and the lack of precision in any new set tended to make Canadian officers even more dependent on the British to do their thinking for them. In 1935, for example, when it was well known that the artillery of the British Territorial Army (the reserve) would be mechanized, the chief of the general staff in Ottawa would not make a decision for or against mechanizing Canada's militia gunners without first clearing it with the War Office.[59] Similarly, he approached the chief of the imperial general staff in 1936 to ask whether the Dominion's mounted cavalry division should be organized as a mobile mechanized formation on the British pattern.[60] And in 1938 headquarters announced that the question of artillery support for tanks would not be studied at the Canadian Armoured Fighting Vehicle School until the relevant pamphlets had arrived from London.[61] This attitude was undoubtedly responsible for the general conservatism about modern developments that is so apparent in the *Canadian Defence Quarterly* articles written by regular officers. Reluctant to work out solutions before they saw the British answer, they were also hesitant to use their imagination. It was not a good environment for producing a Canadian J.F.C. Fuller or Basil Liddell Hart.

It should not be surprising, therefore, to find that the sharpest criticism of British doctrine came from those who knew it least or were opposed to the regular army's commitment to fight a continental war in Europe alongside British forces. These included civilians such as Loring Christie, who thought that the Angle-Canadian military alliance 'must always completely discourage original thinking ... and block the chance to stimulate native inventive genius.'[62] Included too were friends of Brigadier Sutherland Brown, among them Major G.B. Soward, who was angry that instead of recognizing that 'our own needs should come first,' Canadians were 'slavishly follow[ing] organizations that have been based upon requirements for warfare outside the [North American] continent.'[63] Finally, there were a few young non-permanent active militia officers like Lieutenant W.W. Goforth who still thought in the traditional terms of mobilizing a levée en masse to defend Canada in North America. Because geographic and climatic factors limited the possibility of European-style warfare in Canada, he pointed out, 'army reorganization ... particularly along mechanized lines, should be subjected more to indigenous experiment than to following the kaleidoscopic changes of Imperial models ... largely in the paper stage.'[64]

Had the army been given a clear commitment to a role in which imperial co-operation was unimportant, it might have produced more independent military thought in Canada, as officers would have been forced to prepare for operations they would both plan and direct. But that called for an uncharacteristically firm and focused decision on defence policy by the government. Moreover, most of these non-imperial contingencies were so hypothetical that they did not lend themselves to serious consideration and rigorous study: by 1930 the United States had long since been abandoned as a potential enemy; there was minimal political support for military service in aid of the League of Nations; and invasion from overseas was unthinkable. Left with but one raison d'etre – to fight alongside the British army in a major war – the general staff drew the obvious conclusions. Operational planning would be in the hands of the British, who would control the Canadian army once war broke out, and British doctrine was accepted as given.[65] By the time the government gave home defence unquestioned priority in 1937 it was too late to stop the momentum for imperial standardization. Beyond that, conditions in Europe had deteriorated to such an extent that the army was sure it would soon be in action there. Thus pressure to adhere to British concepts was considerably reinforced.

Integration of British and Canadian formations proved relatively easy during the Second World War because of their common organization and operational procedures. But the price of the army's largely uncritical borrowing from the United Kingdom may have been high: a dangerously unimaginative approach to military operations on the part of most Canadian commanders, and deference to British military leadership that went beyond the requirement for proper subordination to higher military authority.

That even very senior Canadian officers would tend to respect the judgment of their British colleagues was natural enough. They had been raised in an environment that glorified the exploits of the British soldier, and from a purely practical standpoint it was obvious that British officers had far greater experience of command and were much more familiar with the conduct of operations than Canadians of comparable rank. It would take time, as the Great War had shown, for officers from the Dominion to overcome this initial disadvantage. Unhappily, however, the personnel policies instituted by McNaughton when he became chief of the general staff in 1929 seem to have aggravated the problem of uneven experience. A strong advocate of formal education, especially in the sciences and engineering, he was criticized soon after his appointment for favouring officers with good academic backgrounds and high marks in their written, theoretical military examinations – super-staff officers and students, they were called – at the expense of those with proven ability to lead men in the field.

Some of the carping was undoubtedly directed at McNaughton himself. Considered by many to be a 'super-engineer and college professor,' not a soldier, despite his own limited command experience he had risen to the top ahead of several more senior officers with good records as colonels and brigadiers in France, and this caused considerable resentment. Beyond that, as Sutherland Brown observed, the coterie of officers the new CGS gathered about him had 'entirely too much of the university, gunner, and engineer complex,' with scarcely an infantryman or cavalryman to be found. It seemed that McNaughton had embarked upon a course many in the army had struggled against for years: abstract, theoretical studies – and worse yet, civilian academic achievement – would be rated higher than demonstrated military ability.[66]

A review of the appointments, promotions, and nominations to the Staff College and other institutes of higher professional education bears out the allegations made by McNaughton's critics. The proportion of engineer and artillery officers making their way to Camberley, Quetta, and the Imperial Defence College was far in excess of their representation within the officer corps as a whole, and most of these individuals had no command experience when they left Canada.[67] Furthermore, once they returned home, duly qualified, they tended to remain on the staff, seeing no further service with troops, becoming 'so absolutely engrossed in ... general staff routine,' grand strategy, and the maintenance of military properties that they had little time left for operations. Their focus was on the great issues of peace and war, not the battlefield; yet these were the men, by virtue of their qualifications, upon whom McNaughton would call to lead the army against the enemy. Those who had done this before, and well, were left in the military districts, where their responsibilities were entirely administrative.[68]

Sutherland Brown was always worried that academic qualifications would be the criteria for selecting the brigade and divisional commanders of the next Canadian expeditionary force,[69] and the appointment list for the overseas corps drawn up in 1936 indicates that this was precisely the case. Only one of the six infantry brigades was to be commanded by a serving regular army infantry officer and fourteen of the nineteen senior staff positions were given to gunners and sappers.[70] When the army did mobilize in 1939, formal staff qualifications were essential for all senior appointments abroad. As a result, a number of engineer and artillery officers with no appreciable experience of command beyond the squadron or battery level, but who had passed Staff College, found themselves in charge of brigades, divisions, and later even corps. After several years of staff work, no practice of battle, and only a little wartime training, they were expected to understand military operations sufficiently well to command all-arms formations.

It was the studied way in which McNaughton ignored infantry and cavalry officers in the 1930s, and not the notion that wartime commanders must invariably be selected from these two branches, that underlay Brown's complaints. The simple fact that infantry and cavalry officers were bypassed in the selection for Staff College meant that they were ineligible and unready for senior commands in 1939. Furthermore, despite the criticisms made of these officers by the director of militia training in 1936 and the umpire staff at the Camp Borden concentration of 1938 (in which the super-staff officers did not participate), the infantrymen and cavalrymen were still much more in tune with the rigours and problems of the combat arms than men who served at headquarters, often without break, for five, ten, or fifteen years at a stretch.

The question, then, is whether McNaughton understood this and minimized its significance, or whether he was confronted by obstacles and restraints which forced his hand and made it impossible to further the careers of these infantry and cavalry officers. Sutherland Brown himself admitted that the talent in the infantry was not uniformly good; several of the officers selected by Currie and MacBrien in 1920, for example, proved to be 'mediocre,' 'lacking in character,' and consequently unfit for higher command.[71] McNaughton's choice was therefore limited. The structure of the regular force had also to be taken into account. The infantry and cavalry cadres were so small that officers from these branches could rarely be spared from regimental duty or the militia schools for Staff College or extra-regimental employment at headquarters.[72] This also restricted the chief of the general staff's freedom. As for the alleged failure on McNaughton's part to post staff-trained gunners and engineers out of head-quarters, it is easy to understand his reluctance to lose effective memorandum and essay writers such as Crerar, Pope, and Stuart when the army's ability to secure larger budgets depended so heavily on its paper campaign within the federal bureaucracy. These men were exactly the kind of officers who should have been dealing with External Affairs, the cabinet, and the prime minister. Sutherland Brown, it is clear, was not.

But implicit in McNaughton's policies was the belief that adjustment to military command in wartime would be easy for a well-educated engineer or gunner – a variation on the theme introduced by Sam Hughes twenty or more years before. He was convinced, it seems, that the next war would be a techno-logical conflict in which victory would go to the side whose officers had re-ceived the soundest scientific education, because they would better understand and apply the weapons and techniques required to master the modern battle-field. At the same time, however, McNaughton tended to treat military experi-ence as something to be absorbed along the way like osmosis. The art of high command was similarly demilitarized. Undoubtedly reflecting on his own ca-reer and that of Sir Arthur Currie, McNaughton defined command simply as the ability to select experts and handle men, leaving out all reference to exper-tise in managing a battle. Indeed, he believed that the art of military command could be developed just as easily in civilian life as in a professional army, and that given a quick and basic military education after mobilization, successful businessmen would prove 'very adaptable to military life in war' and probably become good senior officers.[73]

In short, McNaughton argued against the existence of a unique profession of arms if that entailed full-time, life-long, and concentrated study on the part of its members to learn how to manage violence in war. Accordingly, he had no doubt that at least one, and perhaps more, Arthur Curries would emerge from

209 Training and education

a group including himself, Crerar, Pope, Stuart, and Burns. That in the end none did is no reflection on the potential competence of these officers: instead, through no fault of their own, they simply had insufficient opportunity to learn their profession before they became senior commanders. Unfortunately, they failed because of this.

Epilogue

The Canadian army of 1939–45 was a citizen army enlisted for the duration of the war. Although all the regular units saw action, and the militia served as the mobilization base for the rest of the active service force, there was little continuity between the regiments and battalions on the order of battle on 10 September 1939 and those fighting in Europe four years later. The ranks of the professional army were swelled by new recruits required to fill war establishment positions left vacant during peacetime, while many militia units were at least two-thirds under strength when they were called out. Officer cadres were less affected at the time of mobilization, but their character (along with the rest of the army) changed even more dramatically because of postings, promotions, and the replacement of unit or over-age personnel during their long stay in England. Training casualties also took their toll. As a result, little is to be gained by relating the performance of specific units (including those of the regular force) with the training they had received before the war.

It is nevertheless clear that while most Canadian units were not ready to meet the German army when they fought their first battle, they did improve steadily as time went on. This may say something about the inadequacy of their training in Canada and England after the war began, but it seems reasonable to suggest as well that first-hand experience of combat was particularly important in the development of an army whose officer corps had so few opportunities to practice real soldiering in peacetime. Although it affected all ranks, the lack of such experience was felt most keenly among those promoted beyond their level of competence to command brigades, divisions, and corps early in the war because no one better was available.

The army was not entirely to blame for its inability to train realistically in the 1920s and 1930s, but in the event General McNaughton's views on what constituted a sound officer development system were to be proved wrong. It took more than a keen mind, a scientific education, and attendance at British army staff courses to make good generals out of majors and colonels who may have commanded a platoon or company in the Great War, but who had not been in the field since. McNaughton and Crerar, for example, were on the staff in Ottawa or elsewhere for most of the inter-war period. Things were even harder on engineer officers like E.L.M. Burns and C.R.S. Stein, who found themselves commanding divisions without having led so much as a sub-sub-unit from one of the traditional combat arms in battle. It is hardly surprising, therefore, that eight of the twenty-two major-generals and above who commanded divisions, corps, or the army overseas were fired for incompetence before they saw action; that two more were relieved after their first battle; and that another survived only nine months. Nor is it shocking that the record of regular officers who commanded brigades early in the war was, if anything, worse.

These shortcomings were recognized at the time, and attempts to correct them were incorporated into the army's post-war plans. A permanent Canadian Army Staff College was to be established at Kingston, Ontario, not only to educate more than the handful of officers who had gone each year to Camberley and Quetta, but also to involve the army more intimately in the teaching and development of military doctrine. In addition, headquarters hoped that the post-war regular army would be large enough and sufficiently well equipped to undertake realistic training at the brigade level, considered the minimum to prepare officers to plan and direct the all-arms operations likely to dominate the battlefield in the next war.

Even so, the centrepiece of the army's post-war planning harked back to proposals put forward by Willoughby Gwatkin twenty-seven years before. Despite the furor following the government's imposition of conscription for overseas service in November 1944 – a decision forced on Mackenzie King by the army's initial ignorance of the manpower implications involved in building a six-division army and its subsequent failure to monitor casualty rates accurately – the general staff dusted off Gwatkin's 1919 draft for universal military training, substituted the Soviet Union for the United States as the most likely potential enemy, reduced the maximum size of the army from fifteen to six divisions, and apparently submitted the scheme fully expecting its approval.[2]

Given the circumstances in which conscription had been adopted in 1944 – and more significantly, Mackenzie King's belief that he had been the victim of a generals' revolt[3] – the staff's action looks ludicrous today. Yet in 1945 there was reason for thinking that the army's image had improved to the point where its advice would be followed. The pre-war mobilization plan had, after all, determined the size of the expeditionary force; there had been little or no political interference in promotions and appointments overseas; and to the soldiers, at least, the controversy of November 1944 had more to do with the government's allegedly broken promise to rely on volunteers than it did with conscription itself. Indeed, it was argued that the shock value of having to send conscripts abroad just when the war appeared to be won lay at the root of the government's difficulties. The solution seemed to lie in implementing an equitable system of national service in peacetime so that a wartime call-up would be no surprise. Finally, the most promising and encouraging sign to the general staff was the close and cordial relationship that had developed between army headquarters and officials from the Department of External Affairs engaged in post-hostilities planning. Indeed, External Affairs actually went further than the soldiers in warning the government of the possibility of Soviet expansion after the defeat of Germany and Japan and the further possibility that Canada, along with other Western democracies, might have to deter the Russians by a show of force.[4]

The six-division army to be produced by compulsory service seemed admirably suited to this purpose, but the cabinet could not be won over. Hostile to the army and hopeful that the superpowers would work together amicably, the prime minister was reluctant to follow any course that might be interpreted by the Russians as being directed against them; and maintaining a large army in Canada, whether by voluntary enlistment or conscription, could only be interpreted in this light. The government was also preoccupied with transforming the country's super-heated war economy into a stable producer for the domestic market, and this ruled out continued commitments to an overblown military establishment.[5] Finally, the atomic bomb left too many questions unanswered about the nature of future wars. General Charles Foulkes, the first postwar CGS, was convinced that after the Russians had been 'frighten[ed] to death with atomic bombs,' it would still be necessary 'to get down to conventional warfare and seize parts of his country and bring him to his heels.'[6] Mackenzie King admitted his ignorance on this score, but was inclined to take the opposite view: nuclear weapons had rendered traditional warfare obsolete.[7] Now, if not in the 1930s, expeditionary forces really did appear to be things of the past. For all these reasons, Canadian defence policy in 1946 mirrored that of the 1920s. Conscription was rejected; the regular army amounted to a little more than a brigade; and small budgets and limited opportunities to train placed Canadian soldiers in a poor position to maintain the expertise acquired in Italy, France, the Low Countries, and Germany.

As it happened, the army did not suffer for as long as many predicted. The outbreak of a shooting war in Korea and the cold war in Europe produced a revolution in Canadian defence policy which served the interests of all three services. For the first time the country joined military alliances while at peace; defence spending increased substantially; and the number of men in uniform grew to well over one hundred thousand. In the army's case, the most significant development was the government's decision to station a brigade of regular soldiers in Europe on a permanent basis, as part of the front line of deterrence and to counter any Soviet move west. Training for the rest of the army at home was intensified as well, and with its larger establishment the regular force was finally able to hold divisional manoeuvres by the mid-1950s.

All this resulted from the fundamental harmony existing between the government and its military advisers. Soldiers and politicians alike agreed on the nature of the threat and what was required to deter it, while the general staff's advice was listened to carefully because of the army's acknowledged competence and expertise. There were still some frustrations and disappointments, of course, but few could deny that the military profession had at last become a respected institution.

This period from 1951 to 1964 represented the army's happiest years, but it was also an aberration born of the Russian threat to Western Europe and nurtured by the belief that the next war would be much the same as the last. By the late 1950s this paradigm had begun to crumble. The advent of tactical nuclear weapons suggested the the atomic threshold would be crossed even if the fighting was originally limited to Germany, and once this happened it was assumed that intercontinental attacks would soon follow. Moreover, by the late 1950s both sides had enough nuclear weapons, and the delivery systems, to annihilate each other. Placed between the two superpowers, Canada was obviously at risk, but there was little she could do to defend herself. Under all these circumstances, war between East and West, even if it began as a land battle in Europe, seemed irrational, a view which undermined the rationale for maintaining Canada's brigade group there.

There were alternatives to preparing for war on the central European front. Peacekeeping operations in support of the United Nations were one way of preventing local quarrels from becoming arenas for superpower involvement. For a time the idea of outfitting the Canadian forces to fight small, brush-fire wars on the periphery also found favour as a substitute for general war. But as the American experience with 'containment' in Vietnam went sour, this notion was demolished, leaving peacekeeping as the one defence program likely to win widespread public support. The soldiers responded to these changing perceptions dutifully enough, but not without concern about the erosion of their ability to fight the armies of the Warsaw Pact.

The army vanished as a separate entity in 1968, a victim of the integration-unification process which saw the amalgamation of the three independent services into one. The reasons for this reconfiguration of the country's military organization seemed clear enough at the time. Streamlining was essential, Defence Minister Paul Hellyer declared, to save money to buy new capital equipment and to facilitate co-ordination among the land, sea, and air forces in peacekeeping operations and small wars. The disappearance of the army, navy, and air force and their distinctive uniforms caused great anguish, much of it emotional, but other elements of the government's plan should have been more troubling. The creation of a unified Canadian armed forces in which certain trades and specialties no longer belonged to one of the corps or branches of the army challenged long-standing arrangements aimed at guaranteeing battlefield support to the combat arms. Furthermore, the government's inclination to find alternatives to the decade-old policy of outfitting the army to fight a major war in Europe (hinted at in Hellyer's emphasis on small wars and peacekeeping) threatened the raison d'être of Canada's relatively large military establishment and its continental commitment to Europe.[8] And it was precisely this commitment that had played such a large part in improving the army's image and status over the previous fifteen years.

Trouble lay ahead after the general election of 1968. Paul Hellyer had promised that unification would provide more money for equipment, so that even if the armed forces were somewhat smaller than in the 1950s, they would still be better prepared for action. But he was no longer defence minister, and the new prime minister, Pierre Elliott Trudeau, saw the world differently than his predecessors. Having little faith in the value of NATO's conventional deterrent, philosophically opposed to participation in brush-fire wars against national liberation movements, and taking a different view of the imperatives guiding Soviet policy, he launched a review of Canada's foreign and defence programs which put the armed forces on notice to expect substantial cuts in strength and expenditure. Protection of sovereignty, vaguely defined and often with economic overtones, national development, and the promotion of national unity became the new catch phrases, while 'collective security' more or less passed from the lexicon. (Even Mackenzie King had paid lip-service to this principle, providing Canada could avoid active partnership in the collective acting to secure.) The country's commitment to NATO was eventually halved, with the threat of worse to come, and the cabinet took great care to avoid the purchase of equipment designed primarily for major war. Indeed, the government's preoccupation seemed to be the creation of a constabulary force useful for aiding the civil power and building bridges in the North.[9]

These were shattering blows for the armed forces, who had enjoyed the prestige they had won in the 1950s and who for the most part remained convinced of the validity of the strategic appreciations that had produced

Canada's commitment to Europe in the first place. Yet, while the chief of the defence staff reminded the government that 'the primary purpose of defence forces is to contribute to deterring war by being militarily capable,' he also called for a new sense of professionalism within the armed forces that would welcome non-traditional roles to fit the new, less friendly environment. The armed forces would acquire relevance, and budgetary support, by showing the flag, assisting national development, and protecting sovereignty even if they lost their focus on genuine military preparedness.[10] Successive CDSs seem to have adhered to this view, perhaps from the conviction that the very survival of the military establishment was at stake.

Changes in departmental and headquarters organization followed to encourage better management of military and non-military programs alike. These were not misguided efforts, but the opening up of so many general staff functions to civilians that accompanied this reorganization suggested that the armed forces' status as a distinct profession had disappeared too. Decisions of a technical, professional nature were influenced by bureaucrats to an even greater extent than in the 1920s and 1930s, and it was rare for capital expenditures to be made on what soldiers would have regarded as their military merit. Too often the selection of equipment appeared to depend on which part of the country needed the jobs that could be created by production-sharing agreements.[11]

Pessimists expected the military profession and its ethos to vanish altogether under Trudeau, to be replaced by a concept of the armed forces as public servants in uniform. But economic pressures from Canada's allies eventually forced his government to embark upon a modest rearmament program, while the Soviets' intervention in Afghanistan suggested that the USSR was more of a threat than was widely believed in the early 1970s. Small increases in the size of the armed forces were allowed, and by the late 1970s the army was once again permitted to include wartime requirements in its budget submissions – a practice looked upon with disfavour for the previous ten years.

As this is being written, the major political parties have all declared their intention to revitalize and strengthen the armed forces even if the roles of the army, navy, and air force change. Distinctive uniforms have returned, and although it is unlikely that this will be followed by complete de-unification, the army is freer to act as a separate entity now than at any time since 1968. Still, a return to the happy years of the 1951–64 era seems unlikely. The country's spending and consumption habits have changed drastically since then, and social programs have become so entrenched that the monies required to support a larger army are simply not to be found without unacceptably high levels of taxation. More to the point, the 1951–64 period was the product of a specific set of characters and circumstances. A threat to Western (and Canadian) security existed that called for a military solution to which soldiers could make a useful contribution: the deterrence (or winning) of a limited, controlled, and (it was hoped) conventional land war in Europe. But as long as this kind of role seems irrelevant (who cares how well Canadian soldiers fight in Germany if their homeland is destroyed by nuclear attack in the mean time?), the army will have great difficulty in establishing its credibility. And without credibility it can hardly expect to be treated with the same consideration, sympathy, and respect it enjoyed in the 1950s.

This book has examined the growth of a professional army in Canada and its development along the lines established in Europe and modified in Great Britain. Its thesis is that the transformation of A and B batteries of artillery and the infantry and cavalry school corps into a modern, reasonably competent, and reasonably well-equipped professional army representing the country's first line of defence in the mid-1950s was not a sure thing because for most of the period under review this was the very antithesis of what Canadians wanted. Most were satisfied and comfortable with the part-time citizen militia that grew out of the country's colonial experience, in part because it was cheap, and in part because of the exaggerated accounts of the militia's prowess during the War of 1812. All the time the threats to Canadian security remained abstract and hypothetical, and there was a British garrison in North America, governments had no reason to anger their constituents by initiating fundamental reforms of the country's military system.

Less sweeping changes were possible in so far as they did not threaten the status quo. The creation of the volunteer companies in 1855 was one such measure; the institution of formal qualifying examinations in John Sandfield Macdonald's military schools after 1862 was another. Indeed, the latter reflected a continuing challenge to Canadian politicians of the era: how to adopt some of the trappings of professionalism demanded by modern war while remaining loyal to an essentially amateur military ethos.

Confederation in 1867 and the withdrawal of the British garrison in 1872 were turning points at which Canada's military history failed to turn. Despite George Etienne Cartier's admonition that self-respecting nations had to maintain armed forces of more than symbolic value, neither the government of which he was a member nor the Liberal administration of Alexander Mackenzie was willing to establish a standing army. The mood of the country was not right. All that was possible was the extension of the military schools system to the artillery through the two batteries formed to man the fortresses at Kingston and Quebec in 1873.

British pressure on Canada to do more for its own defence intensified over the decade, but neither this pressure nor a change in the country's strategic situation offer satisfactory explanations for the appearance of the infantry and cavalry school corps in 1883. The flurry of excitement accompanying the rumours that Russian warships were off the coasts in 1878 had died down; relations with the United States were good; and the government cannot be credited with prescience in preparing for the outbreak of the Riel Rebellion two years later. Instead, it seems that the concept of educating the militia had caught on, while the minister had discovered a way in which his party could reap important political advantages from the creation of a small regular force. It was simply a matter of following the civil administration's well-entrenched practice of trafficking in lands and offices when the time came to find an officer corps. This is precisely what happened. Although the prime minister was able to block the most odious patronage appointments in 1883, by and large Adolphe Caron offered commissions to men for reasons other than their military abilities. At the same time he emphasized that the scattered school companies must not regard themselves as the nucleus of the country's field army.

This was not the standing army the British had been looking for. The Canadian permanent force also had little in common with the professional armies emerging in Europe, the United Kingdom, and the United States. There, soldiers and politicians alike were beginning to realize that a distinct body of military knowledge, experience, and expertise existed which had to be acquired before an officer could be considered fully competent to undertake the responsibilities of his commission. It was also seen that since the complexity and scope of these responsibilities increased with each step up in rank, it followed that the more senior an officer's appointment, the more he had to have learned and experienced. While other factors such as ethnic origin, socioeconomic background, religious affiliation, or party political loyalties might, under some circumstances, make it easier for an individual to win acceptance as a leader, by themselves these attributes were not substitutes for knowledge and experience in determining his competence nor sufficient to justify promotion to increasingly senior appointments during his career. At some point, and the earlier the better, an officer's advancement had to be based upon professional merit; that is, upon his demonstrated talents and abilities.

This is usually easiest in wartime, when an officer can be judged by his success or failure on the battlefield. Moreover, wars afford officers the opportunity to acquire knowledge, experience, and expertise first hand. In peacetime, by comparison, success and failures are often less dramatic, while the routine of administering regiments and battalions in barracks rarely offers senior officers of the future the chance to learn what they must know. As armies embraced the concept of professionalism in the 1880s, therefore, so they created specialized institutions – military academies, technical schools, and staff colleges – to teach officers at all levels what they needed to succeed in peace and war. So, too, they recognized the importance of realistic manoeuvres, as opposed to staged, sham battles, for the practice of tactics and operations. Consequently an officer's performance at these institutions and on field exercises was included among the criteria used to judge whether he deserved to be promoted.

As we have seen, however, the Canadian permanent force lacked such a professional infrastructure. Appointments were not made according to the rules of military merit and competence, but instead adhered to the dictates of political patronage. And, apart from those offered commissions in 1883, officers could gain promotions without once having to attend any military school or college or having their fitness to lead and command tested in the field. The impact of this environment on the permanent force was considerable. Having benefited from patronage in the first place, and understanding the rules that governed their future, regular officers during the two decades after 1883 had no reason to apply rigid professional standards to themselves or to ask for the introduction of such criteria. Given the widespread view that the permanent force should have no aspirations to do more than teach, it is easy to understand how initiative was stifled and why so many officers were caught in a cycle of mediocrity that led them to treat their position as sinecures. Although regular units were used in the suppression of Riel and his followers, once the fighting was over the injunction against conducting field exercises was repeated. Similarly, appointments and promotions were again clearly aimed at securing political rewards for the minister, not military efficiency.

That a professional army grew, in time, from such shallow and undernourished seeds resulted from a complex aggregation of military, political, and economic factors and involved a bitter debate about the fundamental character of civil-military relations in Canada. For it was the British general officers commanding the militia in these years who wanted, above all else, to create an army (regular and reserve) capable of 'real soldiering.' But to succeed required that they break into the cycle trapping the officer corps, cut out the dead wood, and promote those who deserved to advance regardless of their political connections. Unhappily, this threatened the status quo in a number of ways. The worst permanent force officers wanted nothing to do with the introduction of merit as the basis for promotion; the militia feared any reform that might lead the regulars to usurp the citizen soldier's pride of place in Canada's military establishment; and ministers were loath to give up any of the practices and prerogatives that let them help friends and political benefactors through military appointments. The more the generals urged reform, the more the ministers protested; and the more the ministers protested, the more the generals complained of unwarranted political interference in military affairs. The delicate civil-military balance was upset further by the suspicion that the GOCs were motived by a desire to serve imperial rather than Canadian interests. This was especially true of their carping at the lack of military planning and materiél readiness for war in the Dominion. Canadians were not about to pay for preparations that would reduce Britain's obligation to defend Canada.

The mediocrity imposed upon the permanent force externally and from within was broken at last following the Boer War. Frederick Borden was affected by Canadian casualties in that conflict and understood the disastrous effects of incompetent military leadership. He seems, as a result, to have emerged more positively disposed toward the permanent force and was willing, through military reform, both to ask more of the regulars and do more for them. The removal of the office of general officer commanding eased civil-military tensions, but the gains made in the ensuing seven years had much to do with the arrival of Percy Lake as chief of the general staff. Co-operation between Borden and Lake produced more rigorous assessment standards, increased training, and an end to blatant influence-peddling in personnel matters. Beyond that, the general staff was encouraged to draft mobilization plans, and to ensure that these were well done, Frederick Borden approved the employment of British officers until sufficient numbers of Canadians had passed through the British army's Staff College at Camberley.

The importance of personality in Canadian politics should never be underestimated. Sam Hughes's treatment of the permanent force proved that the army's growing professionalism had not yet become so firmly entrenched that it was immune from attack. The minister humiliated the regulars whenever he could, ridiculed them in public, and when war broke out rejected their mobilization plan with ill-concealed glee and contempt. Then, asserting his superior military knowledge, he ruled the Canadian Expeditionary Force from Ottawa.

Hughes's behaviour wont he enmity of the regulars and much praise from the militiamen whose interests he was protecting. However, the flight from Hughes in the Canadian Corps marked the beginning of the end for the traditional Canadian military system and its amateur ethos. Regulars, militiamen, and civilians under arms for the duration all demanded that personnel selection be governed by merit and that field commanders be allowed to conduct operations as they saw fit. Mediocrity would no longer be self-imposed. At the same time, Hughes's successors admitted both the need for merit and the army's professional competence. The necessary precondition for further professionalization existed.

The inter-war years did not see the fulfilment of this trend, despite the concerted efforts of the general staff to foster change. Although the Liberal and Conservative governments between the wars were quite willing to let the army govern itself according to strictly professional criteria, once again the mood of the country was not right to give the general staff a significant voice in the making of defence policy or to support major increases in defence spending. This despite the fact that Canadians by now expected their army to be competent. For its part, the army became so involved in manoeuvres aimed at strengthening its influence that it forgot about soldiering.

It would take one more world war, the threat of aggressive communism, and the forging of military alliances outside the framework of the empire-commonwealth in the early 1950s before the regular force obtained the credibility and legitimacy it had been seeking for so long. Yet fluctuations in the level of support for the armed forces since the mid-1960s cast doubt on how deeply this legitimacy had been entrenched. The ease with which recent governments have questioned the relevance of the armed forces in providing for the country's security suggests that the need to develop and nurture a professional army able to undertake the responsibilities commonly shouldered by other professional armies has, in fact, never been taken completely to heart. Perhaps the professional army, as an institution, is still not welcome, as it was not welcome to those who espoused the militia myth one hundred years ago.

Some of the trappings of professionalism – the merit principle and a formal system of professional education, for example – have been transplanted successfully; others, like preparing and equipping the army in peace either for specific contingencies or as a general-purpose force of more than token value, have not. Only in 1939 was a pre-existing mobilization plan adhered to when the country went to war. In 1870, 1885, 1898, 1914, 1950 (when a special service force was sent to Korea), and again in 1953 (when another special service contingent was raised as Canada's initial commitment to NATO), Canada has preferred to respond to crises with ad hoc, improvised arrangements. If the Second World War and the years from 1951 to 1964 are accepted as aberrations, then for most of their history since Confederation Canadians have followed the practice of colonial times, both French and English, when the local *milice*, flank companies, and service militia were called out in response to crises of the moment.

In short, there appears to have been a consistent and fundamental disharmony between the requirements of maintaining a modern professional army in Canada and the way Canadian society has developed, influenced by its geographical isolation, its relatively small population, and its dependence first upon Great Britain, and then upon the United States, as a defender of last resort. Under these circumstances it seems reasonable to suggest that the late-Victorian GOCs, who strove to create in Canada a military profession with which they were familiar at home, failed because they were unable to make it sufficiently Canadian to take root. The Canadians who succeeded them, and who were also reared in the British tradition, fared little better. As a result, the task of improving the Canadian army's professional image and credibility as well as its capabilities has not been easy, and probably never will be. Officers who understand this, and set realistic goals and expectations accordingly, should, however, find that much can still be accomplished. Indeed, the greatest threats to the army's status as a profession are fatalism and despair – and the mediocrity they produce.

Notes

Unless otherwise noted all documents or manuscripts cited are from collections at the Public Archives of Canada.

Introduction: Military professionalism

1 A.M. Carr-Saunders and P.A. Wilson, *The Professions* (Oxford: Clarendon Press 1933)
2 See the extensive bibliography in Kurt Lang, *Military Institutions and the Sociology of War: A Review of the Literature with Annotated Bibliography* (Beverly Hills: Sage Publications 1972), 158–280.
3 Harold D. Lasswell, *The Analysis of Political Behavior: An Empirical Approach* (Hamden, Conn.: Shoestring Press 1966), 152
4 Lieutenant-General Sir John Winthrop Hackett, *The Profession of Arms*, The 1962 Lees Knowles lectures given at Trinity College, Cambridge (London: The Times Publishing Co. n.d.)
5 Colonel T.N. Dupuy, *A Genius for War: The German Army and General Staff, 1807–1945* (Englewood Cliffs, NJ: Prentice-Hall 1977), 105
6 Samuel Huntington, *The Soldier and the State: The Theory and Politics of Civil-Military Relations* (New York: Random House 1957), 16; Amos Perlmutter, *The Military and Politics in Modern Times: On Professionals, Praetorians and Revolutionary Soldiers* (New Haven: Yale University Press 1977), 14 ff; and Bengt Abrahammson, *Military Professionalism and Political Power* (Beverly Hills: Sage 1972), 13 ff
7 Huntington, *Soldier and the State*, 57–8

1 Beginnings: The militia schools and the creation of the permanent force, 1860–83

1 General Sir Hastings Doyle to Secretary of State for War, 28 Nov. 1861, quoted in J. Mackay Hitsman, *Safeguarding Canada, 1763–1871* (Toronto: University of Toronto Press 1968), 169
2 Lieutenant-General Sir W. Fenwick Williams to Secretary of State for War, 13 June 1864, quoted in ibid., 187
3 See C.P. Stacey, *Canada and the British Army, 1846–1871: A Study in the Practice of Responsible Government*, rev. ed. (Toronto: University of Toronto Press 1963), and Kenneth W. Bourne, *Britain and the Balance of Power in North America, 1815–1908* (London: Longmans, Green 1967).
4 George F.G. Stanley, *Canada's Soldiers: The Military History of an Unmilitary People*, rev. ed. (Toronto: Macmillan 1960) and Desmond Morton, *A Military History of Canada* (Edmonton: Hurtig Publishers 1985) are the two best survey accounts.
5 J. Mackay Hitsman, 'Militia of Nova Scotia, New Brunswick and Prince Edward Island,' Report No. 7, Canadian Forces Headquarters, Directorate of History, 4 July 1966, 13–15
6 Gwynn Harries-Jenkins, *The Army in Victorian Society* (Toronto: University of Toronto Press 1977), 15, 116–21; Jay Luvaas, *The Education of an Army: British Military Thought, 1915–1940* (Chicago: University of Chicago Press 1964), 101–28; Brian Bond, *The Victorian Army and the Staff College* (London: Eyre Methuen 1972), 7–51; Samuel P. Huntington, *The Soldier and the State: The Theory and Politics of Civil-Military Relations* (New York: Random House 1957), ch. 8; and C. Robert Kemble, *The Image of the Army Officer in America: Background for Current Affairs*, Contributions in Military History No. 5 (Westport, Conn.: Greenwood Press 1973), 22–97
7 Desmond Morton, *The Canadian General: Sir William Otter* (Toronto: Hakkert 1974), 3–37
8 Adjutant General circular, 4 May 1860, British Military Records, C Series, RG 8, vol. 810, 3. For the musketry instructors, see Newcastle to Monck, 4 Dec. 1861, RG 8, vol. 1284, 69–70.
9 The proposed regulations are in clauses 31, 42, and 43 of the commission's report, RG 7 G21, vol. 74 #165 (1). Drafts of the report are in RG 9 IC8, vol. 20.
10 Denison to Macdonald, 28 Apr. 1862, Macdonald Papers, vol. 99, 39085–7
11 John Sandfield Macdonald, circular letter, 26 Aug. 1862, RG 9 ICI, vol. 29. See also 'Report of the Executive Council in reply to Newcastle to Monck,' 21 Aug. 1862, RG 7 G21, vol. 74 #165(1). The general order promulgating the new instructions was issued 13 Nov. 1862.
12 Fenwick Williams to Military Secretary, Horse Guards, 2 Nov. 1860, RG 8, vol.

1284, 69–70

13 Lieutenant-Colonel Walker Powell to John Sandfield Macdonald, 29 Nov. 1862, RG 9 ICI, vol. 115
14 'An Upper Canadian' [H.B. Willson], *The Military Defences of Canada* (Quebec: Morning Chronicle 1862).
15 Province of Canada, Legislative Assembly, *Debates*, 3 Mar. 1863
16 Peacocke to Monck, 25 May 1863, RG G19, vol. 10, letter 1109
17 Newcastle to Monck, 25 May 1863, Newcastle Papers, letterbook B3, 47–52
18 Province of Canada, Legislative Assembly, *Debates*, 3 Mar., 16 Sept., and 9 Oct. 1863. Officers from the volunteer rifle battalions were not permitted to attend the militia schools, but had to pass a separate set of examinations before a board of officers.
19 'Report of the Executive Council,' 31 Jan. 1865, in Monck to Cardwell, same date, RG 8, vol. 818
20 Colonel W.F.D. Jervois to Secretary of State for War, 7 Jan. 1865, RG 7 G21, vol. 74 #165(2). For Wolseley's comments see Canada, Department of Militia, *Annual Report* (Ottawa: King's Printer 1869), 105 (hereafter cited as *Militia Report*).
21 *The Volunteer Review*, 21 Jan. 1867, 9; 1 July 1867, 8
22 Correspondence on the withdrawal may be found in Canada, House of Commons, *Sessional Papers*, 1871, no 46. See also Deputy Minister to Adjutant General, 5 Mar. 1870, RG 9 IIAI, vol. 527, docket 1712, and Adjutant General to Minister of Militia, 14 Nov. 1870, RG 9 IIAI, vol. 37, docket 4083.
23 Complaints about conditions facing French-speaking officers may be found in RG 9 IIAI, vol. 1, docket 52, and vol. 525.
24 See RG 9 ICI, vol. 33, and RG 9 IIKI, vol. 9, 'Military Schools General, 1866–1868.'
25 Adjutant General's circular, 16 July 1868, RG 9 ICI, vol. 288A
26 Adjutant General to Minister of Militia, 10 Mar. 1870, RG 9 IIAI, vol. 25, docket 2577, and same to same, 14 Nov. 1870, RG 9 IIAI, vol. 37, docket 4083
27 G.H. Parry to G.T. Denison, 8 July 1871, Toronto Public Library, George Taylor Denison Papers (RCMI), bundle 10
28 Colonel H.C. Fletcher, *Memorandum on the Militia System of Canada* (Ottawa: n.p. 1873).
29 *Militia Report*, 1872, xxxiii–xxxvii, and *Militia Report*, 1874, vii–ix. See also Colonel Walker Powell to Governor General, 22 Nov. 1873, Dufferin Papers, 'Ordinary Canadian Correspondence,' memorandum 37, microfilm reel A420.
30 Richard A. Preston, *Canada's RMC: A History of the Royal Military College* (Toronto: University of Toronto Press 1969), 3–20. See also Alexander Mackenzie to Dufferin, 5 Aug. 1878, Dufferin Papers, microfilm reel A411.
31 Selby Smyth to Minister of Militia, 15 Feb. 1875, RG 9 IIAI, vol. 188, docket 03488; *Militia Report*, 1878, iv–xi

32 Colonel E.O. Hewitt (Commandant, RMC) to Adjutant General, 19 July 1876, RG
9IIA11, vol. 112, docket 12603
33 Selby Smyth to Dufferin, 30 July 1878, RG 7 G1, vol. 30. See also Adrian W. Preston, 'The Russian Crisis and the British Army Origins of Professionalism in Canada, 1874–1880,' *Army Quarterly* LXXXVI (1968), 88–98, 241–52.
34 Mackenzie to Dufferin, 2 July 1878, Dufferin Papers, microfilm reel A411
35 Selby Smyth to Minister of Militia, 22 Oct. 1879, RG 9 IIA1, vol. 118, docket
03488, and RG 9IIA2, vol. 4, docket 2595, and Macdonald to Sir Stafford North-
cote (Chancellor of the Exchequer), 1 May 1878, Macdonald Papers, 31056–66
36 Luard to Minister of Militia, 8 Sept. 1880, RG IIA1, vol. 604, docket 06783, and
Lorne to Kimberly, 12 Sept. 1880, Kimberly Papers, microfilm reel A313
37 Minister of Militia to Executive Council, 8 Sept. 1880, RG 9 IIA1, vol. 604, docket
06783, and Lorne to Kimberly, 26 Oct. 1880, Kimberly Papers, microfilm reel
A313
38 Owen A. Cooke, 'The Training of the Central Canadian Militia' (MA thesis,
Queen's University 1974), 83
39 Colonel Walker Powell to Lorne, 24 Oct. 1882, Lorne Papers, microfilm reel A716

2 The permanent force and 'real soldiering,' 1883–1914

1 Canada, House of Commons, *Debates*, 10 Apr. 1883, 27 Mar. 1884, 14 May 1886,
4 May 1888
2 Lieutenant-Colonel George Maunsell to Adjutant General, 10 Jan. 1885, and
Lieutenant-Colonel W.D. Otter to Adjutant General, 11 Jan. 1885, RG 9 IIB1, vol.
86, docket 08423. Otter, commanding the school at Toronto, set different examinations for first and second class certificates, while Maunsell, commanding at
Fredericton, set only one exam, and awarded those who did well a first.
3 Major-General Ivor Herbert, memorandum, 1894, RG 9 IIB1, vol. 208, docket
49569
4 Luard to Caron, 26 Apr. 1883, RG 9 IIA1, vol. 182, docket 09548 and, for Luard's
initial selection, RG 9 IIA1, vol. 150, docket 07048. Caron's first hint that a regular
force might be formed came in Caron to Luard, 18 Feb. 1881, Caron Papers, vol.
1, letterbook, p. 21.
5 Luard to Caron, 12 May 1883, RG 9 IIA1, vol. 183, docket 09601, and same to
same, 13 June 1883, RG 9 IIA1, vol. 185, docket 09697.
6 Luard to Lorne, 21 June 1883, Macdonald Papers, vol 83, and Luard to Walker
Powell, 23 June 1883, RG 9IIA1, vol. 185, docket 09697
7 Walker Powell to Caron, 27 July 1883, Caron Papers, vol. 64, letter 3086
8 RG 9, IIA1, vol. 315, docket A9473, vol. 353, docket A11869, vol. 410, docket 16373,
RG 9 IIB1, vol. 408, docket 1476/02, and Luard to Lorne, 21 June 1883, Mac-

donald Papers, vol. 83

9 Macdonald to Lorne, 10 July 1883, Macdonald Papers, vol. 83

10 Mackenzie Bowell to Macdonald, 11 Sept. 1889, Macdonald Papers, vol. 201

11 See Desmond Morton, *The Canadian General: Sir William Otter* (Toronto: Hakkert 1974), 206 ff.

12 *Canadian Military Gazette*, 1 Nov. 1893, 207; 1 Apr. 1895, 1; 15 Apr. 1896, 2; and 15 Dec. 1893, 355

13 Ibid., 15 Feb. 1895, 4–5

14 Thomas Scoble to Hutton, 8 Nov. 1898, RG 9 IIBI, vol. 284, docket 77730

15 Commandants received $4.00 a day in 1883, captains $3.00, and lieutenants $2.50. By 1889 pay had increased by only fifty cents.

16 In 1893 majors in the United States army earned $209–$291 Canadian a month, majors in the British army $117, and majors in the Canadian permanent force $90–$105. Officers in the mounted police having the status of majors were paid $133. All but Canadian militia officers qualified for some form of pension. RG 24. vol. 6564, file HG 1064–1.

17 Mary Otter to Caron, 21 Aug. 1888, Caron Papers, vol. 116, letter 12082

18 Deputy Minister to General Officer Commanding, 11 June 1886, RG 9 IIA1, vol. 250, docket A3826

19 Hughes to Hutton, 18 Aug. 1899, RG 9 IIBI, vol. 404, docket 1091/02

20 Middleton to Caron, 26 Jan. 1888, Caron Papers, vol. 115, letter 11997

21 Middleton memorandum, 4 Feb. 1886, RG 9 IIBI, vol. 113, docket 13865

22 Middleton to Caron, n.d., Caron Papers, vol. 133, letter 13215

23 Herbert to Minister of Militia, 19 Feb. 1891, RG 9 IIBI, vol. 191, docket 35537; same to same, 11 Oct. 1892, RG IIBI, vol. 190, docket 43294

24 Herbert to Minister of Militia, 10 May 1894, I.J.C. Herbert Papers, vol. 12, 'Memorandum file,' and same to same, June 1895, RG 9 IIBI, vol. 76, docket 05464

25 Herbert minute on Lieutenant-Colonel J. Homes to Herbert, 25 Jan. 1892, I.J.C. Herbert Papers, vol. 2, 255

26 See *Militia Report* for each year.

27 Herbert to Caron, 27 Apr. 1892, RG 9 IIBI, vol. 185, docket 40731

28 Herbert memorandum, Jan. 1894, RG 9 IIBI, vol. 208, docket 49569

29 Herbert to Minister of Militia, 10 May 1894, I.J.C. Herbert Papers, vol. 12, 'Memorandum file'

30 Herbert to Minister of Militia, 4 Apr. 1892, RG 9 IIBI, vol. 184, docket 40365

31 Herbert to Colonel Gordon, 18 Apr. 1894, I.J.C. Herbert Papers, vol. 5, letter-book 1, 455–6

32 Colonel Percy Lake (Quartermaster General) to Minister of Militia, 14 May 1895, RG 9 IIBI, vol. 227, docket 56061

33 Minister of Militia, memorandum, 5 Aug. 1893, RG 9 IIA2, vol. 15, docket 9654

34 Lieutenant-Colonel R.H. Davis, 'The State and Condition of Rural Battalions of Infantry,' *Selected Papers from the Transactions of the Canadian Military Institute* VI (1984–5), 52 (hereafter cited as *Selected Papers, CMI*)

35 Herbert to Minister of Militia, 27 Apr. 1892, RG 9 IIBI, vol. 185, docket 40731

36 Herbert to Minister of Militia, 10 May 1891, I.J.C. Herbert Papers, vol. 5, letterbook I

37 Herbert to Minister of Militia, 10 May 1894, I.J.C. Herbert Papers, vol. 12, 'Memorandum file'

38 Desmond Morton, *Ministers and Generals: Politics and the Canadian Militia, 1868–1904* (Toronto: University of Toronto Press 1970), 100–1

39 Canada, House of Commons, *Debates*, 30 Mar. and 8 Apr. 1892, 6 June 1895

40 Morton, *Ministers and Generals*, 106, 117

41 Carmen Miller, 'Sir Frederick Borden and Military Reform in Canada, 1896–1911,' *Canadian Historical Review* L (September 1969), 265–84

42 Quoted in Morton, *Ministers and Generals*, 122

43 Gascoigne minute, 8 June 1893, RG 9 IIBI, vol. 271, docket 73432

44 Maunsell to Adjutant General, 21 Sept. 1897, RG 9 IIBI, vol. 247, docket 64737

45 Hutton to Adjutant General, 16 Jan. 1899, RG 9 IIBI, vol. 285, docket 78290; Hutton to Borden, 18 July 1899, RG 9 IIBI, vol. 287, docket 18661

46 Hutton to Theodore Roosevelt, 17 Oct. 1901, Hutton Papers, microfilm reel C1218, 774–5

47 Hutton to Borden, 21 Dec. 1899, RG 9 IIBI, vol. 210, docket 86765

48 Hutton to Minto, 14 Apr. 1900, Minto Papers, vol. 60, box MM #33, 11–16

49 Canada, House of Commons, *Debates*, 26 June 1900, 15 Apr. 1902. See also C.F. Winter, 'Some Reflections upon Recent Experience and How Our Militia May Profit Thereby,' *Selected Papers, CMI* XII (1902), 45–65.

50 A.K. Blackadar, Inspector of Insurance, to Borden, 8 Mar. 1901, RG 9 IIBI, vol. 667, docket 97263. Bill C-133 was introduced on 2 May 1901. O'Grady-Haly to Minister of Militia, 30 Dec. 1901, RG 9 IIBI, vol. 396, docket 200/02.

51 Canada, House of Commons, *Debates*, 15 Apr. 1901

52 RG 9 IIBI, vol. 379, docket 4296/01, and *Canadian Military Gazette*, 12 Sept. 1905, 26

53 *Militia Report*, 1903

54 Adjutant General circular, 20 Nov. 1902, RG 9 IIBI, vol. 447, docket 6038/02

55 Adjutant General report, n.d., RG 9 IIBI, vol. 448, docket 6120/02

56 Adjutant General to Commandant, RMC, 23 June 1903, RG 9 IIBI, vol. 665, docket C1/03

57 Minutes of Militia Council, Report 3, 3 Jan. 1906, and Report 47, 28 Nov. 1906, RB 9 IIA2, vol. 25

58 Ibid., Report 24, 27 Apr. 1905, RG 9 IIA2, vol. 24

59 *Militia Report*, 1905, 12–15
60 Minutes of Militia Council, Report 27, 24 Dec. 1890, RG 9 IIA2, vol. 27
61 Ibid., Report 4, 30 Jan. 1906, RG 9 IIA2, vol. 25; Minister of Militia, circular letter, 1 Feb. 1906, RG 24, vol. 4468, files HQC 372 and C11-5-1
62 Morton, *Ministers and Generals*, 188 ff
63 Lake to Otter, 9 Feb. 1906, Otter Papers, vol. 2, file 7, 'January 1901–December 1906'
64 Minister of Militia, circular letter, 18 Oct. 1911, RG 24, vol. 4469, file C/11-5-1
65 Wilson to Chief Staff Officer, 5 Feb. 1906, RG 9 IIJ2, vol. 49
66 Chief of the General Staff to Minister of Militia, 10 Apr. 1911, approved 2 May 1911, RG 24, vol. 6504, file HG 31-9-13, part 1
67 Lieutenant-Colonel Victor Williams to Secretary, Militia Council, 26 Mar. 1912, RG 24, vol. 6504, file HG 313-9-13, part 2

3 Politics, planning, and the staff, 1860–98

1 George Taylor Denison, *Soldiering in Canada: Recollections and Experiences* (Toronto: G.N. Morang 1900), 96–9
2 Jay Luvaas, *The Education of an Army: British Military Thought, 1815–1940* (Chicago: University of Chicago Press 1964), 101–29
3 C.P. Stacey, *Canada and the British Army, 1846–1871: A Study in the Practice of Responsible Government*, rev. ed. (Toronto: University of Toronto Press 1963), 93 ff
4 J. Mackay Hitsman, *Safeguarding Canada, 1763–1871* (Toronto: University of Toronto Press 1968), 156–60
5 Colonel Patrick MacDougall to John A. Macdonald, 15 July 1865, RG 9 IDI, vol. 2
6 Order-in-Council, 6 Jan. 1866, RG IIA6, vol. 8, 99–100
7 *Militia Report*, 1867–8, 1 ff; MacDougall to General Sir John Michel, 28 Mar. 1867, RG 9 ICI, vol. 274, docket 1425
8 Hitsman, *Safeguarding Canada*, ch. 10; Richard A. Preston, *The Defence of the Undefended Border: Planning for War in North America, 1867–1939* (Montreal: McGill-Queen's University Press 1977), ch. 5
9 Luvaas, *The Education of an Army*, 129 ff
10 Lindsay to Secretary of State for War, 19 Aug. 1870, RG 8, vol. 1287, 485–7; Hastings Doyle to Lisgar, 25 Nov. 1870, RG 8, vol. 1372, 10–13
11 Desmond Morton, *Ministers and Generals: Politics and the Canadian Militia, 1868–1904* (Toronto: University of Toronto Press 1970), ch. 2
12 Adrian Preston, 'The Russian Crisis and the British Army Origins of Professionalism in Canada, 1874–1880,' *Army Quarterly* LXXXVI (1968), 89, and Lisgar to

Kimberly, 20 Feb. 1871, RG 7 G12, vol. 7, 2–3

13 Quoted in Morton, *Ministers and Generals*, 26. See also Richard A. Preston, *Canada and 'Imperial Defense': A Study of the Origins of the British Commonwealth's Defense Organization, 1868–1919* (Durham, NC: Duke University Press 1967), chs. 5 and 7.

14 W.S. Hamer, *The British Army: Civil-Military Relations, 1885–1905* (Oxford: Clarendon Press 1970), 1–76, 118–21, 132

15 Dufferin to Carnarvon, 20 Mar. 1874, in C.W. de Kiewet and F.H. Underhill, eds., *The Dufferin-Carnarvon Correspondence* (Toronto: Champlain Society 1955), 17–19

16 Desmond Morton, *The Canadian General: Sir William Otter* (Toronto: Hakkert 1974), 82

14 RG 9 IIAI, vol. 112, docket 02638, and vol. 141, docket 06142

18 *Militia Report*, 1870, 4, and *Militia Report*, 1871, 39

19 Selby Smyth to Dufferin, 21 Nov. 1874, Dufferin Papers, 'Ordinary Canadian Correspondence,' memorandum 30, microfilm reel A420

20 Selby Smyth to Minister of Militia, 5 Jan. 1876, RG 9 IIAI, vol. 103, docket 01392

21 Quoted in Preston, *Canada and 'Imperial Defense*,' 122–3

22 Luard to Walker Powell, 4 Apr. 1881, RG 9 IIAI, vol. 600, docket 8

23 Report of Major G.E. Walker (RE), 20 Apr. 1882, RG 9 IIAI, vol. 181, docket 19467

24 Canada, House of Commons, *Debates*, 10 Apr. 1883

25 Deputy Minister of Militia to Luard, 16 Aug. 1883, RG 9 IIA2, vol. 6, docket 3893; Luard to Caron, 19 Aug. 1883, Caron Papers, vol. 64, letter 3076; same to same, 28, 29, and 30 Aug. 1883, RG 9 IIB2, vol. 660, 'Headquarters Memoranda' file; Caron to Luard, 30 Aug. 1883, Caron Papers, vol. 5, 442; Luard to Caron, 6 Sept. 1883, RG 9 IIBI, vol. 660, 'Headquarters Memoranda' file.

26 Morton, *Ministers and Generals*, ch. 4

27 RG 9 IIAI, vol. 202, docket A699, vol. 542, docket 12364, and vol. 267, docket A6285, RG 7 G21, vol. 76 #165(5)

28 Morton, *Canadian General*, 137

29 Middleton to Caron, 11 Oct. 1884, 28 Oct. 1884, RG 9 IIBI, vol. 84, docket 07525

30 Herbert to George Taylor Dennison III, 21 Jan. 1913, George T. Denison Papers, vols. 3–4, 6027–30. See also Wolseley to Denison, 5 Dec. 1890, copy in ibid., 1881.

31 Herbert memorandum, n.d., RG 7 G21, vol. 29 #165(1), and Stanley to Caron, 6 Apr. 1891, RG 9 IIAI, vol. 350, docket 11667-1/2

32 Herbert memorandum, 26 Jan. 1892, I.J.C. Herbert Papers, vol. 2, folder 4, 258–61 (emphasis in the original)

33 Stanley to Bowell, 18 Feb. 1892, Mackenzie Bowell Papers, vol. 10, 4783–4800

34 Herbert to Patterson, 19 Jan. 1893, I.J.C. Herbert Papers, vol. 5, 181–2

35 Herbert to Patterson, 7 Oct. 1893, I.J.C. Herbert Papers, vol. 5, 316–18

36 Walker Powell to Patterson, 17 July 1894, and Herbert to Sir Reginald Gibbs (Military Secretary to the Commander-in-Chief), 4 Aug. 1894, I.J.C. Herbert Papers, vol. 8, '1894' file

37 Herbert to Duke of Cambridge, 8 July and 8 Dec. 1894, I.J.C. Herbert Papers, vol. 8, '1894' file

38 Lake to Herbert, 12 Apr. 1895, I.J.C. Herbert Papers, vol. 8, '1895' file; Lake to Major Hubert Foster, 4 June 1895, RG 9 IIHI, vol. 3, 80–1

39 Herbert to Caron, 9 Mar. 1891, RG 9 IIAI, vol. 207, docket A6285

40 Herbert to Major-General E.R. Chapman (Director of Military Intelligence at the War Office), 16 Nov. 1891 and 25 May 1892, I.J.C. Herbert Papers, vol. 7, '1891' file, 2822–7, and '1892' file, 2851–5

41 Herbert to Bowell, 13 June 1892, I.J.C. Herbert Papers, vol. 12, folder 5, and Herbert to Patterson, 3 Nov. 1892, RG 9 IIAI, vol. 350, docket A12109

42 Lieutenant-General H. Brackenbury (Director of Military Intelligence at the War Office) to Herbert, 22 Jan. 1891, I.J.C. Herbert Papers, vol. 7, '1891' file, 2778–9. Herbert to Chapman, 29 May 1892 and 15 Feb. 1893, I.J.C. Herbert Papers, vol. 8, '1893' file, 2930–3, 2936–7

43 Herbert memorandum, 1894, and Brackenbury to Herbert, 22 Jan. 1891, I.J.C. Herbert Papers, vol. 12, 4995–5005, and vol. 7, '1891' file, 2778–9

44 Lake to Herbert, 23 Jan. 1898, I.J.C. Herbert Papers, vol. 8, '1898' file, 3236–9

45 Gascoigne to Gibbs, 13 Nov. 1895, RG 9 IIBI, vol. 660, 34–6, and Gascoigne to Adjutant General, Horse Guards, 5 Feb. 1896, Public Record Office, WO 32/725A, 246–55 (hereafter PRO)

46 Gascoigne to Minister of Militia, 23 June 1896, RG 9 IIAI, vol. 393, docket 14867

47 RG 9 IIH2, vol. 3, and RG 9 IIAI, vol. 414, docket 16739

48 Captain A.H. Lee (RA), memorandum, 15 Jan. 1896, RG 9 IIBI, vol. 238, docket 59909

49 Gascoigne to War Office, 9 Mar. 1896, PRO, WO 106/40, BI/6

50 Colonial Defence Committee, 'The Defence of Canada' (Memorandum 59M) 2 Mar. 1896, in Colonial Office circular, 14 May 1896, RG 7 G21, vol. 79 #165(3), 'additions.' See also Colonial Defence Committee memorandum 57 (M), 18 May 1896, revised 13 July 1897, in RG 7 G21, vol. 798 #165(2) and (3).

51 Montgomery-Moore to Laurier, 3 Dec. 1897, RG 7 G21, vol. 77 #165(7)

52 Chamberlain to Aberdeen, 13 Apr. 1898, RG 7 G21, vol. 77 #165(6c), and Preston, *Canada and 'Imperial Defense,'* 238 ff

4 Politics, planning, and the staff, 1898–1911

1 See Richard A. Preston, *Canada and 'Imperial Defense': A Study of the Origins of the British Commonwealth's Defense Organization 1867–1919* (Durham, NC:

Duke University Press 1967), 244–9, 326–9.

2 Chamberlain to Aberdeen, with enclosures, 26 June 1898, RG 9 IIA6, vol. 5, 2066–7

3 Hutton to Minto, 30 Mar. 1889, Minto Papers, vol. 15, 15–17; 'Minto Narrative,' Hutton Papers, microfilm reel C1218, 836–7; Chamberlain to Aberdeen, 24 July 1898, RG 7 G21, vol. 77 #165(7); Leach to Secretary of State for War, 20 Nov. 1898, PRO WO 32/275A, 258–9

4 Leach Report, part I, RG 24, vol. 1855, file 73; part II, vol. 1856, file 74

5 RG 9 IIB2, vol. 22; RG 9 IIB2, vol. 292, docket 79824. See also Hutton to Wolseley, 12 Feb. 1899, Hutton Papers, microfilm reel C1218, 6–11; Hutton to Director-General Medical Services, 8 Mar. 1899, Toronto Public Library, E.W. Banting Collection, 'A.'

6 *Canada and 'Imperial Defense,'* ch. 9

7 Hutton to Minto, 27 Mar. 1901, Minto Papers, vol. 17, 34–43; Hutton to Borden, 6 Oct., 7 Oct. 1898, RG 9 IIB1, vol. 280, docket 77015; Hutton to Borden, 20 Aug. and 2 Nov. 1898, and 30 May 1899, Hutton Papers, microfilm reel C1218, 218–33, reel C1219, 1017–27, 1223–4; and Hutton to Borden, 6 Feb. 1899, RG 9 IIB1, vol. 285, docket 77954

8 Borden to Hutton, 2 Nov. 1898, Hutton Papers, microfilm reel C1218, 236–7

9 Hutton to Wood, 4 May 1899, Hutton Papers, microfilm reel C1218, 58–61

10 Desmond Morton, *Ministers and Generals: Politics and the Canadian Militia, 1868–1904* (Toronto: University of Toronto Press 1970), 151–7

11 Colonel Hubert Foster (Quartermaster General) to Hutton, telegram, 25 Jan. 1900, RG 9 IIB1, vol. 304, docket 84084; Hutton to Foster, telegram, 26 Jan. 1900, Foster to Lieutenant-Colonel George White, 29 Jan. 1900, and Deputy Minister to Hutton, 3 Feb. 1900, RG 9 IIB1, vol. 304, docket 84084

12 Desmond Morton, *Ministers and Generals*, 146–8

13 Borden to Deputy Minister, 9 Feb. 1900, Public Archives of Nova Scotia (PANS), F. Borden Papers, vol. 93, 905

14 Chamberlain to Minto, 17 Apr. 1900, PRO, CO 42/876, 166–9; ibid., Privy Council Report, 9 June 1900

15 Sir Montagu Ommaney (Permanent Undersecretary, Colonial Office) to Minto, 6 Apr. 1901, quoting Leach to Ommaney, 1 Mar. 1901, Minto Papers, vol. 12, 153–4

16 Minto to Chamberlain, 8 Feb. 1900, Minto Papers, vol. 16, 2–6; ibid., Minto to Privy Council, 3 Feb. 1900, and reply, 9–16, 17–37

17 Morton, *Ministers and Generals*, 160 ff

18 Canada, House of Commons, *Debates*, 10 Feb. 1900

19 Minto to Privy Council, 20 Feb. 1900, RG 9 IIA1, vol. 432; Minto to Chamberlain, 28 June 1900, PRO WO/32/815/058/2397, 236

20 Laurier to Chamberlain, 24 Apr. 1900, Laurier Papers, microfilm reel C775,

44489–90, and Laurier to Minto, 9 June 1900, Minto Papers, vol. 2
21 St John Brodrick (Secretary of State for War) to Minto, 31 Mar. 1901, Minto Papers, vol. 12, 100–101; O'Grady-Haly to Minister of Militia, 25 Feb. 1901, RG 9 KKBI, vol. 660, 'Headquarters Memoranda'
22 Kitson to Minto, 6 Aug. and 2 Dec. 1901, Minto Papers, vol. 21, 191–3, 194–7
23 Chamberlain to Minto, May 1901, RG 7 G21, vol. 78 #165(9), and Brodrick to Minto, 23 Nov. 1901, Minto Papers, vol. 12, 103–5; Borden to Minto, 22 Mar. and 5 June 1901, RG 9 IIAI, vol. 440, docket 18828
24 Dundonald to Minto, 20 Aug. 1902, Minto Papers, vol. 21, 12–14; Dundonald to Lieutenant-Colonel E.A. Altham (Assistant Quartermaster General, War Office), 6 Mar. 1903, RG 24, vol. 1885, file 67; Canada, House of Commons, *Debates*, 22 Mar. 1903
25 RG 24, vol. 1885, file 67
26 Minto to Brodrick, 11 Apr. 1903, Minto Papers, vol. 12, 109–11
27 Chamberlain to Minto, 20 Apr. 1903, Laurier Papers, vol. 753(2), 215662; Borden to Minto, 4 Apr., 13 Apr. 1903, Minto Papers, vol. 8, 313, vol. 9, 54
28 E.A. Altham, minute 24, 24 Mar. 1903, on Dundonald to Director of Military Intelligence, 6 Mar. 1903, printed in Colonial Defence Committee, 'Canadian Command and Efficiency,' memorandum 306M, PRO CO 16448/08 and WO 32/1418/058/2748
29 John Anderson to Ommaney, 16 Apr. 1903, ibid.
30 Major F.S. Maude, minute 4, 18 June 1903, ibid.
31 Colonial Defence Committee memorandum, 28 July 1903, ibid.
32 Ibid.
33 Brodrick minute, 29 Aug. 1903, ibid.
34 Dundonald minute, 19 Aug. 1903, ibid.
35 Maude memorandum, 26 Nov. 1903, ibid.
36 Colonial Office memorandum, 'Summary of Conference, 3 December 1903,' and War Office memorandum, 21 Dec. 1903
37 W.S. Hamer, *The British Army: Civil-Military Relations, 1885–1905* (Oxford: Clarendon Press 19780), ch. 7
38 Borden to Minto, 29 Mar. 1904, Minto Papers, vol. 9, part II, 62
39 Altham to Director of Military Operations, War Office, 9 Apr. 1904, PRO, WO 32/1418/058/2801
40 Minto to Lyttleton, 11 Apr. 1904, Altham minute, 20 Apr. 1904, Grierson minute, 23 Apr. 1904, and Army Council to Colonial Office, 26 May 1904, PRO, WO 32/1418/058/2804
41 Borden to Minto, 15 Apr. 1904, ibid.
42 Report of Privy Council, 14 June 1904, RG 24, vol. 6528, file HGS 511–12. See also Morton, *Ministers and Generals*, 188 ff.

43 Borden to Lake, 1 July 1904, and Borden to Sir Edward Ward, 1 July 1904, PANS, F. Borden Papers, vol. 70, 947–9, 950

44 Canada, House of Commons, *Debates*, 11 July 1904

45 Borden to Lake, 1 July 1904, PANS, F. Borden Papers, vol. 70, 947–49

46 Borden to Minto, 21 Nov. 1904, and Sladen to Minto, 13 Feb. 1905, Minto Papers, vols. 9 and 23

47 Lake to Borden, 28 Nov. 1904, RG 24, vol. 6537, HG 650-12-21, part I; Lake to Borden, 29 Nov. 1904, approved 2 Dec. 1904, RG 9, IIA2, vol. 24. See also Minutes of Militia Council, Report 12, 7–8 Feb. 1905, RG 24, vol. 6537.

48 Minutes of Militia Council, Report 24, 27 Apr. 1905, RG 24, vol. 6537

49 Lake to Borden, 11 Jan. 1905, RG 24, vol. 2488, file HQC 772

50 Military Members of Militia Council, memorandum, 14 June 1950, Laurier Papers, vol. 396, 98494–9

51 Canada, House of Commons, *Debates*, 10–11 July 1905

52 Borden to Minister of Finance, 17 Feb. 1906, Laurier Papers, vol. 656, 178022–7

53 Chief of the General Staff to divisional commanders, 16 Aug. 1906, and to militia commanding officers, 28 June 1907, RG 24, microfilm reel C5052, file HQS 484. See also RG 24, vol. 2488, file HQC 748 for Gwatkin's plans.

54 Lake to Borden, 10 Jan. 1908, RG 24, vol. 2488, file HQC 772

55 Borden to Laurier, 15 June 1908, PANS, F. Borden Papers, vol. 123, 115–16; Borden to Laurier, 14 Nov. 1908, 12 Jan. 1909, Laurier Papers, vol. 545, 147925–6, vol. 555, 150298–301

56 RG 24, microfilm reel C5052, file HQC 365-11

57 Report of the Royal Commission on the Public Service, Canada, House of Commons, *Sessional Papers*, 1908, no. 29(a), 740 ff; see also Minutes of Militia Council, report 14, 17–21 Apr. 1908, RG 24, vol. 6537.

58 Order-in-Council, 6 Nov. 1908, PC 2448, Privy Council records, RG 2, 1. vol. 1088

59 Grey to Lake, 4 Nov. 1908, Grey of Howick Papers, vol. 28, drawer 4, file 3, 7311

60 Desmond Morton, *The Canadian General: Sir William Otter* (Toronto: Hakkert 1974), passim

61 War Office to Colonial Office, 27 Sept. 1909, to Governor General, 23 Oct. 1909, RG 234, vol. 6606, file HQ 6890-1, part I. See also Morton, *The Canadian General*, 294–5, and Preston, *Canada and 'Imperial Defense,'* 424–6.

62 Otter to Militia Council, 27 June 1910, and Militia Council to Otter, 14 Sept. 1910, RG 24, vol. 6606, file HQ 6890-1, part I

63 RG 24, vol. 6401, file HQ 93-1-3, and vol. 2498, file HQS 1050, part I

64 Canada, House of Commons, *Sessional Papers*, 1911, no. 35; Lake's response is *Sessional Paper* 35(a).

65 Canada, House of Commons, *Debates*, 5 May 1911

66 General Staff memoranda, 3 Oct. and 10 Oct. 1911, RG 24, vol. 4263, file HQC 2-4,

and vol. 231, file HQC 2-1-6
67 RG 9 IIBI, vol. 395, docket 90/01
68 Otter to Militia Council, 13 Oct. 1908, RG 24, vol. 6506, file HQ 33-33-1, part I
69 Adjutant General to District Officers Commanding, 8 Mar. 1911, ibid., part IV

5 Politics, planning, and the staff, 1911–14

1 C.P. Stacey, *Canada and the Age of Conflict: A History of Canadian External Policies, Vol. I, 1867–1921* (Toronto: Macmillan 1977), 125–37, 155–61
2 Loring Christie memorandum, n.d., Loring Christie Papers, vol. 2, file 3, 'War'
3 General Sir Ian Hamilton, *Report on the Military Institutions of Canada* (Ottawa: King's Printer 1913)
4 Richard A. Preston, *The Defence of the Undefended Border: Planning for War in North America, 1867–1939* (Montreal: McGill-Queen's University Press 1977), 181–6
5 Kenneth Bourne, *Britain and the Balance of Power in North America, 1815–1918* (London: Longmans, Green, 1967), 350
6 See, for example, Committee of Imperial Defence, Oversea Defence: Probable Scales of Attack against Oversea British Ports, No. 109-C, 21 Apr. 1914.
7 See Carl Berger, *The Sense of Power: Studies in the Ideas of Canadian Imperialism, 1967–1914* (Toronto: University of Toronto Press 1970), 163–73.
8 Gwatkin to Lieutenant-Colonel P.E. Thacker, 13 May 1913, RG 24, vol. 6531, file HQ 590-10
9 RG 24, vol. 2507, file HQC 1219, vol. 302, file HQ 33-1-218, vol. 2432, file HQC 484, and vol. 1855, file 70
10 Lieutenant-Colonel George Paley, 'The Defence of Canada against the United States,' 13 Jan. 1912, RG 24, microfilm reel C5059, file HQC 1276
11 Lieutenant-Colonel G. Gordon-Hall, 'The Defence of Canada against the United States,' 12 Jan. 1913, RG 24, vol. 2509, file HQC 1432
12 'Extract from the proceedings of the inter-departmental committee on defence,' Sir Joseph Pope Papers, vol. 131, file 118
13 Ibid. Duke of Connaught to Borden, 31 Dec. 1913 and to Sir William Harcourt, 15 Jan. 1914, RG 7 G21, vol. 228 #343, part VI(a); Gordon-Hall to A.F. Duguid, 18 Nov. 1936, RG 24, vol. 1503, file HQ 683-1-30-5, part III
14 Canada, House of Commons, *Debates*, 19 Mar. 1912
15 See Ronald Haycock, 'The Public Career of Sir Sam Hughes' (PHD thesis, University of Western Ontario 1975), and *Sam Hughes: The Public Career of a Controversial Canadian, 1885–1916* (Waterloo: Wilfrid Laurier University Press 1986).
16 Hughes to Hutton, 18 Aug. 1898, RG 9 IIBI, vol. 404, docket 1092/02
17 Desmond Morton, *Ministers and Generals: Politics and the Canadian Militia*

1868–1904 (Toronto: University of Toronto Press 1970), 152 ff
18 Hughes to Hutton, 18 Aug. 1898, RG 9 IIBI, vol. 404, docket 1092/02
19 Secretary of State for War to Lord Roberts, 19 June 1900, and Roberts's reply, 28 June 1900, RG 7 G21, vol. 142 #265, part I
20 Canada, House of Commons, *Debates*, 11 July 1905
21 Minutes of Militia Council, 10 Apr. 1912, RG 9 IIA2, vol. 31; minutes of conference of militia officers, Nov. 1911, RG 24, vol. 150, file HQ 9879-2
22 Hughes to Mackenzie, 6 Feb. 1912, Hughes to Borden, 12 Feb. 1912, and Mackenzie to Borden, 6 Feb. 1912, in Borden Papers, vol. 7, 742-2H
23 Hughes to Borden, 12 Feb. 1912, ibid.
24 Mackenzie memorandum, n.d., Borden Papers, vol. 109, 'RLB 88,' 91825-31
25 Minutes of Militia Council, Report 13, 7 May 1912, RG 9 IIAI, vol. 31, and Hughes to Chief of the General Staff, 9 July 1912, RG 7 G21, vol. 142, file 265A part I
26 Mackenzie to Hughes, 15 July 1912, ibid.
27 Colin Mackenzie, 'A brief resumé of Militia affairs in Canada during 1912,' ibid.
28 Minutes of Militia Council, Report 9, 19 Mar. 1913, RG 9 IIA2, vol. 32
29 Mackenzie to Adjutant General, 14 Apr. 1912, to Lieutenant-Colonel H.C. Lowther, 10 Mar. 1913, and to Governor General, 9 Apr. 1913, RG 7 G21, vol. 142, file 265(A)
30 Borden Papers, vol. 7, 796-6D
31 Mackenzie to Borden, 25 Apr. 1913, RG 7 G21, vol. 142, file 265(A)
32 Hughes, 'Memorandum on Mackenzie,' June 1913, ibid.
33 Lieutenant-Colonel H.C. Lowther (Military Secretary to Governor General) to Sir William Harcourt, 19 Dec. 1913, ibid.
34 Borden to French, 18 Aug. 1913, Borden Papers, vol. 7, 'OC 55,' 732 ff
35 Duke of Connaught to Borden, 3 Dec. 1913, and reply, 8 Dec. 1913, RG 7 G21, vol. 141, file 265A, part I
36 Government House, 'Notes on Colonel Hughes,' sent to Colonial Secretary, 19 Dec. 1913, ibid.
37 Duke of Connaught to Borden, 15 May 1913, Borden Papers, vol. 7
38 Hughes to Connaught, 30 Jan. 1914, RG 7 G21, vol. 142, file 265A
39 Memorandum by F.D. Farquhar (Secretary to Governor General), n.d., ibid.
40 Hughes, 'Memorandum on Mackenzie,' June 1913, ibid.
41 RG 24, vols. 2510 and 1509
42 RG 24, vol. 4263, file C-2-4
43 Gordon-Hall to A.F. Duguid, 18 Nov. 1936, RG 24, vol. 1503, HQ 683-1-30-5, part III
44 G.W.L. Nicholson, *Canadian Expeditionary Force, 1914–1919* (Official History of

the Canadian Army in the First World War) (Ottawa: Queen's Printer 1962), 14–32
45 D Hist, Walter Bapty Diary, part II, 40.
46 Frederic C. Curry, *From the St. Lawrence to the Yser: With the 1st Canadian Brigade* (Toronto: McClelland, Goodchild, and Stewart 1916), 2
47 B.G. Tuxford to A.F. Duguid, 1 Sept. 1936, and Gordon-Hall to A.F. Duguid, 18 Nov. 1936, RG 24, vol. 1503, file HQ 683-1-30-5, parts I and II
48 Sutherland Brown to Chief of the General Staff, 7 Jan. 1921, RG 24, vol. 1754, DHS 10-9; see also his 'Lecture on mobilization,' ibid.
49 Currie to Sam Matson, 29 Sept. 1914, Borden Papers, vol. 361, 'Currie' file
50 Borden Papers, vol. 31, 'OC 165(I),' 12463–13043
51 Gwatkin to Hazen, 8 Oct. 1914, Borden Papers, vol. 196, 'RLB 724,' 109471 ff; Borden to Hughes, 19 Oct. 1914, Borden Papers, vol. 49, 'OC 225–227,' 28850
52 Connaught to Borden, 1 Nov. 1914, Borden Papers, vol. 1, 'OC 69,' 2113–14
53 Borden to Hughes, 16 Dec. 1914, Borden Papers, vol. 37, 'OC 187–191(2),' 15687–9
54 Hughes to Borden, 22 Dec. 1914, 11 Jan. 1915, Borden Papers, vol. 37, 'OC 187–191(2),' 15689–92, 19696–9
55 Roger Graham, *Arthur Meighen: A Biography* (Toronto: Clarke, Irwin 1960), I, 108–9; D.J. Goodspeed, *The Road Past Vimy: The Canadian Corps 1914–1918* (Toronto: Macmillan 1969), 11; John Swettenham, *To Seize the Victory: The Canadian Corps in World War I* (Toronto: Ryerson 1965), 38
56 Quoted in Anthony J. Trythall, *'Boney' Fuller: The Intellectual General, 1878–1966* (London: Cassell 1977), 33
57 Alderson to Connaught, 4 Dec. 1914, Borden Papers, vol. 49, 'OC 223–235(I),' 22857
58 Creelman Diary, 17 Nov. 1914, 19 Dec. 1914, Creelman Papers, PAC
59 Currie to Sam Matson, 29 Sept. 1914, Borden Papers, vol. 36, 'Currie' file
60 Hughes to Borden, 22 December 1914, Borden Papers, vol. 37, 'OC 187–191,' 15689–92
61 Department of Militia and Defence, *Militia List*, 1914; A.F. Duguid, *Official History of the Canadian Forces in the Great War, 1914–1919*, vol. I, *Appendices and Maps* (Ottawa: King's Printer 1939), 428–31; RG 24, vol. 1843, file GAQ-10-50; K. Eyre, 'Staff and Command in the Canadian Corps' (MA thesis, Duke University 1967)
62 Duguid, *Official History*, I, 52
63 Director of Military Training to Chief of the General Staff, 13 Feb. 1914, RG 24, vol. 6504, file HQ 313-9-13, part III
64 Gwatkin to Adjutant General, 9 Sept. 1914, RG 24, vol. 1259, file HQ 593-2-2
65 Alderson to Connaught, 4 Dec. 1914, Borden Papers, vol. 49, 'OC 223–235(I),' 22857; Carson to Hughes, RG 25 A7, vol. 4789, file 100

6 Sam Hughes and the Canadian Expeditionary Force, 1914–16

1 Richard A. Preston, *Canada and 'Imperial' Defense: A Study of the Origins of the British Commonwealth's Defence Organization, 1867–1919* (Durham, NC: Duke University Press 1967), 462 ff

2 Gwatkin to Loring Christie, 3 Mar. 1915, Gwatkin Papers, folder 1. See also G.W.L. Nicholson, *Canadian Expeditionary Force 1914–1919* (Ottawa: Queen's Printer 1962), ch. 7.

3 Currie to Duguid, 24 Apr. 1926, copy in Urquhart Papers, vol. 2, folder 3. See also McNaughton to G.W.L. Nicholson, 25 Apr. 1961, McNaughton Papers, vol. 315, 'Historical Section, General Staff' file.

4 Gwatkin to Deputy Minister, 2 Feb. 115, RG 24, vol. 1273, file HQ 593-2-51; Gwatkin to Military Members of Militia Council, Mar. 1915, RG 24, vol. 2518, file HQC 1550

5 Gwatkin to Deputy Minister, 9 Sept. 1916, and to Adjutant General, 23 Oct. 1916, RG 24, vol. 1126, file HQ 54-21-50-11

6 Gwatkin to Loring Christie, 25 June 1915, RG 24, vol. 2533, file HQC 1700

7 J.L. Granatstein and J.M. Hitsman, *Broken Promises: A History of Conscription in Canada* (Toronto: Oxford University Press 1977), 84

8 The story of the Canadian Defence Force is told best by John Griffith Armstrong, 'Canadian Home Defence, 1914–1917: The Role of Major-General Willoughby Gwatkin' (MA thesis, Royal Military College of Canada, 1982).

9 See ch. 5 above.

10 See Nicholson, *Canadian Expeditionary Force*, 18–28.

11 Ibid., 545–50; see also RG 24, vol. 2537, file HQC 1782.

12 Report by Brigadier-General P.E. Thacker, Adjutant General, Overseas Military Forces of Canada, 27 Feb. 1917, RG 24, vol. 2545, file HQ 2069B; Report by General Staff Branch, Overseas Military Forces of Canada, 1 June 1918, RG 24, vol. 1883

13 RG 24, vol. 6536, file HQ 650-1-65; RG 24, vol. 308, file HQ 33-1-235-15; Borden Papers, vol. 62, 'OC 271–282,' and vol. 69, 'OC 318(1)(2), all show Gwatkin's concerns.

14 MacDougall to Hughes, 9 Feb. 1915, RG 24, vol. 1273, file HQ 593-2-51; Nicholson; *Canadian Expeditionary Force*, 201–35; Desmond Morton, *A Peculiar Kind of Politics: Canada's Overseas Ministry in the First World War* (Toronto: University of Toronto Press 1982), 34–75

15 Carson to Hughes, 23 Feb. 1915, and reply, 19 Mar. 1915, RG 9 III, vol. 44, file 8-5-10; Thacker memorandum, 27 Feb. 1917, RG 24, vol. 2545, file HQ 2069B; Alderson to Carson, 16 Feb. 1916, RG 9 III, vol. 44, file 8-5-8D; Alderson to Adjutant General, Home Forces, 29 Aug. 1915, RG 9 III, vol. 44, file 8-5-8H. See also the correspondence in RG 9 III, vol. 45, file 8-5-10H.

16 Major-General R.W. Whigam (DCIGS) to Carson, 13 June 1916, RG 9 III, vol. 44, file 8-5-8F
17 MacDougall to Carson, 23 Mar. 1915, and reply, 26 Mar. 1915, and Carson to Hughes, 26 Mar. 1915, RG 9 III, vol. 34, file 8-1-87
18 War Office notes to Canadian government, Apr. 1915, RG 24, vol. 2518, file HQC 1550
19 Borden to Hughes, 26 May 1915, and reply, Borden Papers, vol. 231, 'OC 165(1)' and vol. 62, 'OC 271–282'
20 PC 2138, 16 Sept. 1915, agreed to earlier
21 Carson to Steele, 23 July 1915, and to MacDougall, 23 and 27 July 1915, RG 9 III, vol. 34, file 8-1-87
22 Steele to MacDougall, 24 July 1915, and to Carson, 28 July and 22 Aug. 1915, ibid.
23 Carson to Alderson, 26 Aug. 1915, and to Steele, 26 Aug. 1915, ibid.
24 Carson to Hughes, 30 Sept. 1915, ibid.
25 Carson to MacDougall, 1 June 1916, ibid., file 8-1-87A.
26 Currie to Carson, 21 Dec. 1915, RG 24, vol. 1246, file HQ 593-1-64
27 Turner to Carson, 7 Dec. 1915, RG 9 III, vol. 34, file 8-1-87
28 Reid to Carson, 12 May 1916, RG 9 III, vol. 2883, file 0-44-33
29 Hughes to Cabinet, 15 Jan. 1916, RG 24, vol. 1125, file HQ 54-21-50-1
30 Hughes to Carson, 30 Nov. 1915, and Max Aitken to Borden, 3 Dec. 1915, Borden Papers, vol. 75, 'OC 337,' 39325-34
31 Borden to Hughes, 30 Nov. 1915, RG 9 III, vol. 29, file 8-1-22
32 Kenneth C. Eyre, 'Staff and Command in the Canadian Corps' (MA thesis, Duke University 1967), 114 ff; Nicholson, *Canadian Expeditionary Force*, 128
33 Gwatkin to Adjutant General, 24 Jan. 1916, RG 24, vol. 1126, file HQ 54-21-50-1; Carson to Hughes, 19 Jan. 1916, RG 9 III, vol. 43, file 8-5-8B; Alderson to Carson, 25 Apr. 1916, RG 9 III, vol. 44, file 8-5-8E
34 B.B. Cubitt (War Office) to Secretary of State for Colonies, 12 May 1916, sent to Canada 23 May 1916, copy in RG 24, vol. 1125, file HQ 54-21-50-1
35 Hughes to Caron, 26 May 1916, RG 24, vol. 1125, file HQ 54-21-50-1
36 Villiers Diary, 17 Aug. 1916, Villiers Papers, vol. 4. Villiers was a staff officer in France.
37 Morton, *A Peculiar Kind of Politics*, 72–5
38 Ibid., 152–6
39 Currie to Carson, 21 Dec. 1915, RG 24, vol. 1246, file HQ 593-1-64; Carson to Reid, 2 Jan. 1916, RG 9 III, vol. 28, file 8-1-2, proves Currie was right.
40 Odlum to Carson, 1 Apr. 1916, RG 9 III, vol. 31, file 8-1-70
41 Watson to Currie, 12 May 1916, RG 9 III, vol. 44, file 8-5-8E
42 Alderson to Perley, Alderson to Borden, 31 Dec. 1915, Perley Papers, vol. 4, folio

119, and Borden Papers, vol. 75, 'OC 337,' 39325–34

43 Currie to Alderson, 11 Dec. 1915, RG 9 III, vol. 43, file 8-5-8B

44 Mercer to Alderson, 11 Dec. 1915, ibid.

45 Turner to Alderson, 11 Dec. 1915, ibid.

46 B.B. Cubitt (War Office) to Carson, 5 Jan. 1916, including Haig to War Office, 13 Dec. 1915, copy in RG 9 III, vol. 28, file 8-1-2

47 Bennett to Perley and to Borden, 7 Dec. 1915, Perley Papers, vol. 5, folio 132

48 Newton Rowell to Borden, 18 Sept. 1916, copy in Kemp Papers, vol. 157, file 4-9

49 Perley to Borden, 25 Jan. 1915 and 9 Mar. 1915, Perley Papers, vol. 3, folios 44 and 53

50 Quoted in Morton, *A Peculiar Kind of Politics*, 84

51 Perley to Borden, 12 Oct. 1916, Perley Papers, vol. 6, folio 173

52 Borden to Perley, 2 Nov. 1916, RG 25 A2, vol. 270, file P-6-94

53 Perley to Borden, 24 Nov. 1916, Borden Papers, vol. 58, 'OC 260,' 38976–7

54 A.C. Macdonnell to Greenfield, 12 Dec 1915, Public Archives of Ontario, A.C. Macdonnell Papers

55 Creelman Diary, 19 Nov. 1916, Creelman Papers

56 McNaughton, quoted in John Swettenham, *McNaughton* (Toronto: Ryerson Press 1968), I, 174

7 The Canadian Expeditionary Force after Hughes, 1917–18

1 See William Stewart's admirable MA thesis, 'Attack Doctrine in the Canadian Corps, 1916–1918' (Fredericton: University of New Brunswick 1982).

2 McNaughton to Colonel G.W.L. Nicholson, 26 Apr. 1961, McNaughton Papers, vol. 315. See also Lieutenant-General E.L.M. Burns, *General Mud: Memoirs of Two World Wars* (Toronto: Clarke, Irwin 1970), 8–15, 52.

3 Currie to Minister Overseas Military Forces of Canada, 7 Feb. 1918, Currie Papers, vol. 37, file 166; same to same, 21 Feb. 1918, RG 9 III, vol. 104, 'Fifth Division' file

4 G.W.L. Nicholson, *Canadian Expeditionary Force, 1914–1919* (Official History of the Canadian Army in the First World War) (Ottawa: Queen's Printer 1962)

5 John Swettenham, *To Seize the Victory: The Canadian Corps in World War I* (Toronto: Ryerson Press 1965), 202

6 Borden to Perley, 12 June 1917, Perley Papers, vol. 8, folder 252

7 See Perley to Borden, 8 Dec. 1916, RG 9 III, vol. 97, file 10-14-2.

8 Perley to Borden, 2 Jan. 1917, RG 9 III, vol. 73, file 10-8-16

9 Perley to Borden, 30 Apr. 1917, Perley Papers, vol. 8, folder 252

10 Steele to Rogers, 18 June 1917, Turner Papers, vol. 10, file 67

11 Perley to Borden, 28 June 1917, ibid.

12 See John English, *The Decline of Politics: The Conservatives and the Party System* (Toronto: University of Toronto Press 1977), 193–205.

13 Perley to Kemp, 26 Apr. 1918, Perley Papers, vol. 11, folder 332

14 Odlum to Carson, 1 Apr. 1916, RG 9 III, vol. 31, file 8-1-70

15 Director of Military Training to Chief of the General Staff, 14 Jan. 1917, RG 24, vol. 2543, file HQC 2043

16 Gwatkin memorandum, 2 Feb. 1917, ibid.

17 Kemp to Perley, 29 Jan. 1917, and reply, 3 Feb. 1917, ibid.

18 F.F. Montague (Acting Military Secretary, Overseas) to Turner, 4 May 1917, RG 9 III, vol. 53, 'May 1917' file

19 J.L. Biggar to W.N. Ponton, 7 June 1917, Ponton Papers, vol. 15

20 Adjutant General memorandum, 29 Mar. 1917, RG 24, vol. 1132, file HQ 54-21-50-43

21 Turner to Perley, 16 and 20 Dec. 1916, RG 9 III, vol. 90, file 10-12-11. For negative comments on the schools see RG 9 III, vol. 3101, file 8-7-31.

22 B.B. Cubitt to Carson, 5 Jan. 1916, RG 9 III, vol. 28, file 8-1-2

23 Adjutant General circular, 15 Dec. 1916, RG 9 III, vol. 2882, file 0-36-33

24 Adjutant General circular, 13 Dec. 1916, RG 9 III, vol. 2881, file 0-29-33; Adjutant General memorandum, 4 Aug. 1917, ibid.

25 Minister of Overseas Military Forces of Canada to War Office, 17 Mar. 1917, RG 9 III, vol. 2739, file C-944-33

26 Haig to War Office, 17 June 1917, RG 9 III, vol. 2739, file C-944-33

27 Sims to Turner, 13 June 1917, and reply, 16 June 1917, RG 9 III, vol. 2904, file 0-276-33

28 Perley to Borden, 28 Nov. 1916, Perley Papers, vol. 7, folder 212

29 Ibid.

30 Turner Papers, vol. 7, file 39, and Currie Papers, vol. 38, folder 172

31 Desmond Morton, *A Peculiar Kind of Politics: Canada's Overseas Ministry in the First World War* (Toronto: University of Toronto Press 1982), 125, 170–2

32 Perley to Borden, 7 Sept. 1917, RG 9 III, vol. 55, file 'Our Boys Overseas'

33 Perley to Borden, 22 Nov. 1917, Perley Papers, vol. 7, file 205

34 Daniel G. Dancocks, *Sir Arthur Currie: A Biography* (Toronto: Methuen 1985), 81–2, 100

35 Turner to Perley, 30 Nov. 1916, quoted in Sweetenham, *To Seize the Victory*, 147; Dancocks, *Sir Arthur Currie*, 100

36 Dancocks, *Sir Arthur Currie*, 99–105

37 Perley memorandum, 14 Jan. 1917, RG 24, vol. 2543, file HQC 2043

38 Dancocks, *Sir Arthur Currie*, 101–2; Nicholson, *Canadian Expeditionary Force*, 283–4

39 Currie to Perley, 4 Aug. 1917, RG 9 III, vol. 72, file 10-8-7 (emphasis in original)

40 Kemp to Turner, 17 Nov. 1917, RG 9 III, vol. 71, file 10-8-3
41 Thacker to Turner, 20 Nov. 1917, Turner Papers, vol. 8, file 52
42 Thacker to Kemp, 26 Nov. 1917, RG 9 III, vol. 71, file 10-8-3
43 Currie to Overseas Military Forces of Canada, 25 Feb. 1918, RG 24, vol. 6540, file HQ 650-55-10
44 Turner memorandum, 12 June 1918, ibid.
45 Kemp to Mewburn, 8 Jan. 1918, 1 Apr. 1918, Kemp Papers, vol. 150, file M-5, vol. 152, file O-6; Kemp to Borden, 1 Apr. 1918, Borden Papers, vol. 105, 'OC 525,' 57576-8
46 Dancocks, *Sir Arthur Currie*, 101
47 Kemp to Mewburn, 8 Jan. 1918, 243 Feb. 1918, 26 Mar. 1918, 16 May 1918, Kemp Papers, vol. 150, file M-5
48 Kemp to Borden, 1 Apr. 1918, Kemp to Mewburn, 1 Apr. 1918, Kemp Papers, vol. 152, file O-6
49 C.S. Harrington, memorandum, 3 June 1918, RG 24, vol. 176, file DHS 10-52
50 Currie to Overseas Military Forces of Canada, 25 Feb. 1918, 6 Mar. 1918, RG 9 III, vol. 910, file C-41-3; Morton, *Peculiar Kind of Politics*, 161-9
51 Kemp to Borden, 1 Apr. 1918, Borden Papers, vol. 105, 'OC 525,' 57576-8; Walter Gow to Kemp, 14 Mar. 1918, Kemp Papers, vol. 162, file T-7
52 Currie, draft memorandum to Embury, RG 9 III, vol. 72, file 10-8-7, part I; Morton, *Peculiar Kind of Politics*, 166-8
53 This is the thesis of Morton's *A Peculiar Kind of Politics*.
54 Borden to Acting Prime Minister, 9 Dec. 1918, Borden Papers, vol. 12, 'OC 515,' 55588

8 Post-war reconstruction and the higher organization of national defence

1 Gwatkin memorandum, 1 Nov. 1917, RG 24, vol. 6402, file HQ 95-1-12
2 Currie to Elmsley, 31 Jan. 1918, Currie Papers, vol. 1, file 1; Currie to Turner, 25 Aug. 1918, Urquhart Papers, vol. 3, folder 6
3 Gwatkin to Deputy Minister, 20 Nov. 1918, and Mewburn minute, RG 24, vol. 2571A, file HQC 862, part I
4 Macdonell to Currie, 9 Feb. 1919, RG 9 III, vol. 78, file 10-8-58
5 MacBrien memorandum, 'The Future Military Force of Canada,' 1919, RG 24, vol. 6522, file HQ 420-18-52, part I
6 Gwatkin memorandum, 1 Nov. 1917, RG 24, vol. 6402, file HQ 95-1-12; Gwatkin to Deputy Minister, 20 Nov. 1918, RG 24, vol. 2571A, file HQC 862, part I; MacBrien, 'The Future Military Force'
7 MacBrien, 'The Future Military Force'

8 MacBrien to Currie, and reply, 15 Mar. 1920, Currie Papers, vol. 11, file 34
9 Churchill to Borden, 9 May 1919, PRO, WO 32/5355/091/2663
10 Perley to Harrington, 20 May 1919, ibid., and RG 9 III, vol. 789, file 10-8-63
11 Kemp to Deputy Minister, Overseas Military Forces of Canada, 10 Dec. 1918, RG 9 III, vol. 78, file 10-8-57
12 Director of Military Operations (War Office) to Chief of the Imperial General Staff, 4 July 1919, and Deputy CIGS to CIGS, 5 July 1919, PRO, WO 32/5355/091/2663
13 MacBrien to Deputy Minister, Overseas Military Forces of Canada, 14 May 1919, 14 July 1919, and to Minister, Overseas Military Forces of Canada, 27 Aug. 1919, Kemp Papers, vol. 146, T-7; MacBrien to Currie, 6 Oct. 1919, MacBrien Papers, vol. 1; and MacBrien, 'Interim Memorandum on the Future Organization and Distribution of the Military Forces of the Empire,' Oct. 1919, RG 24, microfilm reel C5061, file HQC 3149
14 Daniel G. Dancocks, *Sir Arthur Currie: A Biography* (Toronto: Methuen 1985), 197–206
15 Currie to MacBrien, 28 Aug. 1919, Currie Papers, vol. 11, file 34
16 MacBrien, 'The Future Military Force of Canada,' 1919, RG 24, vol. 522, file HQ 420-18-52, part 1
17 Currie to MacBrien, 15 Mar. 19200, Currie Papers, vol. 11, file 34; MacBrien to Currie, 21 May 1920, MacBrien Papers, vol. 3
18 Currie to MacBrien, 12 Apr. 1920, MacBrien Papers, vol. 1
19 RG 9 III, vol. 2777, file E-17-33; RG 24, microfilm reel C5046, file HQC 1-1-89; Currie Papers, vol. 39, file 76
20 Currie to Farmer, 5 Jan. 1920, Currie Papers, vol. 11, file 34
21 Currie to Radcliffe, 6 July 1920, Currie Papers, vol. 5, 'Correspondence P–R'
22 J.L. Granatstein and J.M. Hitsman, *Broken Promises: A History of Conscription in Canada* (Toronto: Oxford 1977), ch. 4; Mewburn to Kemp, 6 Aug. 1919, Kemp Papers, vol. 141, file E-9; Canada, House of Commons, *Debates*, 16 June 1919, 16 June 1920; James Eayrs, *In Defence of Canada*, vol. 1, *From the Great War to the Great Depression* (Toronto: University of Toronto Press 1964), ch. 1
23 Eayrs, *In Defence of Canada*, I, introduction
24 Canada, House of Commons, *Debates*, 16 June 1920
25 Currie to MacBrien, 13 Dec. 1919, MacBrien Papers, vol. 1
26 Canada, House of Commons, *Debates*, 16 June 1920
27 O.M. Biggar, memorandum, 13 Dec. 1918, 21 June 1919, RG 24, vol. 2572A, file HQC 2862, part 1
28 Currie to MacBrien, 15 June 1920, and to McNaughton, 9 Dec. 1920, Currie Papers, vol. 11, file 34 and 18
29 Eayrs, *In Defence of Canada*, I, 237

30 Norman Hillmer and W. McAndrew, 'The Cunning of Restraint: General J.H. MacBrien and the Problems of Peacetime Soldiering,' *Canadian Defence Quarterly* 8 (Spring 1979), 40-7

31 MacBrien, report to Currie, n.d., Currie Papers, vol. 11, file 34

32 Maurice Pope, *Soldiers and Politicians: The Memoirs of Lieutenant-General Maurice Pope* (Toronto: University of Toronto Press 1962), 132-4

33 C.E. Callwell, *Field Marshal Sir Henry Wilson: His Life and Diaries*, II (London: Macmillan 1927)

34 MacBrien report to Currie, n.d., Currie Papers, vol. 11, file 34

35 Ibid.

36 MacBrien to Currie, 1 Jan. 1920, ibid.

37 See ch. 4, 76

38 Gwatkin to O.M. Biggar, 29 Jan. 1920, RG 24, microfilm reel C5052, file HQC 365-11. See also Queen's University, Douglas Library, J. Sutherland Brown Papers, box 8, folder 163.

39 PRO, CAB 16-45

40 Currie to Meighen, 5 Aug. 1920, Currie Papers, vol. 11, file 35

41 Hose to Gwatkin, 24 Aug. 1921, quoted in Eayrs, *In Defence of Canada*, I, 225

42 King Diary, 15 Dec. 1921; Fiset to King, 15 Dec. 1921, King Papers, J1, vol. 60, 51762-5; MacBrien to Minister of Militia, 19 Dec. 1921, ibid.

43 MacBrien memorandum, 19 Dec. 1921, McNaughton Papers, vol. 109, 'NDHQ Reorganization'

44 Hose, memorandum, 19 Dec. 1923, quoted in Eayrs, *In Defence of Canada*, I, 241 ff

45 Lieutenant-Colonel R. Orde, memorandum, 31 Dec. 1923, McNaughton Papers, vol. 109, 'NDHQ Reorganization'

46 Hose, memorandum, 19 Jan. 1923, quoted in Eayrs, *In Defence of Canada*, I, 241

47 MacBrien to Desbarats, 30 Apr. 1923, and reply, 2 May 1923, McNaughton Papers, vol. 109, 'NDHQ Reorganization'

48 Hose to Adjutant General, 8 Nov. 1924, Hose Diary, D Hist, Naval File, 1440-5

49 See ch. 10 below.

50 Hillmer and McAndrew, 'The Cunning of Restraint,' 45-6

51 Ralston's minutes of meeting with Thacker, 5 and 8 Feb. 1927, Ralston Papers, vol. 8, 'MacBrien'; Thacker to McNaughton, 23 Sept. 1928, McNaughton Papers, vol. 107, 'Change of Appointment'

52 Thacker to Ralston, 27 Dec. 1928, RG 24, vol. 6541, file HQ 650-77-1

53 McNaughton to Lascelles (Secretary to Governor General), 8 June 1935, McNaughton Papers, vol. 104, 'Government House 1935'

54 Ibid.

55 McNaughton to Minister of National Defence, 24 Oct. 1932, McNaughton Papers,

vol. 16, folder MCN(M) 87.

56 John Swettenham, *McNaughton* (Toronto: Ryerson 1968), I, 251
57 A.C. Macdonell to Currie, 17 Aug. 1933, and reply, 18 Aug. 1933, Currie Papers, vol. 11, file 33
58 Eayrs, *In Defence of Canada*, I, 261 ff
59 McNaughton to Lascelles, 8 June 1935, McNaughton Papers, vol. 104, 'Government House 1935'
60 McNaughton to Minister of National Defence, 24 Oct. 1932, McNaughton Papers, vol. 16, folder MCN(M) 87.
61 McNaughton to H.L. Keenleyside, 31 Mar. 1939, McNaughton Papers, vol. 111, 'Royal Visit'
62 Vancouver *Sun*, 20 Nov. 1935
63 Eayrs, *In Defence of Canada*, II
64 Swettenham, *McNaughton*, I, 314-16
65 McNaughton to Lascelles, 8 June 1935, McNaughton Papers, vol. 104, 'Government House 1935'
66 Ashton to Minister of National Defence, 6 Dec. 1935, Ian Mackenzie Papers, vol. 30, file X-13; Joint Staff Committee, 'The Higher Direction of War,' 20 Apr. 1938, RG 24, vol. 2684, file HQS 5199
67 Defence Council minutes, 12 Sept. 1938, Ian Mackenzie Papers, vol. 32, file X-52
68 G.N. Hillmer, 'O.D. Skelton: The Scholar Who Set a Future Pattern,' *International Perspectives* (Sept./Oct. 1973), 46-9; 'The Anglo-Canadian Neurosis: The Case of O.D. Skelton,' in P. Lyon, ed., *Britain and Canada: A Survey of a Changing Relationship* (London: Frank Cass 1976), 61-84; and 'Defence and Ideology: The Anglo-Canadian Military "Alliance" in the 1930s,' *International Journal* 33 (Summer 1978), 588-613, especially 599
69 Christie to Lord Lothian, 30 May 1935, Christie Papers, vol. 12 file 40; Christie memorandum on Geneva Protocol, 1924, Christie Papers, vol. 10
70 Christie to King, 20 Feb. 1936, Christie Papers, vol. 27, folder 8
71 Christie, 'Defence policy and organization,' 26 Feb. 1937, Christie Papers, vol. 27, folder 9.
72 Thacker, memorandum, 27 Dec. 1928, RG 24, vol. 6523, file HQ 462-18-1
73 McNaughton to Ralston, 25 Nov. 1928, McNaughton Papers, vol. 111, 'Ralston'; Stuart, 'The problems and requirements of Canadian defence', n.d., Ian Mackenzie Papers, vol. 34, file B-30; drafts of Defence Scheme No. 3, RG 24, vol. 2643, 2646, 2648
74 See Maurice Pope, 'The Organization of the Department of National Defence,' 9 Mar. 1937, RG 2 18, vol. 2, file D-19; Crerar to Pope, 11 April 1936, D Hist 000.8(D 5)
75 Mackenzie to King, 7 Jan. 1936, King Papers, JI, vol. 220, 189607

76 King Diary, 18 Aug. 1936
77 King to Mackenzie, 22 Apr. 1937, RG 24, vol. 2759, file HQS 6615
78 Ashton to Mackenzie, 14 Aug. 1937, ibid.
79 Escott Reid to Deputy Minister of National Defence, 15 Dec. 1937, and Christie to Skelton, 4 Feb. 1938, Christie Papers, vol. 27, folder 9
80 Deputy Minister to Chiefs of Staff, 21 Mar. 1938, RG 24, vol. 2759, file HQS 6615
81 Christie to Skelton, 4 Feb. 1938, Christie Papers, vol. 27, folder 9
82 Deputy Minister to Chiefs of Staff, 21 Mar. 1938, RG 24, vol. 2759, file HQS 6615, and Chief of the General Staff to Colonel M. Pope, 13 Dec. 1938, ibid.
83 C.P. Stacey, *Arms, Men and Governments: The War Policies of Canada* (Ottawa: Queen's Printer 1970), 69; RG 24, vol. 2084, file HQS 5199-3
84 Stacey, *Arms, Men and Governments*, 71
85 Norman Hillmer, 'O.D. Skelton and the Declaration of War,' in R. Bothwell and N. Hillmer, eds., *The In-Between Time: Canadian External Policies in the 1930s* (Toronto: Copp Clarke 1975), 180
86 Stacey, *Arms, Men and Governments*, 41

9 Military planning, 1919–39

1 James Eayrs, *In Defence of Canada*, vol. I, *From the Great War to the Great Depression* (Toronto: University of Toronto Press 1964), 3–26, 70–84
2 Christie to Lord Lothian, 30 May 1935, Christie Papers, vol. 12, file 40. See also Norman Hillmer, 'Defence and Ideology: The Anglo-Canadian Military "Alliance" in the 1930s,' *International Journal* 33 (Summer 1978), 599.
3 Eayrs, *In Defence of Canada*, I, 70–7. For a more sympathetic view see Charles Taylor, 'Brigadier James Sutherland Brown,' in *Six Journeys: A Canadian Pattern* (Toronto: Anansi 1977), 1–38.
4 Donald Cameron Watt, *Too Serious a Business: European Armed Forces and the Approach to the Second World War* (London: Temple Smith 1975), 95–6
5 Richard A. Preston, *The Defence of the Undefended Border: Planning for War in North America* (Montreal: McGill-Queen's University Press 1977), xi, 7, 216–7
6 See RG 24, vol. 4686, file G1A42, vol. 2656, file HQS 3568, and microfilm reel C5052, file HQC 363-46-1.
7 McNaughton, 'Epitome of Jellicoe's Report,' McNaughton Papers, vol. 109. 'Otter Committee' file
8 Wilson to Gwatkin, 26 Jan. 1920, RG 24, microfilm reel C5069, file HQC 4529, and Crerar to McNaughton, 29 Jan. 1931, RG 24, vol. 2740, file HQS 5902, part I
9 Colonel J. Sutherland Brown, 'Memorandum on the Direct Defence of Canada,' 12 Apr. 1921, RG 24, vol. 2925, file HQS 3496
10 Queen's University, Douglas Library, Sutherland Brown Papers, Box 3, folder 56

11 Brown to District Officers Commanding, 3 Jan. 1921, D Hist 340.003(D24); same to same, 4 Apr. 1921, RG 24, vol. 2926, file HQS 3496. Defence Scheme No. 1 is found in Queen's University, Douglas Library, Sutherland Brown Papers, Box 9, folder 210.

12 See, for example, Colonel J.P. Landry to Brown, 24 Dec. 1923, Brigadier H.C. Thacker to Brown, 28 Dec. 1923, Colonel J.C. Armstrong to brown, 28 Dec. 1923, RG 24, vol. 2925, file HQS 3496.

13 MacBrien, 'The Military Forces of Canada,' McNaughton Papers, vol. 109, 'Otter Committee' file

14 McNaughton to Ralston, 25 Nov. 1928, McNaughton Papers, vol. 111, 'Ralston' file; McNaughton, 'Memorandum,' 21 Dec. 1931, RG 24, vol. 2740, file HQS 5902, part 1

15 McNaughton to MacBrien, 13 Mar. 1923, McNaughton Papers, vol. 109, 'Otter Committee' file

16 Lieutenant-Colonel H.D.G. Crerar, 'Notes on lecture to War Office,' 3 Nov. 1925, McNaughton Papers, vol. 109, 'Otter Committee file'

17 Taylor, 'Brigadier James Sutherland Brown,' 1 ff; the reconnaissance files are at D Hist, 325.009 (D517 and D518).

18 Report of Special Militia Committee, 19 Jan. 1922, Queen's University, Douglas Library, Sutherland Brown Papers, Box 8, folder 166

19 McNaughton to MacBrien, 21 Sept. 1923, RG 24, vol. 2679 file HQS 4530

20 Brown to MacBrien, 29 Dec. 1923, ibid.

21 Ibid.

22 Director of Equipment and Ordnance Services to Quartermaster General, 16 Sept. 1926, ibid.

23 McNaughton to Quartermaster General, 5 Oct. 1926, ibid.

24 MacBrien to McNaughton, 2 July 1924, ibid.

25 MacBrien to Brown, 15 Oct. 1926, RG 24, vol. 2875, file HQC 3067

26 Brown to MacBrien, 4 Jan. 1927, RG 24, vol. 2679, file HQS 4530

27 MacBrien, 'Memorandum,' 29 Jan. 1927, and letter to Ralston, 23 Apr. 1927, RG 24, vol. 2683, file HQS 5121

28 General Staff memorandum (by Lieutenant-Colonel H.H. Matthews), 24 Oct. 1927, and minutes, Joint Staff Committee, 27 Oct. 1927, RG 24, vol. 2684, file HQS 5199

29 Brown to Thacker, 11 Nov. 1927, Matthews to Lieutenant-Colonel R.O. Alexander, 10 Aug. 1928, Thacker to Brown, 28 Dec. 1928, and Matthews to McNaughton, 26 Jan. 1929, RG 24, vol. 2925, file HQS 3496

30 McNaughton notes on Matthews to McNaughton, 26 Jan. 1929, ibid.

31 McNaughton memorandum, read to Minister 18 Oct. 1929, RG 24, microfilm reel C5077, file HQS 5436

32 McNaughton memorandum, ibid., and McNaughton, 'The Defence of Canada,' 28 May 1935, D Hist 112.3M2009 (D7)
33 MacBrien, 'The Military Force of Canada,' McNaughton Papers, vol. 109
34 Brown, 'An expeditionary force for the "Neutral Zone" in Turkey,' 18 Sept. 1922, RG 24, vol. 2643, file HQS 3498, part I
35 Brown, 'An expeditionary force for service in China,' 26 Jan. 1926, ibid.
36 Deputy Minister of National Defence to O.D. Skelton, 4 Oct. 1926, RG 234, microfilm reel C5075, file HQS 5076; McNaughton to MacBrien, 2 Dec. 1926, RG 24, vol. 2643, file HQS 3498, part I
37 MacBrien to Brown, 8 Feb. 1927, RG 24, vol. 2643, file HQS 3498, part I; MacBrien memorandum, 29 Jan. 1927, RG 24, vol. 2683, file HQS 5121; Matthews report to McNaughton, 23 Jan. 1930, RG 24, vol. 2643, file HQS 3498, part I; minutes, Joint Staff Committee, 27 Oct. 1927, RG 24, vol. 2864, file HQS 5199
38 Ralston to McNaughton, 18 Nov. 1928, and reply, 25 Nov. 1928, McNaughton Papers, vol. 111, 'Ralston' file; McNaughton to Ralston, 19 Feb. 1929, McNaughton Papers, vol. 109, 'Otter Committee' file
39 Colonel H.H. Matthews, 'The Land Forces of Canada,' Sept. 1930, McNaughton Papers, vol. 104, 'Disarmament' file, 'Book C'
40 H.D.G. Crerar, 'The military aspects of the disarmament conference,' 19 Oct. 1931, McNaughton Papers, vol. 103, 'Disarmament' file. L.B. Pearson's note of 28 Oct. 1931, ibid., supported Crerar's positions.
41 McNaughton memoranda, 21 Dec. 1931, 29 Jan. 1932, 21 Feb. 1933, RG 24, vol. 2740, file HQS 5902, part I; see also McNaughton to Director of Medical Services, 12 May 1933, RG 24, vol. 2686, file HQS 5199, part VII.
42 McNaughton, 'Minutes of Cabinet Committee Meeting, 14 June 1933,' 16 June 1933, and McNaughton to O.D. Skelton, 15 June 1933 and 16 Oct. 1933, RG 24, vol. 2686, file HQS 5199, part II
43 McNaughton to Lord Milne, Liaison Letter No. 4, 31 Dec. 1932, Ian Mackenzie Papers, vol. 30. See also Crerar to McNaughton, Nov. 1933, McNaughton Papers, vol. 16, 'McN(M) 88; Defence Scheme No. 3, second revise, 20 Oct. 1933, McNaughton Papers, vol. 16, file McN(M) 87.
44 Brigadier C.F. Constantine, memorandum, 22 May 1931, and Major-General E.A. Ashton, memorandum, 13 June 1931, D Hist 162.009(D43)
45 Defence Scheme No. 3, second revise, 20 Oct. 1933, McNaughton Papers, vol. 16, file McN(M) 87; McNaughton to Adjutant-General, 13 Sept. 1932, RG 24, vol. 2643, file HQS 3498
46 Crerar to Colonel H.H. Matthews, 15 May 1931, RG 24, vol. 2692, file HQS 5199-A; McNaughton to W.D. Herridge, 20 Mar. 1933, McNaughton Papers, vol. 105, 'Herridge' file, 1933–4; McNaughton, 'The Defence of Canada,' 28 May 1935, copy in D Hist 74/256, part I

47 Joint Staff Committee, memorandum, 10 Mar. 1933, RG 24, vol. 2692, file HQS 5199-A; Correspondence with the Department of External Affairs, RG 24, vol. 2693, file HQS 5199-A; Defence Scheme Number 2, 16 Apr. 1938, copy in D Hist, 168.0016(D2)

48 Crerar to Matthews, 25 Mar. 1930, RG 24, vol. 2733, file HQS 5178, and Matthews to general staff, 22 Jan. 1932, ibid. First Draft of Defence Scheme Number 4 is in D Hist, 112.3M2009(D64).

49 McNaughton, 'The Defence of Canada,' 28 May 1935, copy in Ian Mackenzie Papers, vol. 29, file X-4

50 Major-General E.C. Ashton, 'The Requirements of Canadian Defence,' 12 Nov. 1935, Ian Mackenzie Papers, vol. 29, file X-4; Ashton, 'Scheme for the Reorganization of the Canadian Militia,' 5 Dec. 1935, D Hist 112.3M2009(D47)

51 RG 24, vol. 2646, file HQS 3498, part I, and vol. 6604, file HQS 5199, part I, have the working files for the militia reorganization.

52 Christie to Mackenzie King, 20 Feb. 1936, Christie memorandum, 1 Sept. 1936, Christie Papers, vol. 27, folder 9.

53 Ashton to Mackenzie, two memoranda of 22 Apr. 1936, Mackenzie Papers, vol. 29, file X-4, vol. 30, file X-11; Ashton to Mackenzie, 26 Aug. 1936, and Ashton to Mackenzie, 31 Aug. 1931, RG 24, vol. 2693, file HQS 5199D; Matthews to 'Scheme Holders,' 10 Aug. 1936, RG 24, vol. 2645, file HQS 3498, part VIII

54 King Diary, 26 Aug. 1936, Mackenzie King Papers

55 King, memorandum, 29 July 1936, RG 24, vol. 2693, file HQS 5199B

56 Joint Staff Committee to Mackenzie, 31 Aug. 1936, ibid; Joint Staff Committee, 'Appreciation of the Defence Problems Confronting Canada,' 5 Sept. 1936, Ian Mackenzie Papers, vol. 32, file X-5

57 Ian Mackenzie to Cabinet, 16 Nov. 1936, Ian Mackenzie Papers, vol. 29, file X-6

58 Deputy Minister of National Defence, memorandum, 2 Dec. 1936, RG 24, vol. 2500, file HQC 1050

59 Canada, House of Commons, *Debates*, 15–19 Feb. 1937

60 Ashton to Mackenzie, 1 Jan. 1937, Ian Mackenzie Papers, vol. 29, file X-4, and Ashton to Mackenzie, 15 Mar. 1937, RG 24, vol. 2648, file HQS 3498, part XXII

61 Mackenzie to Ashton, 17 Mar. 1937, Ian Mackenzie Papers, vol. 29, file X-4

62 For corroboration, see Mackenzie to Deputy Minister of National Defence, 15 Mar. 1937, Ian Mackenzie Papers, vol. 29, folder 165/6, and Crerar to Joint Staff Committee, 31 Mar. 1937, RG 24, vol. 2684, file HQS 5199/2

63 Pope to Duguid, 3 Nov. 1943, D Hist 314.009(D108)

64 Ashton, 'The Requirements of National Defence,' 24 Sept. 1937, Ian Mackenzie Papers, vol. 29, file X-4; Ashton to Mackenzie, 14 Oct. 1937, D Hist 112.3M2009(D27)

65 Ashton, 'The Defence of Canada,' 7 Jan. 1938, Ian Mackenzie Papers, vol. 29, file

x-4; Ashton, 'A Survey of Militia Requirements,' 10 Jan. 1938, D Hist, 112.3M2009(D27)

66 Defence Scheme No. 3, revised 15 Jan. 1938, RG 24, vol. 2646, file HQS 3498, parts IX and X; 'Interim Plan of Coast Defence,' 31 Jan. 1938, Ian Mackenzie Papers, vol. 30, file X-27

67 Joint Staff Committee, 'Review of Canada's Position with Respect to Defence,' 27 July 1938, RG 24, vol. 2693, file HQS 5199B

68 James Eayrs, *In Defence of Canada*, vol. II, *Appeasement and Rearmament* (Toronto: University of Toronto Press 1965), 148–52

69 Pope to District Officers Commanding, 9 Sept. 1938, RG 24, vol. 2646, file HQS 3498, part IX

70 Pope to Ashton, 21 and 23 Sept. 1938, RG 24, vol. 2646, file HQS 3498, part IX

71 Pope to Colonel J.H. Jenkins, 14 Feb. 1944, Pope Papers, vol. I, 35

72 Lieutenant-Colonel K. Stuart to Ashton 26 Sept. 1938, RG 24, vol. 2646, file HQS 3498, part IX

73 Ashton, 'Principles under which it is considered Military Forces required to a maximum effort in the Defence of Canada should be organized,' 28 Sept. 1938, RG 24, vol. 2646, file HQS 3498, part IX

74 Ashton to Mackenzie, 8 Oct. 1938, RG 24, vol. 2646, file HQS 3498, part XIII

75 Ashton to Mackenzie, 28 Oct. 1928, Ian Mackenzie Papers, vol. 40, file G-11; Ashton to Mackenzie, 29 Oct. 1938, RG 24, microfilm reel C5113, file HQC 7724; Ashton to Mackenzie 4 and 8 Nov. 1938, Ian Mackenzie Papers, vol. 30, file X-38, vol. 39 file D-72

76 K. Stuart, 'The Problems and Requirements of Canadian Defence,' 19 Jan. 1939, with marginal notes by Ian Mackenzie, Ian Mackenzie Papers, vol. 34, file B-30

77 Chief of the General Staff to AG, QMG, and MGO, 4 and 7 Feb. 1939, RG 24, vol. 2646, file HQS 3498, part I

78 Crerar to District Officers Commanding, 24 June 1939, RG 24, vol. 2646, file HQS 3498, part XI; Crerar to Adjutant General, 8 Mar. 1939, ibid.

79 Major-General T.V. Anderson, memorandum, 21 Aug. 1939, RG 24, vol. 2649, file HQS 3498, part XXII

80 O.D. Skelton to Mackenzie King, 24 Aug. 1939, King Papers, J4, vol. 396, file 54

81 Pope to Duguid, 3 Nov. 1943, D Hist, 314.009(D108)

82 Stuart to CGS, 26 Aug. 1939, RG 24, vol. 2648, file HQS 3498, part XIII

83 Anderson, 'Canada's national effort in the early stages of a major war,' 27 Aug. 1939, RG 24, vol. 2648, file HQS 3498, part XXII

84 Ian Mackenzie's notes on ibid.

85 Anderson, 'Canada's national effort in the early stages of a major war,' redrafted, revised, and subsequently signed by the three service chiefs, 29 Aug. 1939, King Papers, J1, vol. 272, 230453–65

86 C.P. Stacey, *Six Years of War: The Army in Canada, Britain and the Pacific* (Ottawa: Queen's Printer 1955), 29–49
87 T.N. Dupuy, *A Genius for War: The German Army and General Staff, 1870–1945* (Englewood Cliffs, NJ: Prentice-Hall 1977)

10 Training and education, 1919–39

1 Currie to MacBrien, 15 Mar. 1920, Currie Papers, vol. 11, file 34; Currie to Radcliffe, 6 July 1920, Currie Papers, vol. 5, 'Correspondence P–R'
2 See RG 24, microfilm reel C8299, file HQC 4347, reel C5046, file HQC 1-1-89, vol. 6422, file HQ 420-18-52, vol. 6415, file HQ 150-8-1.
3 Colonel T.V. Anderson, 'Qualifying for Promotion in the Permanent Force,' *Canadian Defence Quarterly* (hereafter *CDQ*) II (July 1925), 325–30. See also RG 24, vol. 6503, file HQ 313-1-33-6.
4 Lieutenant-Colonel A.C. Garner, 'Impressions of the Militia Staff Course, Western Canada, 1928–1929,' *CDQ* VII (April 1930), 376–82
5 M.P.A. Hankey, 'Institution of a Joint College for Officers of the Three Services,' 16 June 1926, PRO WO 32/3074
6 Lieutenant-Colonel T.V. Anderson (for Director of Military Training) to CGS, 12 Apr. 1921, and Report of Minutes of Militia Council, 4 May 1921, RG 24, microfilm reel C5061, file HQC 3579
7 Richard A. Preston, *Canada's RMC: A History of the Royal Military College* (Toronto: University of Toronto Press 1969), 226 ff
8 PRO, WO 32/4840
9 Chief of the Imperial General Staff to Secretary of State for War, 9 Apr. 1926, PRO, WO 32/4840. For details of the course see RG 9 III, vol. 2740, file C-959-33.
10 Assistant Adjutant General to Adjutant General, Feb. 1922, RG 24, microfilm reel C8299, file HQS 3661
11 H.D.B. Ketchen to R.B. Bennett, 14 May 1929, Bennett Papers, vol. 60, 38322–7; D.M. Sutherland to Alice Miller, 24 Feb. 1934, ibid., vol. 45; Currie to Bennett, 24 July 1933, Currie Papers, vol. 6, file 18
12 [Major K. Stuart], editorial, *CDQ* IX (October 1931), 5–7.
13 General Archibald Montgomery to Major-General A.R. Cameron (Director of Staff Duties, War Office), 30 Mar. 1926, PRO, WO 32/4840
14 MacBrien memorandum, Feb. 1922, RG 24, microfilm reel C8299, file HQS 3661
15 MacBrien to Currie, 21 May 1920, MacBrien Papers, vol. 3, 'Memoranda.' James Eayrs, *In Defence of Canada*, vol. I, *From the Great War to the Great Depression* (Toronto: University of Toronto Press 1964), 85 ff
16 G.R. Stevens, *The Royal Canadian Regiment, 1936–1937* (n.p. 1957), II, 140–1
17 Record of conference of general staff and district commanders, Apr. 1926, RG 24,

vol. 151, file HQ 9879-2, part III

18 *Report* of the Department of National Defence (Ottawa: King's Printer 1927), 8–9
19 J. Sutherland Brown, 'The Canadian Defence Forces,' *Journal of the Royal United Service Institute* LXXV (Feb. 1930), 11–26
20 Chief of the General Staff to Chief of the Imperial General Staff, 17 Jan. 1929, Ian Mackenzie Papers, vol. 30, file X-28
21 McNaughton address to Permanent Force, 20 July 1929, McNaughton Papers, vol. 347, '15 August 1929' file
22 Major H.G. Eady, 'Report on Liaison Trip to Canada,' May 1929, PRO, WO 32/ 2440/058/4830
23 See Department of National Defence, *Report*, 1930, 1934.
24 Stevens, *Royal Canadian Regiment*, II, 8–11
25 'Abridged Report on Permanent Force Collective Training, Camp Borden, 1938,' by Colonel W.H.P. Elkins, D Hist. 324.009(D449)
26 Ibid.
27 James Eayrs, *In Defence of Canada*, I, 27. MacBrien to Overseas Military Forces of Canada, Feb. 1919, RG 24, microfilm reel C5059, file HQC 2593
28 McNaughton to MacBrien, 21 Sept. 1923, RG 24, vol. 2679, file HQC 5046
29 Brown to MacBrien, 29 Dec. 1923, Queen's University, Douglas Library, Sutherland Brown Papers, Box 8, folder 163
30 MacBrien memorandum, 29 Jan. 1927, RG 24, vol. 2683, file HQS 5121
31 'War Office General Organization for War,' RG 7 G21, vol. 670 #54, 713(2); McNaughton to MacBrien, 21 Sept. 1923, and MacBrien to Minister of National Defence, 17 Dec. 1926, RG 24, vol. 2680, file HQC 5041
32 Brown to MacBrien, 21 Sept. 1926, RG 24, vol. 2681, file HQC 5046; Thacker memorandum, 26 May 1928, D Hist 111.2101(DI11)
33 MacBrien, comment on 'Some Modern Tendencies in Training and Mechanization,' by General Ellis, *Selected Papers from the Transactions of the Canadian Military Institute* 26 (1926–9), 105
34 RG 24, vol. 6295, file HQ 38-72-278
35 Major R.S. Timmis, 'Some Lessons from a Four Days' Cavalry Trek,' *CDQ* III (1926), 389 ff
36 Lieutenant W.W. Goforth, 'The Influence of Mechanization and Mobility on the Organization and Training of the NPAM,' *CDQ* X (July 1933), 431–53
37 'The present distribution and strength of the British Army in relation to its duties,' prepared by the General Staff, War Office, 1 Nov. 1927, PRO, WO 32/28/23
38 Quartermaster General to Chief of the General Staff, 19 July 1929, RG 24, vol. 2679, file HQC 5046
39 See Department of National Defence *Report*, 1920–9
40 Ibid., 31 Mar. 1926, 69–70

41 McNaughton to Minister of National Defence, 18 Sept. 1930, D Hist 112.1(D77)
42 McNaughton to W.D. Herridge, 3 June 1933, McNaughton Papers, vol. 105, 'Herridge, W.D.,' vol. 2
43 McNaughton, 'The Defence of Canada: A Review of the Present Position,' 28 May 1935, D Hist 112.3M2009(D7)
44 Ashton, 'The Requirements of Canadian Defence: A Review of the Present Position,' 12 Nov. 1935, Ian Mackenzie Papers, vol. 29, file x-4
45 Colonel N.O. Carr, Director of Mechanization, to McNaughton, 20 July 1934, RG 24, vol. 6294, file HQ 38-72-26
46 McNaughton to Director of Military Training, 6 Aug. 1936, RG 24, vol. 6294, file HQ 38-72-26
47 'Detailed Estimates to Accompany Joint Staff Committee Memorandum,' 5 Sept. 1936, D Hist 112.3M2009(D21)
48 Ashton, 'Report on Remedial Action,' 16 Dec. 1936, RG 24, vol. file HQC 5182
49 McNaughton to Minister of National Defence, 8 Sept. 1937, King Papers, vol. 237, 203869-87
50 Loring Christie memorandum, 1 Sept. 1936, Christie Papers, vol. 27, folder 9; J.W. Pickersgill, 'Principle of Uniformity of Equipment,' 5 Dec. 1938, ibid., folder 8. See also James Eayrs, *In Defence of Canada*, vol. II, *Appeasement and Rearmament* (Toronto: University of Toronto Press 1965), 134-54.
51 Eayrs, *In Defence of Canada*, II, 119-31
52 Ashton to Minister of National Defence, 22 Apr. 1936, Ian Mackenzie Papers, vol. 29, file x-4; Colonel N.O. Carr to Deputy Minister, 17 Jan. 1938, RG 24, vol. 2588, file HQS 3352, part II; Major-General T.V. Anderson to Minister of National Defence, 18 Jan. 1939, Ian Mackenzie Papers, vol. 34, file x-66. The general file on self-sufficiency in the Mackenzie Papers is vol. 47, file 'CNS 48.'
53 Interview with W. Moogk, 17 Jan. 1979; see also G.R. Stevens, *Royal Canadian Regiment*, II, 5.
54 Lieutenant-Colonel E.L.M. Burns, 'A Division that Can Attack,' *CDQ* xv (Apr. 1938), 282-98; Captain G.G. Simonds, 'An Army that Can Attack a Division that Can Defend,' *CDQ* xv (July 1938), 413-17; Lieutenant-Colonel E.L.M. Burns, 'Where Do the Tanks Belong?' *CDQ* xvi (Oct. 1938), 28-31; Captain G.G. Simonds, 'What Price Assault Without Support?' *CDQ* xvi (Jan. 1939), 142-47; Captain G.G. Simonds, 'The Attack,' *CDQ* xvi (July 1939), 379-90
55 Maurice Pope, *Soldiers and Politicians: The Memoirs of Lieutenant-General Maurice Pope* (Toronto: University of Toronto Press 1962), 53
56 Burns, 'A Division that Can Attack'
57 Crerar to Master General of the Ordnance, 28 Mar. 1922, RG 24, vol. 6522, file HQ 462-1-15
58 Currie to Sutherland Brown, 13 May 1919, RG 24, vol. 6534, file HQ 640-1-18, part

1. See also RG 24, vols. 2498–2500, file HQC 1050, and RG 6 G21, vol. 230 #343(9)a
59 Chief of the General Staff to Quartermaster General, 1 Oct. 1935, RG 24, vol. 2679, file HQC 5046
60 Chief of the General Staff to Chief of the Imperial General Staff, 18 July 1936, Liaison Letter 3/36, RG 24, microfilm reel C5088, file HQS 6723
61 RG 24, vol. 152, file HQ 9801-17-5
62 Loring Christie memorandum, 26 Feb. 1937, Christie Papers, vol. 27, folder 8
63 Soward to Brown, Queen's University, Douglas Library, Sutherland Brown Papers, Box 190, folder 8
64 Goforth, 'The Influence of Mechanization,' 431–53
65 The addresses made by McNaughton, Crerar, and Pope to the Imperial Defence College are in McNaughton Papers, vols. 105, 106 and 110.
66 Ketchen to Bennett, 14 May 1929, Bennett Papers, vol. 60, 38322–7; Brown to MacBrien, 29 May 1930, Queen's University, Douglas Library, Sutherland Brown Papers, Box 2, folder 31; Brown to Grote Sterling, 6 Jan. 1932, ibid., Box 3, folder 43; Brown to Colonel W.W. Foster, 31 Dec. 1932, ibid., Box 1, folder 6; Brigadier-General J.L. Embry to Currie, 1 Aug. 1929, Currie Papers, vol. 8, folder 23
67 From 1919 to 1927, when McNaughton was vice-chief of the general staff or director of staff duties, and again from 1928–35, while he was chief of the general staff, fifteen artillery, ten engineer, twelve infantry two cavalry and six other branch officers went to the Staff College. Three gunners, three sappers, and only one infantry officer graduated from Imperial Defence College. Information from the *Militia List, 1939*
68 Pope, *Soldiers and Politicians*, 90, 98
69 Brown to CGS, 28 Nov. 1927, Queen's University, Douglas Library, Sutherland Brown Papers, Box 1, folder 2; the 1936 list is in RG 24, microfilm reel C2645, file HQS 3498, part XVI.
70 Brown to Chief of the General Staff, 11 Nov. 1927, Queen's University, Douglas Library, Sutherland Brown Papers, Box 1, folder 2
71 Director of Military Training to Director of Military Operations, 7 Aug. 1936, RG 24, vol. 2645, file HQS 3498, part VII; CGS to DMT, 1 Apr. 1939, RG 24, vol. 6503, file HQ 313-1-32-16, part I
72 McNaughton to Commandant, Royal Military College of Canada, 25 July 1923, RG 24, vol. 5923, file HQ 74-26-4 part I; McNaughton to Commandant, RMC, 6 May 1937, McNaughton Papers, vol. 5, 'RMC Instructions'; McNaughton, Staff College Paper, 1921, McNaughton Papers, vol. 345, 'Staff College folio'

Epilogue

1 See Director of Staff Duties to Chief of the General Staff, 23 Nov. 1943, D Hist 312. 3S2009(D200), vol. I, and E.L.M. Burns, *Manpower in the Canadian Army, 1939–1945* (Toronto: Clarke Irwin 1956).
2 See Assistant Chief of the General Staff to Director of Military Operations, 10 July 1941, Director of Staff Duties to CGS, 11 Aug. 1944, D Hist, 112.3S2049(D9), and CGS to Minister of National Defence, 11 Aug. 1945, D Hist 112.21009(D19).
3 J.W. Pickersgill and D.F. Forster, *The Mackenzie King Record*, vol. II, *1944–1945* (Toronto: University of Toronto Press 1968), 231
4 Post-Hostilities Planning files, Directorate of History
5 J.W. Pickersgill and D.F. Forster, *The Mackenzie King Record*, vol. III, *1945–1946* (Toronto: University of Toronto Press 1970), 393–4
6 Foulkes's speech to army headquarters, quoted in James Eayrs, *In Defence of Canada*, vol. III, *Peacemaking and Deterrence* (Toronto: University of Toronto Press 1972), 390–6
7 *Mackenzie King Record*, III, 256
8 Canada, Department of National Defence, *White Paper on Defence* (Ottawa: Queen's Printer 1964)
9 Canada, Department of National Defence, *Defence in the Seventies* (Ottawa 1971)
10 Quoted in Colin S. Gray, *Canadian Defence Priorities: A Question of Relevance* (Toronto: Clarke Irwin 1972), 42
11 See, for example, Peter C. Kasurak, 'Civilianization and the Military Ethos: Civil-Military Relations in Canada,' *Canadian Public Administration*, 25 (Spring 1982), 108–29.

Note on sources

The main sources for this study are the records of the Department of Militia and Defence (RG 9) and the Department of National Defence (RG 24) in the Public Archives of Canada, and those records of the two departments still retained by the Directorate of History, Department of National Defence, Ottawa. Together these make up an extensive collection of several thousand volumes. Most of the departmental files contain an extensive record of correspondence with ministers, internal memoranda, and 'private' letters between officers, and it is usually possible to trace memoranda and submissions to cabinet back through their draft stages.

The records of the Department of Militia and Defence and of the Department of National Defence are arranged by subject after 1905. The material for the period before 1905 is much less helpfully organized, mainly because the departmental structure was such as to produce what can only be called 'random' filing. Files were numbered chronologically, according to when the first piece of correspondence was received, but from time to time like files were gathered together, and usually given the number of the last file that made up the set. Most of these files belonged to the adjutant general, general officer commanding, or deputy minister.

Special mention should be made of a set of DND records that has only recently become available: the microfilm series referred to in the notes. These were created in the 1950s, when a records management specialist microfilmed most of the department's older 'Confidential,' 'Secret,' and 'Top Secret' files, and destroyed the originals. These microfilm reels contain some of the most significant and important files for the 1919-22 reorganization proposals, as well as many other things.

Other important departmental records for this study are the Governor General's Office files at the PAC (RG 7) and the War Office and Colonial Office records. The former are a gold mine, because until 1920 the Governor General's Office was both a clearing house for despatches and memoranda passing between the Canadian and British governments and because it often made independent reports to Britain. These records contain the best account of Sam Hughes's struggle with Major-General Colin Mackenzie. Of special note are the WO 32 and WO 106 (Intelligence) files relating to Canada.

The most useful collections of private papers include those of seven officers – Hutton, Dundonald, McNaughton, Crerar, Currie, and MacBrien, all at the PAC, and Sutherland Brown, at the Douglas Library, Queen's University. The papers of the prime ministers and ministers before 1914 were helpful; but what they show clearly is that these men looked to the part-time militia first, and then primarily for partisan advantage, when they made policy. Unfortunately there are no Hughes, Lake, or Gwatkin papers to speak of. For the period after the First World War the 'political' papers are much more helpful. Those of Ian Mackenzie and J.L. Ralston are huge collections, as are the redoubtable Mackenzie King Papers, and they are invaluable supplements to the departmental records.

In terms of published primary sources, the annual reports of the Department of Militia and Defence are extraordinarily full for the period from 1867 to 1900. Many run to over four hundred pages. On the other hand, Canadian officers have not been very prolific. The memoranda and letters in the departmental files or private papers are the best guides to their aspirations and opinions. However, two memoirs stand out – *General Mud*, by E.L.M. Burns, and *Soldiers and Politicians*, by Maurice Pope. Articles, addresses, lectures, and editorials in the *Volunteer Review*, *Canadian Military Gazette*, and *Selected Papers* from the *Transactions* of the Canadian Military Institute, as well as those in the *Canadian Defence Quarterly* after 1919, are extremely useful. The difference between the professional orientation of the latter and the amateur bent of the others is striking. There are a few articles by Canadians in the *Journal* of the Royal United Services Institute.

All historians of recent military affairs expect to have some difficulty with restricted access to records. Happily, relaxation of the Canadian thirty-year rule has opened up almost all of the records dealing with the period under review. The exempt categories are few, and they are concerned primarily with intelligence-gathering methods and courts martial. Not so happily, the rule on access to personnel records is very restrictive. Nothing is available until the individual reaches (or would have reached if he is already dead) his ninetieth birthday. This means that the files on most of the twentieth-century officers are closed; those on nineteenth-century officers are not that useful.

The most useful published accounts of the Canadian army or of military affairs in the Dominion are cited in the notes. There are, however, a number of theses deserving special recognition. Kenneth Eyre's 'Staff and Command in the Canadian Corps' (MA thesis, Duke University 1967) outlines the process of Canadianization in the Corps, while William Stewart's 'Attack Doctrine in the Canadian Corps, 1916–1918' (MA thesis, University of New Brunswick 1982), by far the best treatment yet on the subject, explodes the myth of Arthur Currie as the main innovator of the Corps' tactical doctrine. John Griffith Armstrong's 'Canadian Home Defence 1914–1917: The Role of Major-General Willoughby Gwatkin' (MA thesis, Royal Military College of Canada 1982) illustrates why the general staff of the 1930s had reason to be wary of the government's apparent desire to maintain a large home army in any future war. Roger Flynn Sarty's 'Silent Sentry: A Military and Political History of Canadian Coast Defence 1860–1945' (PHD thesis, University of Toronto 1982) is the authoritative account of home defence policy in Canada. It is also a social history of the military in Halifax and a technical study of the development of coast artillery, and illustrates how responsibility for something concrete and viable on the part of the gunners and infantrymen stationed at Halifax was a professionalizing influence of no little importance.

Picture credits

The permanent force before the First World War:
B Battery near St Helen's Island   Public Archives Canada (PAC) C6330; Infantry
School Corps, Fredericton   Department of National Defence (DND) PMR 87-518;
Royal School of Mounted Infantry, Winnipeg   PAC C44196

The beginnings of the staff:
Old Fort, Toronto   PAC C31371; Staff Ride, Niagara   PAC C31361

Two generals who fell victim to partisan politics:
Earl of Dundonald   PAC C42616; Colin Mackenzie   PAC C16487

A successful partnership:
Borden   PAC PA25996; Lake   PAC PA42299

Ministers at war:
Hughes   PAC C20240; Perley   PAC PA33966; Mewburn, Borden, and Kemp   DND
PMR 87-517

Canadian Brass at war:
Currie and MacBrien   DND PMR 87-520; Canadian Corps Heavy Artillery, Bonn
DND PMR 87-519

Canadian 'spies,' 1921–3:
Hodgins, Prower, and Sutherland Brown   DND PMR 87-516; Brown's party near
Lake Placid   DND PMR 87-512

Toward war, 1937:
Royal Canadian Dragoons   DND PMR 81-382; RCD in cavalry cloaks and gas masks
DND PMR 81-397; Partial mechanization   DND PMR 81-390; RCD armoured cars and
horses   DND PMR 72-21

The manipulators of Defence Scheme No. 3:
Ashton   PAC C49483; Anderson   PAC C25912; Mackenzie   PAC C36646

Index